HORRIBLE HISTORIES

FRIGHTFUL
FIRST WORLD
WAR

TERRY DEARY

ILLUSTRATED BY MARTIN BROWN

Scholastic Canada Ltd.
Toronto New York London Auckland Sydney
Mexico City New Delhi Hong Kong Buenos Aires

To Private John Condon, Royal Irish Regiment.
Died 24 May 1915, aged 14 years old.
The youngest British soldier to die during the
First World War.

Scholastic Canada Ltd.
604 King Street West, Toronto, Ontario M5V 1E1, Canada

Scholastic Inc.
557 Broadway, New York, NY 10012, USA

Scholastic Australia Pty Limited
PO Box 579, Gosford, NSW 2250, Australia

Scholastic New Zealand Limited
Private Bag 94407, Greenmount, Auckland, New Zealand

Scholastic Children's Books
Euston House, 24 Eversholt Street, London NW1 1DB, UK

Library and Archives Canada Cataloguing in Publication
Deary, Terry
Frightful First World War / Terry Deary, author ; Martin Brown, illustrator.
(Horrible histories)
ISBN 978-0-545-99325-8
1. World War, 1914-1918--Juvenile literature. I. Brown,
Martin, 1959- II. Title. III. Series: Deary, Terry. Horrible histories.
D522.7.D43 2008   j940.3   C2007-907185-6

ISBN-10: 0-545-99325-3

Text copyright © Terry Deary, 1998.
Illustrations © Martin Brown, 1998.
First published in the UK by Scholastic Ltd., 1998.
First Canadian edition published 2008.
All rights reserved.

Scholastic Ltd. gratefully acknowledges permission to reprint the extract
from All Quiet on the Western Front by Erich Maria Remarque,
published by The Bodley Head.

6 5 4 3 2 1   Printed in Canada   08 09 10 11 12

CONTENTS

Introduction

History can be horrible. So horrible that some boring old fogies think young people should not be told the whole, terrible truth.

But if you never learn the truth, you'll miss out on some of the most useful things in life. . .

MY GRANDAD SAYS SOLDIERS SOFTENED THEIR BOOTS WITH SWEET PEA MIXTURE. WHAT'S THAT?

SWEET PEAS ARE FLOWERS. NOW GET ON WITH YOUR WORK

And the next time your new leather shoes hurt you, stuff them full of flowers. What happens? Nothing. The shoes stay hard and your feet get blisters.

Why couldn't your teachers tell you the truth about "sweet pea" mixture? Either. . .

a) they don't know, or

b) they know . . . but they are too embarrassed to say.

What you need is a book that's not too embarrassed to tell you about the awful things people used to do. You want a history of the horrible.

And it's no use telling you. . .

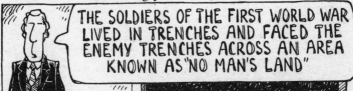

THE SOLDIERS OF THE FIRST WORLD WAR LIVED IN TRENCHES AND FACED THE ENEMY TRENCHES ACROSS AN AREA KNOWN AS "NO MAN'S LAND"

That makes it sound cosy and peaceful, doesn't it? The truth is pretty nasty, but you'll never understand how those people suffered unless you read their own true memories of trenches and no man's land. . .

> Bodies and bits of bodies, and clots of blood and green metallic-looking slime made by the explosive gases were floating on the surface of the water. Our men lived there and died there within a few yards of the enemy. They crouched below the sandbags and burrowed into the sides of trenches. Lice crawled over them in swarms. If they dug to get deeper cover, their shovels went into the softness of dead bodies who had been their friends. Scraps of flesh, booted legs, blackened hands, eyeless heads came falling over them when the enemy fired shells at their position. . .

That's more like the truth because it was written by a soldier who was there.

Of all the history in the world, the story of the First World War—also known as the Great War—is perhaps the most horrible. It's a story of what happens when machines go to war and human beings get in the way. But it's also a story of courage and craziness, brave people and batty people, friendships and fierce hatreds, love . . . and lice.

The Great War gangs

Why did the Great War start? Lots of big, thick history books have been written to answer that question. But, to put it simply, by 1914 the countries of Europe had formed themselves into two big gangs . . . like street gangs. The gang called the "Central Powers" were led by the Germans and the gang we call the "Allies" were led by the French and British.

The two gangs started collecting weapons, making threats and swapping insults, the way gangs do.

All it needed was for one gang member to throw the first stone and a huge punch-up would follow.

The Black Hand bunglers

So exactly *how* did the First World War start? It's never one of the gang leaders that starts the fight, is it? It's always one of the scruffy little kids that hangs around the edge. In this case the scruffy little kid was called Bosnia, in the Allies' gang.

And so, a Serbian gang known as the Black Hand (honest!) waited till the Emperor came to Bosnia. Gavrilo Princip was a Serbian Black Hand freedom fighter. . .

9

NUMBER 2 SWALLOWED POISON AND JUMPED IN THE RIVER TO DROWN RATHER THAN BE CAPTURED

BUT THE CROWD DRAGGED ME OUT OF THE RIVER AND SAVED ME...THEN THEY NEARLY BEAT ME TO DEATH!

FERDI WENT TO THE TOWN HALL AND MADE A SPEECH. HE WAS IN REACH OF 3, 4, 5 AND 6. AND THEY...

ER...DID NOTHING

FERDI HEADED FOR THE HOSPITAL TO VISIT THE BOMB VICTIMS. BUT, BY AN AMAZING CHANCE, HIS DRIVER TOOK A WRONG TURN. THIS ROAD BROUGHT HIM STRAIGHT PAST NUMBER 7...

ME! I JUMPED ON TO THE OPEN CAR AND FIRED TWO SHOTS...

I KILLED FERDI AND HIS WIFE. FERDI'S UNCLE, EMPEROR OF AUSTRIA, WAS FURIOUS. HE WANTED REVENGE AGAINST ALL OF SERBIA'S ALLIES. HE WANTED *WAR*

The first stone had been thrown. Austria declared war on Serbia, and Germany helped Austria so Russia helped Serbia so France helped Russia. Germany marched through Belgium to get to France so Britain helped Belgium.

The First World War had started. It was expected to last about four months but it lasted four frightful years.

But, before the war starts, here are two quick questions.

1 What happened to Ferdi's blood-soaked jacket after his death?

   a) It was taken into battle like a flag for the Austrians to follow.

   b) He was buried in it.

   c) It was put in a museum, so gruesome people can go and gaze at it.

2 What happened to the assassin Gavrilo Princip?

   a) He was shot by the police as he ran away.

   b) He escaped and lived happily ever after.

   c) He was arrested and put in prison.

Answers: **1c)** Franz Ferdinand's death was the start of the bloodiest war seen until that time. So his blood-soaked coat was an important reminder of the terrible event. It is now on display in the Austrian Historical Museum in Vienna. Go and see it . . . if you like that sort of thing.

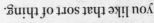

2c) Gavrilo Princip was taken alive. His two shots killed millions and millions of people. Yet he was allowed to live. Just as the First World War reached an end, gunman Gavrilo died in prison, of a lung disease. Pity it didn't get him four years before!

Wacky Willie

Things may have stayed calm and the Serbian trouble could have died down. But some of the leaders of the gangs weren't too bright and weren't too pleasant. Take the German monarch. . .

Title: Kaiser Wilhelm

Job: Monarch of Germany

Peculiarity: Unpopular. Nobody liked poor Willy. His grandmother, Queen Victoria of Britain, couldn't stand him. His (English) mother refused to wish him a happy birthday . . . so he sulked for days. His father thought he would be a dangerous leader—smart dad!

Weakness: He was born with a withered left arm and it embarrassed him. When he was photographed he insisted that he hide his weak arm. People around him hid their strong left arms too.

Nasty streak: German workers went on strike and he ordered soldiers to attack the strikers. "I expect my troops to shoot at least 500," he said.

Most likely to say: I hate everybody.

Least likely to say: Let's talk calmly about this.

1914–The year of the first shot

No one is surprised when a war breaks out in August 1914. Germany smashed France in the Franco–Prussian War of 1871 and it was just a matter of time before France tried to take its revenge. But people are surprised that the war is still going on by the end of 1914. The two sides are like two heavyweight boxers jumping into the ring. Each one expects a quick knockout. But they will end up slugging it out, toe to toe, till they are exhausted.

Timeline 1914

28 June Archduke Franz Ferdinand is assassinated in Bosnia. Austria is very annoyed because he was going to be their next emperor. (Franz is too dead to be annoyed.)

23 July Austria blames Serbia for the death of Ferdi because the assassins were from Serbia. Serbia grovels but apology is not accepted. This means *WAR*.

4 August German army marches through Belgium to attack France, so Britain joins the war to help "poor little Belgium."

23 August Meanwhile, in the east, the German army defeats the Russian army. Round one to Germany.

9 September The French stop the Germans at the Battle of the Marne. Round two to France.

October Millions rush to join the armies. They're afraid it will be over before Christmas and before they can fight. It *will* be over before Christmas . . . 1918.

22 November The Allies and the Central Powers have battered one another to a standstill in northern France. They dig trenches opposite one another . . . and won't move from them much for four years. No winners—only soldiers lose . . . their lives.

25 December Enemies stop fighting for a day or two, and even play friendly football matches. It can't last, and it won't be repeated.

Did you know . . . ?

The first Brits to fight in the First World War fought in London! On 2 August 1914, two days before war was declared, peace marchers clashed with Londoners who wanted war.

True lies

When you go to war you can't fight against nice people, can you? You have to believe the enemy are real slimeballs who would murder your granny and poison your gerbil if they won. You have to learn to *hate* them.

In Germany, a new national anthem was written called the "Hymn of Hate." And when people met a friend in the street they no longer said, *"Güten Morgen"* (good morning), they said, *"Gott strafe England"* (God punish England). These words were rubber-stamped on letters, printed on millions of postcards and engraved on badges and brooches.

Meanwhile, in the UK, the music of German composers was banned. (Since many had died some years before the war, they won't have been too upset.)

And if your enemy *wasn't* nasty enough, what could you do? You could invent a few lies about them. So it was widely believed that German grocers in Britain had poisoned food and that German barbers were cutting their customers' throats and secretly dumping the bodies. Here's what the enemies said about one other . . . but can you spot the lies?

1   Brits believed the German soldiers were monsters. . .

15

2 And the Germans believed the British were just as bad. . . .

3 Germans believed foreign visitors were spies. . .

4 And the Brits didn't even trust their allies!

5 The Brits certainly didn't trust their own business-men. . .

6 While the Germans knew who was to blame for starting the war. . .

7 The Germans also believed the most amazing tales of heroic deeds. . .

8   Brits were sure the Germans were desperate for materials and especially fat. . .

9   They were also sure that Germany was running short of fighting men. . .

Every one of these stories was believed—and every one was false, of course. Some were deliberate lies, but others were simple mistakes. Take the story of corpses being melted to make oil. It appeared in a German newspaper report from the Western Front in April 1917. . .

We are passing the great Kadaver Exploitation Department of this Army Group. The fat that is won here is turned into lubricating oils, and everything else is ground down in the bone mills into a powder which is used for mixing with pigs' food—nothing can be permitted to go to waste.

Brits called corpses "cadavers" and thought the Germans were melting *human* corpses. In German "kadaver" means an *animal* corpse. The corpses being melted down were horses.

The "Fat King"

The Brits needed fat extractors too. Major Ellis—known to soldiers as the "Fat King"—invented a "fat extracting" plant and set it up on the French coast. This factory took waste food, dead horses and animal waste and turned it into fat. This was sent across the Channel to be made into glycerine—an important part of TNT explosives. Nine thousand tons of fat were produced by the Fat King's factory.

So, a horse could be killed by a German shell (no, the army "shells" were not like winkle shells you find on the beach. They were huge exploding bombs fired from large guns), turned into TNT and fired back at them! A perfect revenge!

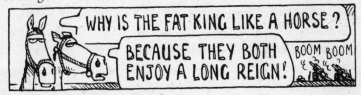

WHY IS THE FAT KING LIKE A HORSE?

BECAUSE THEY BOTH ENJOY A LONG REIGN! BOOM BOOM

Christmas crack shots

The First World War was the first war to see aircraft used. To begin with, they would fly over enemy armies and photograph their positions or bomb them. Then the defenders sent fighters to shoot down these spy planes. War in the air had begun.

Airplanes also meant Brits in their homes were no longer safe in a foreign war. Londoners discovered this after just four months. . .

FOE FLIERS FLEE

Londoners had hopes of a quiet Christmas crushed when two German planes flew up the Thames yesterday. Crowds gathered in the streets to watch as two gallant airmen from our Royal Flying Corps chased the intruders at speeds of up to 70 miles an hour!

"I could hear the gunfire quite clearly," a resident of Chiswick told our reporter. "What if one of those bullets landed on an innocent head?" The aircraft observers had fired rifles at one another—a common sight in the skies over France these days. No one was hurt and the horrid Huns hurried back to Germany with their tails between their legs. But the use of guns is a deadly development of war in the air. In the early days of the war observers would carry a supply of bricks and try to drop one on to the enemy.

Londoners have been ordered to dim their lights this evening in case the unwanted visitors return. It has been reported that the Germans have invented steel darts to be dropped from their aircraft. If these strike a man they will split him in half from head to foot. Is there no end to the atrocious cruelty of this enemy?

"It just makes the people of Britain all the more determined to win," a shop assistant from Wapping told our reporter. "I am sending my Bobby down to the recruiting office today."

The stories of brick bombs and deadly darts were true.

Later aircraft carried machine guns; the pilot aimed his plane at the enemy and pulled the trigger. But there was a danger that the bullets would then hit his own propeller and shatter it. In time, engineers invented a timing gear so the bullets could only fire into the gaps between the turning propeller.

But how did the first machine guns fire forward? If you were an Allied inventor, what simple solution could you come up with?

Answer: The propellers were covered with sheets of steel. If a machine gun bullet happened to hit the propeller it bounced off.

Great idea—and it worked. For a month or two the German airmen were terrified and puzzled by the Allied fighter planes. Finally they captured one, saw how it was done and copied it.

The trouble is there was no way of telling where the bullet would bounce off to if it hit the propeller. It could smash into the pilot's own engine, if he was unlucky—or bounce back and hit him between the eyes if he was really, *really* unlucky!

Did you know . . . ?

In the Second World War (1939–45), there were sirens to warn people of air raids. But when air raids became common in the First World War, many defence chiefs in Britain sent out a letter saying. . .

B7253A/6

It has been decided that no warning of air raids will be given as it is thought this may do more harm than good.

OFFICIAL

So, you could be walking to school and the first thing you know about the air raid is when you wake up dead.

Is this a record?

On 21 December 1914, William Gilligan, aged 41, joined the West Yorkshire Regiment at Hull. The next day, he deserted at York!

1915—The year of total war

From 1915, battles are fought from trenches dug into the ground—where these battles are fought becomes known as the Western Front. Meanwhile, the war spreads around the world. It is also the year of new weapons to kill new targets . . . including people in their homes!

People at home can't fight back, but they can take it out on foreigners living in their country (known as "aliens," but not to be confused with little green beings from Mars!). So, in the East End of London, German shops are looted and, in one riot, German pianos are thrown from houses onto the road. A street concert is held where patriotic songs are sung. The government is forced to imprison enemy aliens for their own protection as well as to stop them spying.

In Germany, anyone with "a well-cut coat, a well-filled wallet and a notably good car" is arrested as a spy. All British people are rounded up and most are imprisoned.

Timeline 1915

19 January First Zeppelin airship raids on Britain. Women and children, cats and dogs are in this war, like it or not.

2 February Germany says it will surround Britain with submarines, sink food supply ships and starve Britain to defeat.

18 March British Government asks women to sign up for war work. Many do and they start doing it better than the men did!

22 April Nasty new weapon,

poisoned gas, first used against soldiers in the trenches.

May Allies try to sneak round the back of the German front by landing in Gallipoli, Turkey. They expect the Turks will be a pushover.

7 May German submarines sink a passenger ship, the *Lusitania*—on board are 128 Americans who are not even part of the war yet. Big mistake, Germany.

7 June Zeppelin airship shot down over Flanders, northern France. That slow-moving bag of gas makes Zeppelins easy targets.

July The Turkish state uses war as an excuse to wipe out an entire race of people, the Armenians. A step on the road to the terrors of the Second World War.

August Food getting short, especially in Germany. Prices go up and taxes go up to pay for the war—£1 million a day in Britain is needed to pay for the fighting.

September At the Battle of Loos, in Flanders, some brave Brits dribble a football toward enemy lines. The ball was found riddled with bullets. Like the foolhardy footballers.

12 October Nurse Edith Cavell is caught helping Brit prisoners to

24

escape in Belgium. She says, "If I had to, I'd do it all over again." Germans shoot her so she can't.

11 November Brit minister Winston Churchill gets sacked because his Gallipoli idea is a disaster. He'll be back.

20 December Allies give up on the Gallipoli attack and retreat. It was a very bloody mistake.

Pests and plagues

Soldiers had more to fear than enemy weapons. Creepy-crawlies and deadly diseases could kill you just as dead.

Fierce flies

At Gallipoli, flies in the summer of 1915 were very bad because of the number of unburied bodies. One soldier of the Australia and New Zealand Army Corps (Anzacs) wrote home about the flies. . .

Some of them must have tin openers on their feet, they bite so hard.

A Brit soldier complained. . .

In order to eat your food you had to wave your hand over it then bite suddenly, otherwise a fly came with it. Any bit of food uncovered was blotted out of sight by flies in a couple of seconds.

That fly had probably had a picnic on a dead donkey a few minutes before, so it's no wonder the troops suffered so much disease in Gallipoli.

Deadly doctors

Since Florence Nightingale's work in the Crimean War of 1856 it was a little safer in war hospitals. Back in Florie Nightie's day, a wound could easily get infected—if the bullet didn't kill you then the germs did. But doctors could still be pretty clumsy. One soldier reported. . .

An Anzac soldier, Private O'Connor, was wounded in the leg and captured. He was taken to Istanbul where an Armenian doctor operated to amputate O'Connor's leg. The doctor sawed halfway through the bone, grew too tired, and snapped off the rest.

Frightful first aid

In the middle of a battle you couldn't pop down to the local shop for an aspirin or call for an ambulance. Soldiers had to look after each other and they all carried a small first aid pack into battle. Brit soldiers also had a book, *The Field Almanac 1915*, that gave some advice.

There are some instructions you may *not* like to follow next time you are flattened in a fierce football match. . .

Broken limbs:
Gently put the broken limb straight after cutting off the clothes. Then fix it in this position by means of a splint made from a rifle, a roll of newspapers, bayonets, swords, pieces of wood.

A roll of newspapers! In a battle? What newspaper could be as tough as a wooden splint? The *Daily Telegraph-pole* perhaps?

By 1918, because of severe shortages in Germany, soldiers were forced to use bandages made from crêpe paper and tied on with thread.

F-f-f-f-frostbite

Frostbite is another problem you may suffer in school sports (especially during cricket matches in Britain). Again, you wouldn't want to suffer the 1915 cure. . .

Frostbite:
Carry the sufferer to a room or place without a fire, remove the clothes and rub hard with a cloth soaked in water or snow.

Brrrr!

And the way of preventing frostbite was even worse. . .

In the winter of 1914–15, anti-frostbite grease was supplied in two pound tins to soldiers on the Western Front. It looked like lard and it contained mostly pork fat. After 1915, whale oil was issued in rum jars. This was little used because of the terrible smell. Army orders said that, before going out on patrol in cold or wet weather, each man was to be stripped and rubbed down with whale oil by an officer. Most men refused to strip . . . and most officers refused to rub!

Putrid poisons

The army listed three types of poisoning. The emergency cure for "corrosive" poisoning looks weird. . .

№ 31a   *British Army Field Almanac 1915*

Corrosive poisons:
Give scrapings from whitewashed walls or ceilings, mixed with water.

Perhaps the advice to eat walls is not so surprising. After all, walls make great ice cream and sausages!

Gruesome gas

A new First World War danger was gas attack. Orders went out from army headquarters. . .

If you are caught in a gas attack:
1 Take out your handkerchief.
2 Urinate into the material till it is soaked.
3 Tie it round your mouth and nose and breathe through it.

fig I

The orders didn't say what you should do if you didn't feel like a pee!

Crafty cordite

Soldiers wishing to appear unwell and thus avoid duty would chew cordite, an explosive taken from their rifle bullets. Cordite gave the soldier a high temperature, but the effect soon wore off.

Lovely lice

At the Gallipoli battles the soldiers were forced to wear the same clothes for weeks without even taking them off. One Australian soldier finally got to take his socks off and saw a ghastly sight. . .

> And, Ma, I swear that as I dropped my socks on the floor I saw them start to move! They were a seething mass of lice!

In the trenches, the soldiers found "chatting" was a peaceful way to pass the quiet times. But "chatting" didn't mean talking. It meant getting rid of the "chats," or lice, from the seams of their tunics.

One soldier compared lice to an army that had invaded his body. . .

The Little Soldiers of the Night

Though some hundreds you may kill,
Still you'll find there's hundreds still,
For they hide beneath each other
And are smart at taking cover;
Then you have an awful bite,
They've a shocking appetite.

> *There are families in dozens,*
> *Uncles, mothers, sisters, cousins,*
> *And they have their married quarters*
> *Where they rear their sons and daughters;*
> *And they take a lot of catching*
> *Cause an awful lot of scratching.*

German soldiers described another way of dealing with their bloodsucking friends. They took the lid from a boot polish tin and held it by a piece of wire over a candle. When the lid began to glow they'd simply drop the lice on the red hot tin. The sizzle of the frying lice was a sweet sound to their ears.

Did you know . . . ?
British soldiers suffered from lice that were a pale fawn colour, but German soldiers had red lice. If they'd bred the two together they could have had pretty pink lice!

Seriously spooky
When your life is in danger then you start to believe in luck. People in danger can be very superstitious. A few new beliefs sprang up in the First World War.

Super superstitions
Bulletproof Bibles
Pocket-sized copies of the New Testament suddenly sold

tens of thousands of copies. They were being bought by anxious Brit mothers for their sons. There were stories of bullets being stopped by these little Bibles. There may have been one or two true cases of Bibles stopping "spent" rifle bullets. They were not a lot of good against high explosive shells and machine gun bullets.

God's people

Each side believed that they were in the right; that meant that God would be on their side. The Germans even went to war with a belt buckle that read, "*Gott mit uns*" (God with us). British soldiers saw the word "*uns*" and thought that proved what they knew—they were fighting the *Huns*! One very popular belief was that either God had your name and number on a bullet . . . or he didn't. So, you may as well charge that machine gun. After the war one soldier said. . .

I was most amazed by the bullets that missed *me!*

But the most dangerous superstition of all was that "Prayer can turn bullets aside."

For the soldiers who didn't believe in God or luck, there was always this common sense advice. It was a notice passed around the trenches. . .

31

Don't worry

When you are a soldier you can be in one of two places:

A dangerous place or a safe place.

If you're in a safe place . . . don't worry.

If you're in a dangerous place you can be one of two things:

One is wounded and the other is not.

If you're not wounded . . . don't worry.

If you are wounded it can be dangerous or slight:

If it's slight . . . don't worry.

If it's dangerous then one of two things will happen:

You'll die or you'll recover.

If you recover . . . don't worry.

If you die . . . you can't worry.

In these circumstances a soldier never worries.

The third man

The reason for this belief was that it was a dangerous thing to do in the trenches where an enemy sniper might be watching.

First light will catch his eye, second light he'll fix his sights on the light and third light . . . he'll pull the trigger.

Mascots

Animals bring you luck. Regiments collected them as mascots: a bulldog mascot and the regiment is saying, "We're tough"; a goat mascot says, "We'll charge head-down and fearless." What would your school mascot be?

A SNAIL . . . 'COS WE'RE HARD AS SNAILS HERE!

GRRRR

A HAMSTER BECAUSE WE'RE SO FURRY NICE

But Bella and Bertha were an unusual choice for the Scots Guards. In late 1914, two cows were found near Ypres (pronounced "ee-pruh" . . . though most Brit soldiers called it "Wipers"), Flanders, by the regiment. They were the only survivors from a herd that had been hit by shellfire. (Yeah, all the udders were dead.) The cows—soon named Bella and Bertha—became the battalion's mascots, providing fresh milk for the men in the trenches. After the war, the cows were taken to Scotland for retirement. When the Scots Guards marched through London on the Victory Parade, they were accompanied by Bella and Bertha.

The blasted statue

In the town of Albert, Flanders, there was a fine church with a golden statue of the Virgin Mary on top. Early in 1915 the tower was damaged and the statue toppled over, but didn't fall. For months it hung there as the war dragged on, and the British defenders in Albert invented a strange superstition. . .

WHEN THE STATUE FALLS THE WAR WILL END!

If the statue fell the British soldiers would be terribly discouraged, so the army set up strong cables to hold the Virgin Mary in her perilous place. For over three years the Germans failed to knock her off her perch and for three more years the war went on.

In 1918, the Germans finally captured the town and started using the top of the church tower as an observation post. From that high point they could guide their shellfire toward the British. So it was the British who fired back and ended up demolishing the tower and brought the Virgin Mary down to Earth. The Germans were happy.

HAH! *OUR* SUPERSTITION IS THAT WHOEVER KNOCKS THE STATUE DOWN WILL *LOSE* THE WAR, BYE-BYE BRITS!

And, would you believe it? The war ended shortly after . . . but with the defeat of Germany.

I TOLD YOU SO!

Funny fact: After the British knocked the statue down it disappeared—probably sent to Germany to be melted down and turned into weapons.

When the war finished, Albert and its church were rebuilt. An exact copy of the statue stands there now. But . . . it was suggested that the statue should be put back in her famous wartime pose!

The people of Albert said, "*Non!*"

Ghostly tales

With so many people dying in the First World War, it's not surprising that ghosts were reported. In 1916, there was a great rise in "spiritualists"—people who said they had the power to speak to the dead.

In late 1916 (after terrible losses at the Battle of the Somme where 20,000 Brits died on the first day alone), spiritualism became very popular in the UK with mothers trying to contact lost sons. Many fake spiritualists were caught and put in prison, but still the craze continued.

Why would a spiritualist lie to a woman about her dead son and pretend that she could speak to him? For money, of course. In December 1916 during the trial of fake spiritualist Almira Brockway, it was revealed that she was receiving over £25 a week for her work. Workers in the war factories worked 48 hours each week and made just £1.

Whenever there's misery and suffering, you can be sure there is someone to cash in and make a fortune out of it. But some of the spooky stories are harder to explain than frauds and fakes. They are *seriously* spooky. . .

The angel army of Mons

In August 1914, British troops arrived in southern Belgium

to try and stop the German invasion. They were beaten back and slaughtered by the advancing enemy. Over 15,000 died in the early attacks. Yet some survived and reports said this was thanks to a miracle. . .

Arthur Machen, a journalist, turned the rumours into a short story. His story (called "The Bowmen") said it was the English heroes of the 1415 Battle of Agincourt who had come to the rescue. (The battle was fought near by.) Machen's story was published in the *London Evening News* a few weeks after the Battle of Mons and many Brits believed it. Some of the soldiers who returned from the battle then said it was true.

Even when Machen said he'd invented the whole story, there were some people who went on believing in the angels.

Explanations: Some religious people have said the phantom army was made up of the spirits of the soldiers who had just died in the battle.

Some doctors believed that the Allied soldiers had hallucinations—waking dreams—because they were stressed by fear, pain and exhaustion.

But, weirdest of all, German spy chief Friedrich Herzenwirth claimed that he had created the angels. He had sent up airplanes with cinema projectors. These projected images of angels on to the low clouds. He did this to encourage the German soldiers, who would believe God was on their side.

The Montrose ghost

In October 1917, a ghost was seen at Montrose aerodrome in Scotland. One witness said. . .

It glided up to the door of the old aerodrome bar room and then vanished.

It was seen several times afterwards by many officers. They were sure it was the ghost of Lieutenant Desmond Arthur, who had been killed in a flying accident. Why was air-ace Arthur haunting the site of his crash?

An official enquiry had blamed the accident on Desmond Arthur himself. It said. . .

He was killed by his own foolishness.

Yet the other officers knew that Lieutenant Arthur was a good pilot. They believed that his spirit was tortured by the insulting enquiry. Arthur's friends believed the ghost would not rest until his name was cleared by a second enquiry.

When this second enquiry decided. . .

> We blame the fatal accident on a badly repaired machine.

. . .the ghost paid one final visit to the bar room in January 1917, and then was never seen again.

Explanations: Desmond Arthur's friends were angry that he was blamed for his own death. They started the rumours of the ghost to attract the attention of the newspapers. The fascinated public then demanded to know the truth and a second enquiry was ordered.

Or . . . the ghost seemed to spend a lot of time in the *bar room*. Did the "spirits" they poured in their glasses make the officers see "spirits" walk through the door?

The spirit of the Somme

Soldiers in hospital enjoyed swapping stories of their experiences. Some of them were strange and mysterious. . .

WE HAD A CAPTAIN IN THE BATTLE OF THE SOMME. A TALL, HANDSOME BLOKE AND A FINE LEADER. ONE DAY SOME CHAPS GOT THEMSELVES TRAPPED IN A SHELL HOLE. HE FOUND THEM AND LED THEM TO SAFETY. THEY WAS TERRIFIED, BUT HE SAID...

DON'T BE FRIGHTENED MEN. WHENEVER YOU GET YOURSELF INTO A TIGHT CORNER, I'LL BE THERE TO PULL YOU OUT

Explanations: Soldiers would be bored in hospital. They could well get into a competition to tell the most exciting story. And, if their true stories weren't exciting enough, they could make one up! After all, it's hard to prove that the storyteller was lying.

Or . . . the storyteller was led to safety by an officer who looked like the dead officer. When the storyteller lost sight of the Captain, he believed he'd seen a ghost.

Or . . . a ghostly captain went on protecting his men even after he'd died. He became their guardian angel.

The dead poet's footsteps

One of the most famous victims of the war was the poet Rupert Brooke. He'd written a poem about the glory of war. (This was a dumb thing to do since he'd never seen the horror of it, but the people back in Britain wanted to believe him.)

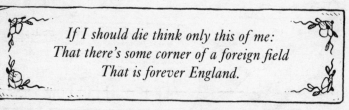

If I should die think only this of me:
That there's some corner of a foreign field
That is forever England.

Rupert used to live in Grantchester Vicarage near Cambridge, and he wrote another famous poem about it. (The poem is called "The Old Vicarage, Grantchester" . . . no prizes for guessing why.)

He was sent off to fight in Gallipoli but never made it. In April 1915, he was bitten on the lip by an insect and died of blood poisoning. (It must have been a dirty insect that forgot to clean its biting teeth. This was probably *not* the glorious end Rupert imagined.) The "corner of a foreign field that is forever England" is his grave in an olive grove on the Greek Island of Skyros, by the way.

When the war was over a doctor called Copeland moved into Rupert's old rooms in Grantchester Vicarage. One frosty evening he sat reading by the fire with his bulldog at his feet. . .

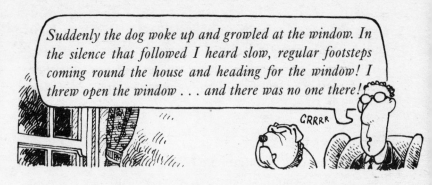

Suddenly the dog woke up and growled at the window. In the silence that followed I heard slow, regular footsteps coming round the house and heading for the window! I threw open the window . . . and there was no one there!

GRRRR

Doctor Copeland's landlord explained that the footsteps had been heard ever since Rupert Brooke was killed four years before. (His phantom feet must have been hurting a bit by 1919!)

Explanations: The dog heard burglars.

Or . . . Rupert didn't like being stuck in "some corner of a foreign field," and wanted to come home.

Or . . . the owners of Grantchester Vicarage wanted to believe that their famous lodger still remembered them. But isn't it strange that only the "famous" Rupert Brooke came back and not some ordinary Joe Blogg?

Or . . . maybe it isn't Rupert's ghost after all. Maybe it *is* Joe Blogg's ghost! This is not as silly as it sounds. In Grantchester churchyard there is a memorial for the local men who died in the First World War. There are usually flowers at the foot of the memorial, put there by poetry lovers who remember the famous Rupert. Is that fair? What

about the other brave men who died? Are they forgotten and do they return to haunt the Vicarage in revenge? Look carefully at the memorial and you will see half a dozen other names on there. And one of the other (forgotten) names is . . . Joseph Blogg.

Simple spymen

Some places were haunted long before the First World War. But the war brought them new horrors and new ghosts. Take the ancient Tower of London, for example. The war brought it back into use in a horrible historical way. . .

Terror in the Tower

"Have you any last requests?" the Major asked the young man in the shabby black suit.

"I have, good sir. I would like to play my violin one last time. Before you shoot me."

The Major nodded and opened a hatch in the steel door and called to the guard outside, "Bring Herr Buschmann's violin from the office." He turned back to the prisoner. "You are honoured, young Fernando. You will be the first to be executed in the Tower of London for hundreds of years."

The young man gave a faint smile. "It is a greater honour to die for Germany," he said.

"It would be better to *live*," the Major pointed out and pulled a wooden chair to the side of the bed and sat facing the German spy.

"My wife and child will suffer back in Germany. I regret being caught . . . but I do not regret spying for my country," he said calmly.

The Major shook his head sadly. "It was Germany that sent you here to die."

"No, they sent me here to *spy*."

"But they prepared you so badly we were *bound* to catch you!" the Major groaned. "Don't you see that?"

"No," the prisoner frowned.

The officer leaned forward and lowered his voice. "You will die at dawn, so there is nothing to lose by telling you this, Fernando. But they trained you in the spy school at Rotterdam. The head of the spy school is Herr Flores."

"Perhaps."

"We *know* it is!" the Major sighed. "And he sent you here with a passport written in his own handwriting. We recognized it at once."

For the first time a small frown of uncertainty crossed the young German's face. The Major went on. "He sent you to a hotel in the Strand where he sends *all* of his secret agents. He gave you a cover story—you were to say you were a salesman of cheese, bananas, safety razors and potatoes . . . but you know hardly anything about those things!"

The spy lowered his head a little in an admission of defeat. "I sent in reports the best I could," he muttered.

"You sent in reports that said we switch on London searchlights at 8:00 p.m. and switch them off again at 10:30 if no Zeppelins appear," the officer said. "That is no great secret to die for."

"You know what messages I sent?"

"Of course! You sent the messages in code to a schoolmaster in Holland. That schoolmaster is a *British* spy. You were an amateur, Fernando. *We* will shoot you . . . but it is *your* spymasters who sent you to your death."

There was a rap on the door and a guard handed a violin to the Major, who passed it across to Fernando Buschmann. For the next three hours the sweet, mournful tones echoed round the ancient walls and stirred the ghosts of long-dead prisoners.

Slowly the sky lightened through the barred window and hobnailed footsteps clattered in the corridor outside. The prisoner played one last melody, but now the notes were wavering and disconnected. "Nice tune," the Major said.

"By Pagliacci," the German said. "The music tells the story of a broken-hearted clown. Maybe that's all I was, Major." He raised the violin to his lips and kissed it. "Goodbye, I shall not want you any more." He laid his precious instrument on the hard bed, straightened his back and faced the men who waited at the door. "I am ready," he said.

Fernando Buschmann faced an eight-man firing squad on the morning of 19 October 1915. He refused a blindfold, saying he wanted to die like a gentleman. He was one of 11 bungling, amateur German spies to die in the Tower during the First World War. A 12th was hanged at Wandsworth Prison.

On 13 November 1997 the papers connected with the case were sold at an auction in London. The saddest was the letter from his wife to his lawyer Henry Garrett that read. . .

Dear Mr. Garrett

I would be grateful if you could send me details of my husband's last moments. Was he at least allowed to keep his violin till his last hours? Had he much to suffer? Will I find his tomb in London to weep at it? My only wish is to visit and to sleep there where my beloved husband is sleeping...

There were many ways to die, and many wasted lives, in the First World War. Fernando Buschmann's was just another one.

Awful agents
In the years before the First World War, Britain was overrun with German spies because they guessed this war would come one day. It wasn't till 1908 that Britain had any spy-catchers—the Secret Service Bureau.[1] Captain Vernon Kell

1. In 1916 this was renamed Military Department 5—the famous MI5. By the end of the war it had 844 members.

was the only member of the Secret Service Bureau and by the start of the war in 1914 he had only nine officers. The Bureau did such a good job that they arrested 21 agents as soon as the war began.

The Bureau had a lot of help from the German spies who were not too clever. In fact, they were awful agents. They got their information from Germans working in Britain—hairdressers and pub landlords were favourites because they heard lots of gossip. And German teachers were a bit treacherous too! (Would you trust a teacher?)

Their code words included. . .
- eggs = foot soldiers
- condensed milk = horse soldiers
- margarine = guns
- Dutch cheese = battleships
- tinned lobster = torpedo boats

Now that code may be hard to crack (except "eggs" which are easy to crack) but you don't have to be James Bond to solve the following genuine German code. Match the code to the real meaning . . . the simple spymen left enough clues in the choice of words!

1 Floating down	a) Dartmouth Naval Base
2 Old folks at home	b) Destroyers
3 Dark melodies	c) Old battleships
4 Chattanooga Rag	d) Southampton
5 Down South	e) Submarines
6 Pirates of Penzance	f) Chatham Base

TOP SECRET

weren't shot.

You'd be arrested and spend the war in jail—if you is you'd make a spy. The bad news is it's a *German* spy. Difficult, eh? If you scored six out of six the good news Down *South* = *Southampton!* *Chattanooga* = *Chatham.*

Answers: 1e), 2c), 3a), 4f), 5d), 6b). How did you score?

That was too easy. So try this quick quiz. . .

Sly spy

Which of the following statements are true?

1   MI5 agents used girl guides to carry their messages . . . but the girls had to promise not to read them.

THEY ARE MOVING ARMY GROUP 'C' UP TO THE FRONT, SECTOR 'NORTH', OUTSIDE ARRAS AND BRINGING THE 4th HIGHLANDERS BACK TO THE RESERVE LINES

HMM...I'D BE INCLINED TO LEAVE GENERAL SMITS WHERE HE IS AND REINFORCE HIM WITH THE ROYAL WESSEX REGIMENT

2   An American (spying for Germany) was arrested as soon as his socks were tested. When they were soaked in water they produced invisible ink.

THESE SOCKS ARE FULL OF INVISIBLE INK!

WHAT SOCKS?

3   A German spy put up a poster in Portsmouth offering £5

to anyone who would give him information about the warships there.

4 British spies in Germany were told, "If someone starts taking an interest in you then you will end up having to kill him. So don't waste time. Do it."

Answer: The above statements are all totally ridiculous. And they are all totally *true*. Girl guides *were* used to carry messages (because they proved more reliable than boy scouts!) and Brit agents in Germany really were "licensed to kill." In November 1997, MI5 published the secret files at last and these wacky facts came to light.

1916–The year of the Somme

In 1914, millions of men had rushed to join their armies and fight for their countries. By 1916, they are trained and ready and are sent off to fight the biggest battle ever. The battleground is around the river Somme in northern France.

This is to be the battle that ends the war for good! All it does is end the war for the million or so captured, wounded or killed. For the rest it goes on . . . and on and on . . .

Timeline 1916

25 January Conscription comes to Britain. That means fit, single men *have* to join the army whether they like it or not.

February The French and Germans begin the longest battle of the war, at the fortress of Verdun in north-eastern France. Even Big Bertha (that's a gun firing one-ton shells, not a woman) can't win it for the Germans.

March German soldiers are told to have one day a week without food to save on supplies . . . but the officers seem to eat well *every* day!

24 April The Irish rebel against British rule and try to seize Dublin *Post Office*! Brits soon *stamp* that out!

May The only great sea battle of the war takes place at Jutland.

49

Germans claim victory but never try to fight the Brit navy again.

5 June Lord Kitchener's face is on a million posters saying "Your country needs YOU!" Today he dies when his ship hits a mine.[1]

1 July The Battle of the Somme begins. Today Brits outnumber Germans seven to one . . . but lose seven men to every one German. Very bloody draw.

10 August A frightful news film, *The Battle of the Somme*, is shown in Brit cinemas even though it's not over yet. It's seen by 20 million shocked Brits.

15 September New Brit super-weapon, the "Willie," enters the war. Luckily someone has changed its name to the "Tank," giving rise to a horrible historical joke. Question: There were two flies in an airing cupboard. Which one was in the army? Answer: The one on the tank.

October In a Brit election the "Peace" candidate is heavily defeated by the one supporting the war. For all the bloodshed, Brits back home still don't want peace.

1. In 1930, a German spymaster said that *he* arranged to have Kitchener killed. He claimed he got Irish enemies of Britain to sneak a bomb on board Kitchener's ship, then he watched from the shore as the bomb was detonated. Don't believe him. It was a mine!

14 November End of the Battle of the Somme. Allied and German losses—over 1.3 million men. Allied gains—six miles. That's 120 men for every yard of ground won. Expensive ground.

7 December Lloyd George becomes new Brit prime minister. Old prime minister Asquith says, "I distrust him."

Silly (but true) story

In the great Somme advance of 1 July 1916, a soldier was given the job of taking a messenger pigeon in a basket to the front. He was told that an officer would use it to send a message when the first target was reached.

Back at headquarters they waited hours and hours for the pigeon and finally it appeared. The anxious commander cried, "Give me the message!" and it was handed to him.

He opened it and read, "I am absolutely fed up with carrying this bloody bird around France."

Daft DORA

Who was DORA? DORA was Britain's Defence of the Realm Act. And DORA could be *very* fussy.

The people of Britain had to live by DORA's rules. But

which rules? Here are some strange regulations. But which are real DORA rules and which are real daft rules?

DEFENCE OF THE REALM ACT

YOU MUST NOT

1... loiter under a railway bridge
2... send a letter overseas written in invisible ink
3... buy binoculars without official permission
4... fly a kite that could be used for signalling
5... speak in a foreign language on the telephone
6... ring church bells after sundown
7... whistle in the street after 10 p.m. for a taxi
8... travel alone in a railway carriage over the Forth Bridge
9... push a handcart through the streets at night without showing a red light at the back and a white light on the front
10... eat sweets in the classroom

One rule which upset children was the one that said, "You must not keep fragments of Zeppelins or bombs as souvenirs." All children hunted for these and ignored the law.

What's a Zeppelin? A huge German airship that flew over Britain and dropped bombs on cities. No one in Britain had ever suffered this sort of attack before and some people feared the dangers a bit too much.

Zeppelin Zep-panic

DORA ordered that no lights could be shown after dark. In 1916, in York, the first person fined was Jim Richardson, who was fined five shillings for lighting a cigarette in the street at night. The Zep-panicking magistrate told him that a lighted match could be seen by a Zeppelin flying 2,000 feet up.

The Rev. Patrick Shaw was arrested for showing a light from his church, despite his plea that it was only a "dim religious light." The Zep-panicking magistrate fined him anyway.

Police also banned loud noises. In York, the Chief Constable told residents. . .

> *Do not laugh in the street, stop your dogs barking and do not bang doors because all these noises can be heard from a Zeppelin listening for its target.*

The man was clearly a Yorkshire *pudding*! But was he any worse than the newspaper that had the bright idea to light a huge area of empty countryside at night to attract Zeppelins, and then destroy them—like moths around a candle flame!

Foul food and worse water

If you think school dinners are bad then you should be glad you didn't live in Europe in 1914–18. It's hard to tell if the food and drink was worse at home or in the army.

Would you like a cup of tea in the trenches? Or would you prefer a drink of milk in your wartime home?

You'd like tea in the trenches? Well, the soldiers' water had chloride of lime added to kill the germs in it. The trouble was the chloride of lime made the water taste *terrible*, even when it was boiled and used to make a cup of tea. It's a bit like drinking your local swimming pool water. Yeuchy. So, would you prefer. . .

Milk at home? In London, William Saxby, a milkman, was sentenced in 1917 to two months' hard labour for selling his customers milk watered down with "foul water obtained from a public lavatory basin." Yeuchier!

Rotten rations

British soldiers were offered a delightful tinned stew called Maconochie. A joke recipe appeared in a soldiers' newspaper. Sadly, it was close to the truth!

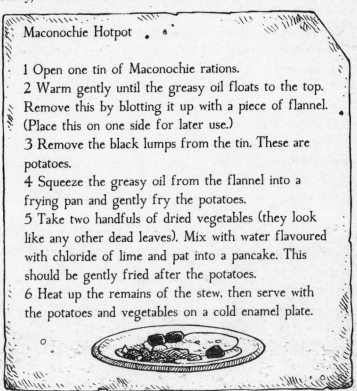

Maconochie Hotpot

1 Open one tin of Maconochie rations.
2 Warm gently until the greasy oil floats to the top. Remove this by blotting it up with a piece of flannel. (Place this on one side for later use.)
3 Remove the black lumps from the tin. These are potatoes.
4 Squeeze the greasy oil from the flannel into a frying pan and gently fry the potatoes.
5 Take two handfuls of dried vegetables (they look like any other dead leaves). Mix with water flavoured with chloride of lime and pat into a pancake. This should be gently fried after the potatoes.
6 Heat up the remains of the stew, then serve with the potatoes and vegetables on a cold enamel plate.

Soldiers were also given bully beef (like corned beef) to which they liked to add raw onions. Sometimes they had to eat this with hard biscuits.

The French peasants who gave rooms to British soldiers were glad of these biscuits . . . they made excellent fire-starters!

Jam was usually plum and apple and arrived in the trenches in tins. Empty tins made useful homemade grenades!

Young soldiers suffered badly. Ernest Parker, a soldier in the 10th Battalion of the Durham Light Infantry, said. . .

> *Army food was monotonous and in the trenches bully beef and bread, often without butter or jam, was the usual fare. Teenagers like myself were always hungry. Alas, when we needed food most it sometimes did not arrive at all, and it was far from pleasant to spend 24 hours or more in the front line with nothing to eat. Sometimes when drinking water did not arrive, we were driven to boiling water from shell holes and this may account for the crop of boils and diarrhea that plagued us.*

Apart from the bully beef and the Maconochie the soldiers had two other big food complaints. . .

One was the cakes that friends and family sent from home! Deadlier than a German bullet some soldiers reckoned.

The other pet hate is explained in a popular poem of the time. . .

Fear

A terror hangs over our heads,
I scarcely dare to think
Of the awful doom that each one dreads
From which the bravest shrink.
It's not the crashing shrapnel shell,
It's not the sniper's shot,
It's not the machine gun's burst of Hell,
These matter not a jot.
It's a far worse thing than that, son,
With which we have to grapple.
It's if we see another one
More tin of Plum and Apple.

Horse sense

The Allied soldiers complained but it was even worse for the German army. One tip sent to the soldiers read. . .

> For tender roast horse flesh, you should boil it first in a little water, before you put it in the roasting pan.

But they only ate horses for the *mane* course.

Suffering civilians

British people may have gone hungry from time to time. But the people of Germany were starving for most of the First World War.

As early as 1915, "Eat less" posters appeared all over Germany with the "Ten food commandments." These included. . .

No.7 Do not cut off a slice of bread more than you need to eat. Think always of the soldiers in the field who would rejoice to have the bread which you waste.

Belly laughs

The British people believed that the Germans would be starved into defeat. In 1914, Germany only produced 80% of its food, 20% had to be imported, so the blockade of Germany by the Royal Navy caused severe shortages and suffering.

By the end of the war Germans *were* starving, but in September 1915 they could still laugh about the British blockade. That month a Zeppelin raid on London dropped 70 bombs, killing 26 people and wounding almost 100. But the crew also dropped a ham bone attached to a parachute. On it was written, "A gift from starved-out Germany."

By September 1918, the German people had stopped laughing . . . and they didn't have spare ham bones for jokes.

Hunger horrors

We all know what it's like to be hungry, but very few people in Europe today know what it's like to be *really* starving, year after year.

Maybe you could try this diet for just *one day* and see how it feels. (Get your friends to sponsor you and give the money to a good cause.) Then remember this is how most Germans ate in the winter of 1916–1917 on a *good* day. It was known as the Turnip Winter because turnip was the only food that was plentiful.

The Turnip Winter diet
You need:
six slices of bread
50g of meat
two teaspoons of sugar
two teaspoons of coffee
50g of cheese
one cup of soup
vegetables (half a turnip, handful of peas, beans, mushrooms); nuts; half a cup of blackberries

Breakfast
Two slices of bread (no butter), one cup of coffee with a spoonful of sugar but no milk
Lunch
Soup with meat and turnip chopped in, peas and beans added. Cup of coffee, two slices of bread
Supper
Cheese, two slices of bread, water
Snacks
Nuts and berries

And, now, the *bad* news. . .
- You would only have the mushrooms, nuts and berries if you'd gone out and picked them in the autumn. (You might have to fight the squirrels for the juicy ones!)
- The meat would probably be horse or dog. (After a day of

the Turnip Winter diet you may look at your pet poodle and lick your lips.) Even the kangaroos in the German zoos were killed and eaten.

- You might not even be able to get dog meat. In April 1916, all Berlin butchers were closed for five days because they had no supplies of anything. In July 1916, women demonstrated outside the Town Hall in Dusseldorf demanding more meat and potatoes. When the Mayor offered them more beans and peas, they rioted and smashed every window in the Town Hall.
- Cream was only obtainable on a doctor's prescription.
- The German newspapers tried to calm things down—one published a long article proving that overeating was the cause of baldness!
- By late 1916, women queued outside food shops all night, bringing camp stools, knitting, etc. (One woman was seen in a queue with a sewing machine to pass the time.)

Hot chestnuts

While Germans were starving, Brits were getting ready for the day when they would have to live with less food. In January 1918, this poster appeared. . .

Healthy advice even today. But some of the recipes look as tasty as a can of vegetarian cat food.

The National Food Economy League Book of Wartime Recipes had this recipe that you may like to try if you really want a taste of the First World War (or if you are the sort of dustbin that would swallow anything).

Chestnut curry
You need:
one pound chestnuts; ½ to ¾ pint curry sauce
Method:
1 Slit and boil the chestnuts for 20 minutes. Remove both outer and inner skins very carefully. (To do this, leave in the hot water and peel one by one.)
2 Place in a casserole dish with curry sauce (made from a tablespoon of curry powder and a tablespoon of flour in ¾ pint of water).
3 Put in a medium heated oven to simmer for two hours, until the chestnuts have taken up all the water and are thoroughly tender.
4 Serve with plain, boiled rice.

No wonder the Brits sang. . .

My Tuesdays are meatless,
My coffee is sweetless,
Each day I get poorer and wiser.
My home it is heatless,
My trousers are seatless,
My God, but I do hate the Kaiser.

But by 1916 it wasn't only the Brits who hated the Kaiser. The Germans were beginning to turn against him. And no wonder. If food was bad in Britain, it was worse in Germany. . .

Fake food

All Germans who lived through the First World War remembered not only the lack of food, but the frightful food *substitutes* that they were forced to eat—known as "ersatz" food. As the war dragged on, exhibitions were held all over Germany to demonstrate the huge range of ersatz food and drinks. For example. . .

Bread soon contained flour made from beans and peas, and often sawdust was added.

Cakes were made from clover and chestnut flour.

Meat was replaced by the rice lamb chop or the vegetable steak (pale green, made from spinach, spuds, ground nuts and eggs substitute).

Butter was "stretched" with starch or made from a mix of curdled milk, sugar and yellow colouring.

Eggs were made from a mix of maize and potatoes.

Pepper was "stretched" with ashes.

Fats—many attempts were made to make fats: from rats, mice, hamsters, crows, cockroaches, snails, worms, hair clippings, old leather boots and shoes. None of those was very successful.

Coffee was first made from roast nuts flavoured with coal tar—with sugar this was OK! Later came coffee-ersatz-ersatz—roasted acorns or beech nuts. Later still, when all acorns had to be fed to pigs, came coffee made from carrots and turnips.

Horrible? At least they filled the stomach. By late 1918, even ersatz foods had run out. For German soldiers struggling to fight, a meal might be turnip stew served with chunks of turnip bread.

Hungry people lose the will to fight. Germans lost that will—the Allies, who hadn't suffered nearly so much, did not lose their will. It's one of the reasons the Germans lost. It was also a reason why the Germans felt so bitter at losing. All that pain for nothing. Ten years after the First World War ended, that bitterness drove them to support Adolf Hitler and a second war.

1917 – The year of the mud

The winter of 1916–17 is bitterly cold, but especially for the French. The Germans hold the north-west where most French coal mines are. One jeweller in Paris places a small lump of coal surrounded by diamonds in his window.

Houses in Paris are allowed only one electric light in each room (anyone caught with more will have their electricity cut off for three weeks!).

In Germany coal is just as short. Berlin lights are to be put out by nine p.m. Elephants from the circus are used in Berlin to pull coal carts from the railway stations—it saves wasting coal on steam trains or using horses that could be working in the army. German workers go on strike, while French soldiers have their own rebellion. Everyone is desperate for peace—but the war goes on . . . and on.

Timeline 1917

January A munitions factory blows up in Silvertown, East London, killing 69.

February The Russian people rebel against their leaders and Russian soldiers lend their rifles to help the revolution. Good news for Germany.

March In Britain, the Women's Army Auxiliary Corps (WAAC) is founded and a new joke is born. . .

April The Doughboys are here! No, not bakers' men, but American soldiers as the USA joins the war.

TROTSKY OVER HERE AND LENIN US A HAND

WHAT IS BETTER THAN A SMACK IN THE EYE?

A WAAK ON THE KNEE!

HO HO

Meanwhile, French troops rebel against their conditions.

May UK horse racing stopped, followed by county cricket and league football.

June Brit ban on rice being thrown at weddings and feeding birds—food is too precious.

July The war now costs Britain nearly £6 million a day. Will they run out of money or men first?

1 August Terrific rainstorms as the British attack in Flanders. The mud is as deadly an enemy as the Germans.

4 September German submarines shell Scarborough, England. Why shell a seaside holiday town when it has a beach full of shells?

October Brit bakers allowed to add potato flour to bread while French bread has become grey, soggy stuff.

November War between Russia and Germany coming to an end as the Russian Bolsheviks start to take over their country.

6 December German Giants reach London. (They're bomber aircraft, not monster men.) They're harder to catch than the old Zeppelins.

Wild Western Front

From November 1914 the two huge armies dug trenches in the ground and faced one another in a line from Belgium to Switzerland. From time to time one tried to attack and push back the other. The defenders usually won in the end . . . but only after both sides had lost large numbers of men.

Lots of books have described trench life on the Western Front. The soldier's only comfort was that it was just as bad for the enemy as it was for himself. Here are five descriptions of trench life from Allied or Central Power soldiers. But which are which?

1 Which side suffered disgusting trenches?

> Lice, rats, barbed wire, fleas, shells, bombs, underground caves, corpses, blood, liquor, mice, cats, filth, bullets, fire, steel; that is what war is. It is the work of the devil.

2 Which side fought till they were exhausted skeletons?

> There were about 20 men. They walked like living plaster statues. Their faces stared at us like those of shrunken mummies, and their eyes seemed so huge that one saw nothing but eyes. Those eyes, which had not seen sleep for four days and nights showed the vision of death. Was this the dream of glory that I had when I volunteered to fight?

3 Which side fought because they thought it was their duty to God and that he was on their side?

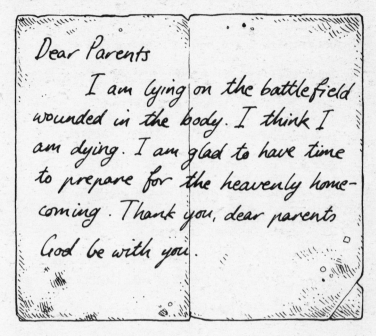

Dear Parents

I am lying on the battlefield wounded in the body. I think I am dying. I am glad to have time to prepare for the heavenly home-coming. Thank you, dear parents God be with you.

4 Which side believed that its heavy shells would destroy the enemy trenches so all they had to do was walk across no man's land and take over?

For some reason nothing seemed to happen to us at first. We strolled along as though walking in the park. Then, suddenly, we were in the midst of a storm of machine gun bullets and I saw men beginning to twirl round and fall in all kinds of curious ways as they were hit—quite unlike the way actors do it in films.

5   Which side sometimes shot the enemy as a sport?

We did some sniping . I had a very good corporal who was an excellent shot. He and I had a shooting competition. We took turns at the enemy in front of us while they were running about and moving around from time to time. That kept our troops amused and took their minds off the mud that was up to their knees.

Terrible toilets

A German writer described the pleasures of being out of the front line. What would you do to relax? Sleep? Write letters to your family? Clean your toenails? Not Erich Maria Remarque, the author of the famous book *All Quiet on the Western Front*, who said that. . .

> *The experienced soldiers don't use the unpleasant, indoor, common toilet, where 20 men sit side by side in a line. As it is not raining, they use the individual square wooden boxes with carrying handles on the sides. They pull three into a circle and sit there in the sun all afternoon, reading, smoking, talking, playing cards.*

In the front line trenches it was different and more dangerous. There were no toilets in the Brit trenches, just buckets. If you upset the sergeant you would be given the job of taking the buckets out after dark. Your job was to dig a hole and empty the buckets. Once you were out of the cover of the trenches you were in danger, but some soldiers still lit cigarettes to hide the smell from the buckets. Enemy snipers were just waiting to aim at the glow of a cigarette end. Emptying toilet buckets could be bad for your health.

THAT ROTTEN SNIPER HIT ME RIGHT IN THE BUCKETS

Even *going* to the toilet shed just behind the trenches was dangerous. The enemy knew men used these toilets at dawn and liked to drop a few shells among the toilet huts to catch the soldiers with their pants down!

Terrible toilet tale no. 1. . .
A major found some deserted houses for his men. He looked at the sign at the end of the street and copied it carefully. Then he sent a message to his soldiers. . .

You will find rooms in "Verbod te wateren"

Unfortunately, he couldn't read Flemish and didn't understand that the sign *wasn't* the street name. It was a warning notice that said, "You must not pee in the street."

Terrible toilet tale no. 2. . .
Army boots had to be tough. The trouble was the leather was so hard it gave men blisters. Old soldiers knew the answer. . .

You probably won't want to try this with your new school shoes. But, if you do, remember to *empty* them before you put them on!

Terrible toilet tale no. 3. . .

In the 1917 battles in Flanders the troops didn't have properly built trenches, just shell holes protected by sandbags. And there were certainly no toilet huts. One officer complained. . .

If you wanted to do your daily job of urinating and otherwise there was an empty bully-beef tin, and you had to do that in front of all your men, and then chuck the contents (but not the bully-beef tin) out over the back.

He forgot to mention one important thing. Find out which way the wind is blowing first!

Frightful fun and gruesome games

If you grew bored with "chatting" you could always try one of the violent entertainments that soldiers used to pass the time. . .

Games you wouldn't want to play

1   Free the prisoner (Australian Rules)

To play:
   • a grenade
   • a German prisoner

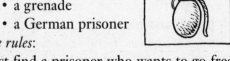

The rules:

First find a prisoner who wants to go free. Take him to the gates of the prison and place a hand grenade in his back pocket. Pull the pin out of the grenade (which will explode in five seconds). Hold the prisoner for a count of "One—two," then release him and tell him to run. If he gets the

71

grenade out of his pocket in the remaining three seconds he is the winner and is free to go. If he gets the grenade out of his pocket and throws it back at you then you are the losers. But that's the risk you take.

HEY LADS, HE MUST'VE HAD A HOLE IN HIS POCKET...

LADS?

There are reports of this happening, so it is probably true, but extremely rare.

2   Beetle racing

You need:
- two or more beetles
- a table
- sugar
- matchsticks

To play:
Each "jockey" chooses a beetle and holds it at one end of the table. A sugar lump is placed at the other end of the table to attract the beetles. Every jockey places one matchstick on the table. On a signal, the beetles are released. The first beetle to reach the sugar wins and the winning jockey collects everyone else's matchsticks. (And the beetles get to eat the sugar.)

I'M A WOOD BEETLE. I'D RATHER EAT THE MATCHSTICK

3   Sea swimming
You need:
- the sea

To play:
At Gallipoli, the chief hobby for Anzac troops was swimming. This took a lot of courage because the Turkish army were shelling the beaches. Troops swam for fun and to keep cool (but also because there was no water for washing in the trenches). Beaches were somewhat spoilt by the sight and smell of dead horses, mules and donkeys.

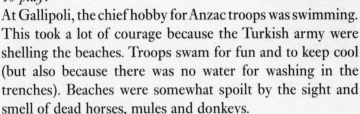

IT'S STILL BETTER THAN AN ENGLISH BEACH

4   Barge boating
You need:
- a wooden box
- two shovels

In 1917, as Sergeant Ernest Parker was sitting reading at the entrance to his dugout in the banks of the Yser canal, he saw an exciting regatta. . .

Lustily plying two oars, a ruffian member of my band was propelling a rectangular box up and down the canal. Shovels were the oars and when rival craft were launched a naval battle began, cheered by the spectators, who were hoping that somebody would take a plunge into the black slime of the canal.

Weird words

If you were a British soldier in the First World War, you would soon learn a new language—army slang. In fact, there were *two* languages to learn—one used by the officers and one by the ordinary soldiers.

Could you learn to "sling the bat" (speak in the local language, that is) with the soldiers or the officers?

Batty bat slinging
What would you do if someone came up to you and said. . .

Of course that will all make perfect sense to you. No? Oh, well, here's an explanation. . .

1 I'd love some nice meat pudding followed by bread and cheese, washed down with a cup of strong tea. For afters (dessert) I'd like jam on bread.

2 Now, my good man, this afternoon (p.m.) we need some tidying up before the mad army chaplain comes to inspect our sleeping bags.

3 I received a wound that will get me sent home when a mortar bomb, a mine and another mortar bomb landed in my dugout.

4 I am itching from all the lice in my shaggy fur coat and I wish I was back in my normal street clothes.

Sometimes the soldiers cheered themselves up by making fun of official army language. Their daily ration of spirits was "service rum, diluted"—SRD. But the sergeant who served it out tended to get to a trench and say, "I'll have mine with you," and pour himself a tot.

He did the same in every trench. If you were unlucky enough to be in the last trench then there was no rum and a very drunk sergeant. So what did SRD stand for? "Seldom reaches destination!"

And the Royal Army Medical Corps (RAMC) became the "rob all my comrades" because soldiers suspected medical staff went through the pockets of the wounded men.

The same RAMC would sometimes be unsure what was wrong with a patient so they labelled him "not yet diagnosed" (NYD). Soldiers swore the letters stood for "not yet dead."

Esses Ink Gee Nuts Ack London—Toc Ack London King!
No, that isn't a secret code to *disguise* the meaning of messages. It's a way of making messages quite *clear* over a crackling phone line. So "Harry – Edward – London – London – Oranges" is "Hello."

Learn the list, impress your friends and confuse your teacher with the Great War code. . .

A = Ack	J = Johnnie	S = Esses
B = Beer	K = King	T = Toc
C = Charlie	L = London	U = Uncle
D = Don	M = Emma	V = Vic
E = Edward	N = Nuts	W = William
F = Freddie	O = Oranges	X = X-ray
G = Gee	P = Pip	Y = Yorker
H = Harry	Q = Queen	Z = Zebra
I = Ink	R = Robert	

76

Nutty names

Any names in the language of the enemy were suddenly unpopular.

France has a perfume called "eau de Cologne" (water of Cologne), but Cologne is in Germany. They tried to change it to "eau de Provence" because Provence is in France, but the idea never caught on.

The name changing went further in Germany. All bars, hotels and shops with English or French names were changed, causing great confusion.

In Breslau, the German military governor went to a sweet shop. . .

In 1915, Italy joined the war against Germany, and Berlin cafés stopped serving "Italian salad". . .

Jolly Germans

Even in the gloom of the war Germany kept its theatres open. But the plays were pretty miserable. The most popular one of 1917 was "Maria Magdalena" about life in a small town. Well, that's not quite true . . . it's more about *death* in a small town!

Which character would you like to be? Can you pick the *two* that stayed alive?

1 Mrs. Magdalena – a hard-working and caring mum
2 Mr. Magdalena – a hard-working and caring dad
3 Maria – their daughter, a beautiful and popular girl
4 The cat – the family's faithful, furry friend
5 Fritz – Maria's lover
6 Hans – a rival for the love of Maria

Want a clue? Of the four who die, one dies in a duel, one suffers a fit on stage, one puts a bullet through their brain and (best of all) one throws themselves down a well.

Answer: The mother dies of a fit on stage, Fritz is killed in a duel with Hans who commits suicide, so Maria jumps into a well. At the end only the father and the family cat are still alive!

Ropey rhymes
Poetry from the First World War is still remembered and enjoyed today by millions of people. Quite rightly.

But there were also some popular rhymes that have been forgotten. The simple poems and songs that soldiers repeated to try and stay cheerful in the bad times. The *bad* news is that most of them are too rude to be printed—even in a horrible history!

But here are a few that you may enjoy.

(Hint: Dig a hole in your back garden, flood it with water and sit there for a few hours while your family throw pots, pans or pianos out of upstairs windows on to you. This will get you in the mood.)

1   This limerick was popular around 1915. . .

There was a young lady of Ypres
Who was hit in the cheek by two snipers.
The tunes that she played
Through the holes that they made
Beat the Argyll and Sutherland pipers.

2   Private Stanley Woodburn wrote his will on a postcard and carried it in his pocket. He wrote it as a poem. . .

My belongings I leave to my next of kin,
My purse is empty there's nothing in;
My uniform, rifle, my pack and kit,
I leave to the poor devil they will fit;
But if this war I manage to clear
I'll keep it myself for a souvenir.

Private Woodburn was killed in France in April 1918.

3   Star of silent films Charlie Chaplin left his home in

England in 1913. When the war started a year later he did not return to join the army. Soldiers made up a popular song. . .

The moon shines bright on Charlie Chaplin,
His boots are cracking, for want of blacking.
And his little baggy trousers they want mending,
Before we send him to the Dardanelles. . .

Charlie didn't see the joke! "I really thought they were coming to get me!" he said. "It scared the daylights out of me."

4   Many Brit soldiers had their own monthly magazines in the trenches. The poems they published were a bit of fun in the misery of the war. . .

There was a young Boche at Bazentin
Who liked the first trench that he went in.
But a 15 inch "dud"
Sent him flat in the mud
And he found that his helmet was bent in.

5   Not all of the poems were funny. There were some things that soldiers said over and over again to cheer themselves up. This simple poem in a trenches' magazine took three of the sayings as its first three lines, then added its own fourth line. . .

It's a long road that has no turning,
It's never too late to mend;
The darkest hour is before the dawn
And even this war must end.

6 Poems were used in the hate-war against the enemy. In a children's magazine there was one to warn of the dangers of German toys which, of course, were supposed to be poisonous!

Little girls and little boys,
Never suck your German toys;
German soldiers licked will make
Darling Baby's tummy ache.
Parents, you should always try
Only British toys to buy;
Though to pieces they be picked,
British soldiers can't be licked.

7 Soldiers were fond of singing. When they couldn't find a suitable song they took a popular one and changed the words. In 1914 they were singing. . .

Though your heart may ache a while
. . .never mind.
Though your face may lose its smile
. . .never mind.
For there's sunshine after rain
And then gladness follows pain,
You'll be happy once again
. . .never mind.

The words were soon replaced by more bitter ones. . .

If you're hung up on barbed wire
. . .never mind.

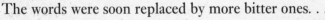

Or. . .

> *If your sleeping place is damp*
> *. . .never mind.*
> *If you wake up with a cramp*
> *. . .never mind.*
> *If your trench should fall in some*
> *Fill your ears and make you dumb*
> *While the sergeant drinks your rum*
> *. . .never mind.*

8   Love songs became war songs. . .

> *If you were the only girl in the world,*
> *And I were the only boy,*
> *Nothing else would matter in the world today,*
> *We would go on loving in the same old way.*
> *A garden of Eden, just made for two. . .*

Became. . .

> *If you were the only Boche in the trench,*
> *And I had the only bomb,*
> *Nothing else would matter in the world that day,*
> *I would blow you up into eternity.*
> *A Chamber of Horrors, just made for two. . .*

9   Even religious songs were made fun of. "What a Friend we Have in Jesus" became. . .

When this lousy war is over, oh how happy I will be,
When I get my civvy clothes on, no more soldiering
   for me.
No more church parades on Sunday,
No more putting in for leave.
I will kiss the sergeant major,
How I'll miss him, how I'll grieve.

(The word "lousy" in the first line was often replaced by a ruder word.)

10 But the song that summed up the First World War the best was the simplest one of all. It was sung to the tune of "Auld Lang Syne" (the one drunken parents join hands to sing at New Year and embarrass you with).

We're here because we're here because
We're here because we're here.
We're here because we're here because
We're here because we're here.

Says it all really.

Horrible historical joke
The soldiers in the front line enjoyed a joke, even in the terror of the trenches. They produced their own magazines and their jokes were often about the senior officers who were miles behind the lines when the shooting started.

   One popular cartoon was this one. . .

Major-General (addressing the men before practising an attack in the training camp behind the lines). "I WANT YOU TO UNDERSTAND THAT THERE IS A DIFFERENCE BETWEEN A REHEARSAL AND THE REAL THING. THERE ARE THREE ESSENTIAL DIFFERENCES. FIRST, THE ABSENCE OF THE ENEMY. NOW," turning to the Sergeant Major, "WHAT IS THE SECOND DIFFERENCE?"
Sergeant Major. "THE ABSENCE OF THE GENERAL, SIR."

Painful punishments

An army, like a school, needs discipline. Men have to learn to obey orders or else. Or else what? There were various punishments that your teachers might like to adopt for your school . . . so keep this page out of their sight.

Field punishment no. 1

In this notorious Brit punishment, the offender is lashed to a gun carriage, tied by wrists and ankles for one hour in the morning and one in the evening for up to 21 days. The intention is to humiliate the soldier. It was rumoured that soldiers were lashed to guns in action.

Toothbrush torture

The Germans had their own way of dealing with problem soldiers. Troublemakers in training were. . .

- made to scrub out the Corporals' room with a toothbrush.
- made to clear the barrack square of snow with hand-brushes and dustpans.

On Sundays (the recruits' only day off) they could be. . .

- forced to parade in full uniform with pack and rifle and then practise attacking and lying down in a muddy field until exhausted and filthy. . .
- . . .then, four hours later, made to report with every item of uniform and kit cleaned, hands bleeding and raw from the cleaning.

Once those trained men were sent to the front they were given a bunch of flowers to wear in their belts.

False fable

Many British soldiers believed that German soldiers were tied to their machine guns to stop them from running away. In fact, German machine gunners wore special belts with which they could carry their machine guns and leave their hands free. If these soldiers were killed whilst carrying their gun, British soldiers would find the bodies "tied" to the guns.

Cruel court martials

If a soldier was accused of a serious crime—like dropping his weapon and running away, or shooting himself in the foot to avoid going into battle—he'd be given a trial, known in the army as a court martial.

Could you be a judge? Try these cases. . .

The case of Bellwarde Ridge

Private Allen and Private Burden were in the same regiment.

In June 1915, their regiment was ordered to move forward to the Bellwarde Ridge, France, which the Germans were defending furiously. Private Peter Allen didn't fancy walking toward machine guns, so he took his rifle and shot himself in the leg. He was sent to hospital to recover and then ordered to serve two years in prison with hard labour.

Private Herbert Burden had joined up the year before. He told the recruiting officer he was 18 but he lied. He was just 16. When he was ordered to attack Bellwarde Ridge he was just 17—the age of many schoolboys today. The attack was a

disaster and Herbert's friends died all around him. He had done his best but, in the end he turned and ran from the battlefield.

He was court-martialled and found guilty. What would you do with Herbert? Remember what had happened to Peter Allen—who didn't even get to the fight. Remember that Herbert was only a boy. And remember that he'd been under heavy fire.

a) Give him a short rest then send him back into battle.
b) Send him home because he had been too young when he joined the army.
c) Give him two years' hard labour, the same as soldiers who wounded themselves.
d) Shoot him.

The case of king's crater
Sergeant Joe Tose and his officer, Lieutenant Mundy, left the safety of their trench to patrol a huge bomb crater in no man's land known as king's crater.

As they reached the crater they were attacked by a larger patrol of German soldiers. Lieutenant Mundy was shot.

Sergeant Tose ran back to the trench and decided to warn the rest of his battalion. To slow down the German attackers, he jammed his rifle across the trench and set off for the rear trenches. As he had no weapon he was charged with "casting away his weapon in the face of the enemy."

Everyone said that he was a good soldier. (One witness said that the Germans spoke good English and, to add to the confusion, had called out "Retreat!") What would you do with Joseph Tose?

a) Give him a medal for his quick thinking in saving his patrol.

b) Take his sergeant's position from him and send him back to fight as a private.

c) Strap him to a gun carriage for two hours a day for 21 days as Field Punishment no. 1.

d) Shoot him.

Answers: In both cases the men were shot (**d.** Men who avoided battle by shooting themselves were not executed. Herbert Burden was one of three 17-year-olds who were shot by the British in the First World War.

Sergeant Tose was disgraced and forgotten. He did not even get his name on his village war memorial until his case was looked at 80 years later. His name was finally added in 1997.

In the First World War the British shot 268 men for deserting their posts. (These are just two examples.) The German records were destroyed but they must have had the same problems. Yet it seems they shot only 48 of their own men. The Russians gave up shooting their own soldiers and the Australians never shot one.

1918–The year of exhaustion

The Allies and the Central Powers have been battering at one another's doors for over three years and are exhausted. The Germans have decided to have one huge attack before they starve to death.

It is like charging with a battering ram at a rotten door. The Allies give way and are pushed back, and back and back. The Germans seem to be the winners!

But the Germans are rushing forward too quickly. Their supplies can't keep up with them and they soon run out. When the Allies stop and turn, the Germans have nothing left to give. The Allies push on and on and on. All the way to Germany. The starved and feeble Germans are the losers . . . and all because they had been the winners.

Timeline 1918

January Britain is forced to have two meatless days a week and no meat for breakfast. Shops with margarine are raided by desperate women!

25 February Meat, butter and margarine rationed in the south of England and the queues (and the fighting shoppers) stop.

21 March Called the "last day of trench warfare." The Germans break out and smash the Allies back from the trenches. Shells fall on Paris.

1 April The Royal Air Force is formed and celebrate by shooting down German ace von Richthofen— the Red Baron—three weeks later.

May The German government wants young people to marry before they are 20 to produce more children for the country (which is running short of people).

June Thirty people die in Lancashire. They had Spanish 'flu. No one has any idea how many millions it's about to kill. Far more than the war, for sure.

18 July At the Marne River the Allies stop retreating. The tide is turning back toward Germany. The Russians massacre their royal family.

8 August German General Ludendorff calls this "the black day for the German army" as they are driven back. Still, no one expects the war to end this year.

29 September Bulgarians have had enough and ask for peace. The beginning of the end for the Central Powers.

October German sailors are ordered to make one great last voyage to destroy the Brit fleet— or be destroyed. Sailors refuse and pour water on their ships' boiler fires.

9 November Kaiser Wilhelm is thrown out of Germany. He retires to Belgium. After what he did to them four years ago it's not

91

surprising they don't want him! He ends up in Holland.

11 November Armistice Day and peace is agreed at last. The peace document is signed at the 11th hour of this 11th day of the 11th month.

28 December Women vote in Britain for the first time. War has changed something, anyway.

PITY IT TOOK FOUR YEARS, FOUR MONTHS AND FOUR DAYS TO GET HERE

Suffering shock

The huge shells that exploded during a battle killed and wounded millions of soldiers. But they had another effect that no one saw and few people understood in 1914–18. It was the effect of days of endless noise and dreadful fear on men's minds. Bombardments broke the minds of some men as surely as they broke the bodies of others.

The popular name for the effect was "shell shock"—the medical name is now "post-traumatic stress disorder." It doesn't matter what you call it really. Men suffered nightmares and fear of loud noises for the rest of their lives. It affected soldiers of all countries, during battles and long after them. Three survivors tell their stories. . .

In 1916, British Lieutenant Frederick Rees explained how shell shock ruined a soldier's common sense. . .

Last night a man had an attack of nerves. He picked up a box of bombs, climbed out of the trench and threw them about in no man's land. He was lucky not to be shot. Either side would have shot him if he had come near when he still had those bombs. However, they got him back safe, poor chap.

92

George Bucher, a German officer in 1917, explained how the illness affected his side too. And some weren't as lucky as the man that Rees saw. . .

> *After four days of the bombardment a very young soldier had had enough. He climbed out of the trench with two hand grenades from which he had taken the safety pins. He told his comrades what he thought about the war. He was going to run toward the British rifle fire and throw his grenades at them. He threatened to throw them at his comrades if they tried to stop him. They let him go…*

Lieutenant A.G. May, British Army, 1917, saw how shell shock could affect different men in different ways. . .

> *The noise was impossible. Shells were bursting overhead. Near our front trench I saw a couple of our lads who had gone completely goofy. It was pitiful. One of them welcomed me like a long-lost friend and asked me to give him his baby. I picked up a tin hat from the ground and gave it to him. He cradled the hat as if it were a child, smiling and laughing without a care in the world, even though shells were falling all around us. I have no idea what happened to the poor chap but if he stayed there very long he must have been killed. A few days later I started to have uncontrollable jerking and shaking of my legs. I was quite upset because I was unable to stop it. The doctor told me I had shell shock but I did not believe this. Later I was told to go to a special hospital for shell shock victims.*

And, when the war had finished, the nightmare of shell shock went on and on, as a French soldier explained. . .

> *The noise of a slamming gate, a flaring gaslight, a train whistle, the barking of a dog or some boyish prank is enough to set off my trembling. Or, sometimes the trembling comes on without a reason. I went to a shop to do an errand for my wife. The crowd, the rustling silks, the colour of the goods—everything was a delight to look on after the misery of the trenches. I was happy and chatted merrily like a schoolboy on holiday. All of a sudden I felt my strength was leaving me. I stopped talking. I felt a shiver in my back, I felt my cheeks going hollow. I began to stare and the trembling came on again.*
>
> *In the tram I feel that people are looking at me and that gives me a terrible feeling. I feel they are looking at me with pity. Some excellent woman offers me her seat. I am deeply touched; but they look at me and say nothing; what are they thinking of me?*

"They look at me and say nothing." That was part of the pain. No one knew how to deal with a shell shocked man.

No one knew *what* to say.

Cruel for creatures

The animals that went to war didn't start the fight and didn't ask to go. But they were shot at and bombed and gassed and diseased as cruelly as their human masters. It was beastly being a beast in the First World War. If you're the sort of person who's pained by the thought of a pet with a prick in its paw, it may be better to skip this section. If you enjoy raw hamster-burgers at school dinners, read on. . .

Creature cwiz

True or false?

1 In the First World War, British dogs were horses.

2 The best horses were saved for the Army priests (the chaplains).

3 German soldiers wiped out a herd of rare European bison in Poland.

4 A British regiment made a miniature steel helmet for their pet dog.

5 The German Army fitted their horses with gas masks.

6 A chick named Dick was used to detect enemy aircraft.

7 Goldfish were banned from the battle areas because water was precious.

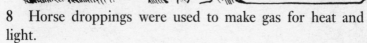

8 Horse droppings were used to make gas for heat and light.

9 Soldiers kept canaries because their song cheered everyone up.

10 The Allies won the war because they had a better supply of horses.

Answers:

1 True. The British Army supplied all the animals they needed but, to keep everything simple, they called these animals "horses" . . . even if they were guard dogs, oxen, reindeer or camels!

2 False. The chaplains were given horses at the start of the war but there was a shortage of horses for the fighting men. The chaplains had their horses taken from them and were given bicycles instead!

3 False. The herd of bison wiped out the Germans! The animals were grazing peacefully and ignoring the soldiers. Then a rifle was fired and the angry bison charged. They gored and trampled the German soldiers to death. Only 20 soldiers survived.

4 True. The dog was a stray that adopted the gunners. It became their lucky mascot. The death of the dog would have meant bad luck, so they protected it from "stray" bullets and shells with a steel helmet.

5 True. The masks (which looked a bit like a nose bag) didn't work very well and didn't protect the animals' eyes from the stinging gas. But at least the kindly Germans were *trying* to help their four-legged friends.

6 True. Driver David Spink rescued a half-starved chicken near St. Quentin in 1918 and christened it Dick. When Allied aircraft flew over it was fine, but it dived for cover (and so did David Spink's company) when an enemy aircraft was overhead. After the war Dick travelled back to Britain in Driver Spink's haversack and enjoyed a happy retirement.

7 False. Goldfish were very useful. After a gas attack the gas helmets were rinsed with water. A goldfish was then dropped into the rinsing water. If the goldfish died then the mask was still poisoned and needed to be washed again. (Sadly, there is no record of a goldfish ever getting a medal for bravery.)

8 True. A horse produced about 14 or 15 kilograms of droppings every day. (Do you ever wonder who gets the job of measuring these things?) The British alone had 870,000 horses in action by the end of the war. That is nearly 13 million kilos of horse muck being produced *every day*! Some was buried, some

burned, some spread on fields as fertilizer. But some was heated to give off a gas that powered lamps and heaters. (Might it have been quicker just to put a lighted match to the horse's bum?)

9 False. Soldiers *did* keep canaries, but they were used in underground tunnels to check for gas. (If the bird fell off its perch then there was gas down there.) Some of the bird handlers became very attached to their canaries and risked their own lives to save the birds during gas attacks. Why bother? They could always find another canary going cheap . . . Cheep! Cheep!

10 True. At least that's what British General Haig said after the war. "If the Germans had a horse service as good as the British then they would have won the war."

Brave beasts

Men and women performed some incredibly brave acts in the face of the enemy. A German hero was covered in Iron Crosses, a British hero was covered in medals and an American hero called Cher Ami was covered in feathers. Because Cher Ami was a pigeon!

Duck, dove!

No, Cher Ami didn't fly over enemy forces and drop bombs on them, stupid. He carried a message from US soldiers in battle and saved dozens of lives. Imagine the sadness when he finally died. . .

DOVE CONQUERS ALL

Cher Ami is dead. The pigeon that won the hearts of all true Americans, has hopped the twig and passed peacefully away to that great pigeon loft in the sky.

It was just a year ago that Cher Ami flew to fame when he joined Major Charles Whittlesey's brigade. In the Argonne Forest, eastern France, the brigade found itself surrounded by enemy forces, starving and exhausted with many dead and wounded. Then shells began to land on the American survivors—but they were American shells aimed at them by mistake. There was only one way to get a message out of the deadly circle of machine guns: a carrier pigeon.

Whittlesey scribbled a note: "Our own forces are dropping shells on us! For heaven's sake stop it!" He took a pigeon from its basket but the frightened bird broke loose and flew for home—the US army base camp. There was just one bird left—one last hope—a bird called Cher Ami. Whittlesey clipped the message to the brave bird's leg and set it free. But Cher Ami

full firepower of the forces towards it. One shot took off part of the battered bird's leg, passed through its chest and knocked out one eye. The peppered pigeon lost height, then, amazingly, recovered and flew on to deliver the message and the brigade was saved. "Without that bird we'd have been wiped out, that is certain," Whittlesey said. "The 384 men who survived owed their lives to Cher Ami's courage."

flew up to the nearest tree and began preening its feathers. The brigade threw sticks and stones but still the perverse pigeon refused to budge. Finally Whittlesey climbed the tree and shook the branch. Cher Ami took the hint and set off for home.

The enemy saw at once that it was carrying a message and turned the

The heroic homing pigeon was patched up and brought back to a hero's welcome in America, where he died peacefully yesterday. He will be stuffed and go on display at the Smithsonian Institute.

Feathered fighters

1 Gallant pigeons like Cher Ami had another use. If soldiers became cut off from their supplies and were starving they could always eat the birds!

2 Pigeon *pies* are very tasty, but pigeon *spies* were also valuable. Baskets full of British pigeons were dropped into

French and Belgian villages that had been captured by the Germans. Villagers could then attach messages to the pigeons who would fly back to Britain. The messages could tell the Allies what the enemy was up to. This is spying, of course, and the punishment for spying in war was to be shot. But it was even more dangerous being a pigeon. Sixteen thousand were dropped but only one in ten returned.

3   The Germans took the problem of pigeon spies seriously. They cleverly planted baskets of German pigeons in the villages. Anyone who attached a message would see the bird fly off to Germany.

4   The Germans also formed squadrons of hawks and falcons to catch any pigeon flying over the English Channel back to Britain. This was rotten luck if you were an innocent pigeon on a day trip to Paris.

5   In the mud and rain of 1917, a group of soldiers were cut off and attached a message to a pigeon. The pigeon was too soaked to fly. It flopped into no man's land . . . then started walking toward the German lines with its message! If the Germans knew the Brits were alone they would have

attacked and finished them off! The Brits had to shoot the plodding pigeon. Their other bird was just as wet. One soldier suggested drying it in the dugout oven, but in the end the soldiers dried it by blowing on its feathers. It worked.

6   A French pigeon saved hundreds of troops at Verdun in 1916. The French were being shelled by Germans but had no heavy guns of their own to fight back. They wanted to get a message out to their gunners to say, "Here are the German gun positions. Aim at them and stop them destroying us." A greyhound got the message through, though he was wounded. And a pigeon got through just before it died of its wounds. The pigeon was given France's highest *human* medal for bravery—the *Legion d'Honneur*. The men and women who won the *Legion d'Honneur* must have been a bit annoyed by this! It's like saying, "Here's your medal. Wear it with pride. You are as brave as a pigeon!"

The tale of a dog

Pigeons weren't the only courageous creatures to help their human masters in the First World War. There were dog heroes too. Heroes like Stubby the American pit bull terrier. . .

Stubby was a poor and homeless stray when Rob Conroy found him on the streets of Hartford, Connecticut. Nothing could separate these pals, not even the First World War. When Rob went to war, Stubby went with him.

Stubby was smuggled all the way to the war zone with the gallant guys in the 102nd Infantry Battalion. But he was no pampered pet, oh no! Stubby was a priceless guard dog with sharper eyes and ears than any sentry.

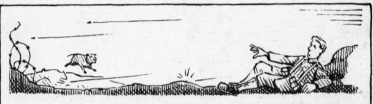

No matter what the enemy threw at him, Stubby ran out on to the battlefield and found the wounded. Then he lay beside them till the stretchers reached him. They called it no man's land, but it wasn't no dog's land!

And while the tired troopers slept, Stubby watched over them. One night he warned them of a gas attack. Another night a sneaking enemy soldier slipped into the US trenches—and left with Stubby's teeth in his butt!

Stubby fought in 17 battles. There was no way they could pin all his medals on his brave little breast—so they had a special blanket made. When the proud pooch met President Woodrow Wilson he wore it.

The First World War ended, but Stubby's work went on. He toured the country with Rob Conroy to raise money for victims of the fighting. What a courageous canine! Stubby! Man's best friend . . . ever!

Daring dogs

1 Dogs made useful messengers. They could be trained to run over the battlefield with messages fastened to their collars. Enemy soldiers watched for messenger dogs and tried to turn them into dead dogs.

2   Of course the Germans had dogs just as brave as Stubby. One was used to carry secret messages backwards and forwards across the trenches. The German dog was the perfect spy courier. The British tried everything to capture him—nets and traps all failed—until the Allied soldiers came up with a devious dodge. They set a female dog to attract him into their hands. One wag of her tail and the German spy dog was caught. (Let this be a lesson to you gentlemen readers . . . if a young lady wags her tail at you then *paws* before you run after her!)

3   Dogs were also put in harnesses and used to drag machine guns around the battlefield. The Italian army used them to pull supply carts over the Alps. In the summer this would have turned them into "hot dogs," I guess.

4   Dogs also had reels of telephone cable strapped to their backs. As they ran along they left a trail of cable behind them and linked the men in the trenches to the support troops behind them. Enemy gunners were always trying to cut these links and would shoot at cable layers. Dogs were faster than men, smaller and harder to hit than men, and it didn't matter so much if a dog was killed . . . unless you were the dog, of course.

5   When the war started, German shepherd dogs in Britain suddenly became unpopular—just because of their name! So the name was changed to "Alsatian" and it's stayed that way ever since. (If you want to test your teacher, tell them of the German shepherd name change then say, "What *other* creatures changed their English name in the First World War?" The answer is . . . the British Royal Family. They changed their family name from the German Saxe-Coburg-Gotha to Windsor. Like the Alsatians they too are stuck with it.)

6 Some dogs went across to the enemy! No, they weren't traitors. Early in the war French and German troops were in trenches just 30 metres apart. They sent each other friendly messages, newspapers and tobacco, tied to the dog's collar. One French corporal had left his wife behind in Germany when the war started. A dog brought him a message from her saying she was quite well and sent her love; the Germans passed it on by puppy post.

7 Terriers were useful for killing rats in the trenches. A devoted soldier wrote a poem to his dog, Jim. . .

Jim

A tough little, rough little beggar,
And merry the eyes on him.
But no German or Turk
Can do dirtier work
With an enemy rat than Jim.

And when the light's done and night's falling,
And shadows are darkling and dim,
In my coat you will nuzzle
Your pink little muzzle
And growl in your dreams, little Jim.

There is no record of what the rats thought of little Jim.

Of course not every company in the trenches had a rat-catcher like Jim. What did these poor soldiers do? They tamed the rats and kept them as pets instead!

Rotten for rats

Rats enjoyed the First World War . . . mostly. There was always plenty to eat because the soldiers brought tons of supplies with them. But most soldiers hated the robbing rodents and spent a lot of their spare time trying to massacre the creepy creatures. Apart from shooting them in the open they also tried some sneaky tricks. The following were all tried in the trenches with great success. . .

Vanquish Vile Vermin!
Method 1

1 If rats have been at your bread then place the ruined loaves on the floor of your dugout.

2 Find yourself a spade and flashlights. Switch out the lights.

3 When you hear the rats swarming over the bread then switch on the flashlights and smash the rats to a pulp.

Method 2

1 Place cordite at the entrance to rat holes and light it. The smoke will drive out the rats.

2 Wait by the exit and smash them with wooden clubs.

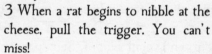

Method 3

1 Put a bayonet on the end of your rifle.

2 Put a piece of cheese on the end of the bayonet. Point it toward the enemy lines.

3 When a rat begins to nibble at the cheese, pull the trigger. You can't miss!

Horrible Histories HEALTH WARNING: Cordite was used as an explosive to propel shells from guns. A group of Australian soldiers smoked out rats this way until the cordite came in contact with an unexploded German mine. Twenty men were injured . . . but the rats were probably pulped!

Soldiers believed that rats knew when a bombardment was coming because the creatures would run away from the trenches that were in danger. They even believed that the biggest rats—usually nicknamed "corpse rats"—could kill a cat or a dog.

German soldiers often kept cats in the front line, not simply to catch rats but because cats also gave early warning of a British gas attack. They became restless, as though they could detect the poison gas in very low concentrations before the main cloud appeared.

Horrible historical joke
In June 1917, it was against British law to feed pigeons. This was part of the plan to save food. Not everyone agreed that this was a smart move.

In one of the soldiers' magazines the following joke appeared. . .

> *A driver has been punished for giving his bread ration to his horse. He certainly deserved it. We are totally against cruelty to animals.*

Women and children

The First World War affected women and children more than any other war had done. Before 1914, wars had been about men fighting men; women and children had been simply victims—they got themselves massacred if they were unlucky enough to be in a battle zone. They were starved, lost husbands and children, but they didn't *give* a lot to war efforts. That was about to change.

Wicked women

In July 1915, 30,000 women paraded in London under the banner, "We demand the right to serve." Women slowly began to take up jobs in war work, especially making weapons and ammunition (munitions).

The miserable men didn't want women in the factories. They thought it would give the women a taste of freedom and change them. They were right! By the end of the war

British women could. . .

- smoke cigarettes openly
- drink in public houses
- openly use cosmetics
- swear
- wear short skirts and bras
- wear short hair (to control the nits)
- go to the cinema without a man
- play football (most factories started girl teams)
- Then, "Land Girls," who'd taken the jobs of farm labourers, began to wear their trousers off duty!

In short, they started doing all the things men had been doing for years. (Oh, all right, you *didn't* see a lot of men in lipstick, short skirts and bras, but you know what I mean!) And women still do these shocking things today!

The German women worked just as hard but didn't earn the same sort of freedom. German men did not approve of freedom for their women. In 1917, a German politician claimed that. . .

Female freedom in England has destroyed all family life there. The women are so bad that more married men than single men offered themselves as recruits for the Army. The married men, in fact, join up to escape from their wives.

In one or two cases he may have been right!

French women were allowed to drink but only very weak wine.

It may sound fun to be a British woman, but the working women paid a high price. They worked in dangerous war jobs where. . .

- 81 died in accidents
- 71 female workers died in explosions
- 61 died of poisoning

. . .and they were only paid half of a man's wages.

It's a fair cop

How did they get poisoned? By working with high explosives like TNT that got into their lungs and blood. The symptoms were. . .

• First your nose hurt, then it bled. Your eyes stung and your throat became sore.

• You would get pains in the chest and stomach, diarrhea and skin rashes.

• If you weren't treated, you'd get sickness, giddiness,

swollen hands and feet, drowsiness and finally death.

But this didn't stop the women taking risks with the TNT. In September 1917, a young munitions worker was fined for stealing TNT from the factory where she worked. She stole it because it was common for workers to use TNT powder to give their hair a chestnut colour. But a redhead could become red hot if you struck a match near her hair!

Britain created its first policewomen during the First World War and one of their duties was to stop women workers taking explosives out of the factories, and to stop them taking cigarettes or matches into the factories. Policewoman Greta East kept a diary of her life on duty at a South Wales Munitions factory. . .

10 April 1917
The girls here are troublesome about bringing in cigarettes and matches. Last week a woman came to the Women Police

Office and asked me to rescue her coat
from the cloakroom as she had a train to
catch. She said I'd recognize the coat
because it had her payslip in the pocket.
But, when I searched the pockets I found
them full of cigarettes. Of course the
poor wretch had to be prosecuted and
fined. She must have forgotten about
them.

A pretty dim worker, but not so dim as the underground
toilets they had to use. Greta went on to describe the
conditions. . .

There are no drains because the ground
is below sea level. The result is the
toilets are a horrible and smelly swamp.
There were no lights in the lavatories
and those same lavatories are often
full of rats and very dirty. The girls
are afraid to go in.

With no lights how did you find the toilet paper? Or how did you avoid reaching out for toilet paper and picking up a rat by mistake? Yeuch!

By the end of war, 30 police forces had appointed women—another First World War idea that is still with us. (Though some, like Manchester, refused.)

Warring women

Not all women were happy to "serve" by making shells. In September 1914, French newspapers reported the story of a 28-year-old laundry woman who had been discovered fighting at the front in the uniform of a French soldier. She was sent back to her old job at the laundry but protested angrily. (Just like most people, she probably hated all the ironing.)

There is a story that a British woman also got as far as the trenches, dressed in the kilts of a Highland soldier. (This was very suitable because the Germans called the Highlanders "ladies from Hell.") She did it for a bet but was caught and returned to Britain. (It was probably the handbag that gave her away.)

By 1917, the Russian Army was so weak it created a women's battalion, "The Battalion of Death," to help. Three hundred women were led by the incredible Maria Botchkareva. Maria had been married at 15 and suffered terribly at the hands of two brutal husbands. War was wonderful compared to what she endured at home! She suffered frostbite and several wounds but survived. (She probably volunteered for the pleasure of being able to shoot at men!)

Battling babes

There are many stories of boys going into army recruiting

offices to join up even though they were under age. Many army recruiting officers were willing to let them join anyway. Of course it was their duty to check on the age and reject the ones who *said* they were under age. This story is true and happened hundreds of times all over the world...

Parents were able to "claim out" their sons if they could trace them, and the boy soldiers were sent home.

- Myer Rosenblum from London joined the London Welsh Regiment in August 1914, aged 13 years and nine months, but was "claimed out" by his father in October 1914. He joined up again and was sent to Gallipoli where he was wounded in June 1915. His father claimed him again when he was sent back to England.
- Private James Bartaby joined the 7th East Surreys, as a volunteer, on 20 January 1915, aged 13 years and ten months. After training, he went to France in late May and was wounded and sent home in October 1915.
- In October 1915, Arthur Peyman—"described as 19 years of age"—was in court, charged with being absent from his regiment since the end of August. During the case, his mother appeared and produced his birth certificate, showing that he was only 14 years old.

At least Arthur Peyman escaped being shot for leaving his regiment. Other boys were not so lucky.

Trench tot

It wasn't just the fighting boys who ended up in the trenches. Sometimes small children were caught up in the battlefields. In early 1916, Philip Impey was going back into the trenches near La Basse, when he found a small girl abandoned in a ditch. He couldn't take her to safety and he couldn't leave her, so Philip picked her up and carried her into the trenches.

During the week, she climbed on to the parapet in full view of the Germans, who were close by. German soldiers shouted to her, offering her sweets and chocolate.

When the soldiers left the front, they took her with them. She was eventually sent to England and survived. Sadly, Philip Impey was killed in action soon after.

Cheeky Charlies

British kids in 1917 were getting out of control. There was a huge increase in vandalism, theft and street crimes among school-aged children.

- Some people blamed the fact that their fathers were away in the army.
- Others blamed the cinema. (Nowadays they'd blame the television, so nothing much changes, does it?)
- A third excuse was weak teachers—old ladies, brought out of retirement, to take the place of the men who had gone off to fight. (Imagine that! Kids taking advantage of their tough teacher being away. You wouldn't do a thing like that, would you?)

In Germany the children had a surprise when the war started. In Berlin all English teachers were sacked! (But that was wartime so don't raise your hopes that it may happen for you!)

I DON'T KNOW. TRYING TO GET OUT OF LESSONS BY STARTING ANOTHER WORLD WAR SEEMS A LITTLE EXTREME TO ME

But by 1917 German children were so hungry they had a desperate new game . . . stealing any food they could find.

Wrinklies at war

- The oldest French soldier was 78 years old.
- Italy's oldest soldier was 74.
- Lieutenant Henry Webber was, at 67, the oldest British soldier killed in action at the Somme in July 1916.
- In December 1915, James White of Sowerby Bridge was sent home from the trenches when it was discovered that he had fought the Zulu War of 1878, and was 70 years old.
- In June 1918, the *Yorkshire Evening Press* told the story of a merchant sailor, William Jessop of Hull. He was 72 years old and had been torpedoed seven times.

William said. . .

Young men sometimes refuse to sail with me because they think I am unlucky.

OK JESSOP, ZIS TIME FOR SURE

- In 1915, Chief Gunner Israel Harding had his left leg broken when his ship was blown up in the Dardanelles, near Turkey. He was 84 years old. He had once been a trawlerman but had run away to join the Royal Navy and first saw active service in the Crimean War of 1853–56.

Frightful 'flu facts

By November 1918, the war had killed about eight-and-a-half million people. But that was nothing to what happened next. Spanish 'flu spread around the world. . .

- People collapsed in the streets, at work and at home.
- It appeared to hit young, healthy people more than the old or very young.
- The deadly virus attacked the lungs, which hardened, making breathing impossible: the victim finally drowned in their own fluid.
- At the moment of death, virus-laden fluid poured out the victim's mouth and nose.
- By May 1919, Spanish 'flu had killed over 200,000 in the UK and 20 million around the world—far more in one year than the war had managed in four.
- It killed more people than the Black Death.
- No one knew where it came from or why it suddenly went away.

Some men survived four years of shells, bullets and bombs only to get home safely . . . and die of the 'flu!

IF I CAN LIVE THROUGH THAT, I CAN LIVE THROUGH ANYTH... BAFF

Strange but true

US soldier Major Harry S. Truman kept his battalion guns firing till the last seconds of the First World War.

Nearly 30 years later, the Major was US President Harry S. Truman. He ordered the dropping of atomic bombs on Japanese towns. This brought the Second World War to an end.

In a strange way you could say the same man fired the last shots in the *two* world wars.

Test your teacher

Try this quick quiz on your teacher and watch as they strain their brain cell to the limit. If they get a question wrong you can jeer because they're a dunce—if they get it right you can jeer because they're probably old enough to remember the First World War!

1   If you lived in Britain in 1916 and wanted to know what it was like in the trenches, you could visit some. Where?
   a) On the French side of the Western Front near the town of Ypres.
   b) Behind the German lines, near Berlin.
   c) In Blackpool.

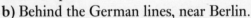

2   A British minister in charge of food production was called what?
   a) The Controller of Potatoes.
   b) The Fat Controller.
   c) Director of Army Food Transportation (DAFT).

3   Soldiers had an average of 20 lice crawling over their bodies. But what was the record?
   a) 428.
   b) 1,428.
   c) 10,428.

I DON'T KNOW WHAT'S WORSE, HAVING THEM OR HAVING TO COUNT THEM

4   French newspapers of 1914 had reports that their soldiers were very comfortable in the trenches with what?
   a) Wine.

BOTTOMS UP!   POP   HICK!   CHEERS!

b) Women.

c) Central heating.

5 What was a "wibble-wobble?"
   a) A soldier's name for a fat general.
   b) Another name for a tank.
   c) A horse with an injured leg.

6 The women who worked with TNT explosive were nicknamed "canaries." Why?
   a) They were so happy they sang like canaries while they worked.
   b) The TNT caused their hair to turn canary yellow.
   c) Because the factory owners were getting "cheep" labour.

7 The First World War changed fashions and almost killed off one fashion. What?
   a) Men wearing top hats to work.
   b) Women wearing knickers.
   c) Children wearing wooden clogs.

8 Kaiser Wilhelm of Germany was a powerful but crazy king. What was his hobby?

a) Pulling the wings off flies.

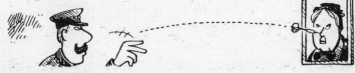

b) Throwing darts at pictures of his grandmother, Queen Victoria.

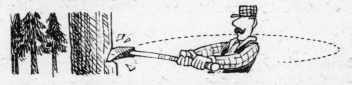

c) Chopping down trees.

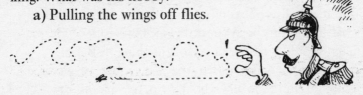

9 Brit Patrick Gara was arrested for trying to dodge joining the army. His excuse was. . .

a) His mum wouldn't let him.

b) He was a coward and was afraid of getting hurt.

c) He didn't know there was a war on.

10 Brits with hard tennis courts were suspected by the police. Why?

a) Police believed they had been prepared as gun platforms for an invasion.

b) Tennis parties were a good cover for two spies to meet and swap messages hidden in tennis balls.

c) Police thought they were up to some secret racket.

Answers:

1c) That's right, Blackpool. Soldiers recovering from wounds built replicas of the trenches at Loos. (That was a battlefield on the Western Front, not a toilet.) German people could visit the same sort of thing in Berlin.

2a) Imagine being called the Controller of Potatoes! Think of all the jokers who'd write to you and say, "My potatoes are very naughty. Can you control them for me?"

3c) As well as having 10,428 lice in his shirt, there were about 10,253 lice eggs waiting to hatch. The same man would have had thousands more in his trousers, socks and hair. It's surprising he had any blood left after the lice had had their lunch!

MAN WITH LICE
(OR LICE WITH MAN)

4c) The truth is the soldiers in the trenches had to be very careful about lighting fires. The smoke gave enemy gunners something to aim at. So you could light a fire and be shelled to death, or not light a fire and freeze to death!

5b) The army name for a tank was a "landship," but they collected lots of other names too: Slug, Whale, Toad, Tortoise, Land crab, Behemoth, Boojum. Newspapers couldn't give away the secret by showing pictures, so Brit writers described a "long, low, dust-coloured tortoise," while French newspapers reported they were equipped in front with "some kind of cow catcher." But to most soldiers it looked like a water tank and that name stuck.

6b) TNT caused nasty skin rashes and its fumes turned

the girls' hair bright mustard yellow—the colour of canaries. These unfortunate girls were often refused service in restaurants whose owners said, "You are *unsightly*. Go away because you are putting the other customers off their food!"

7a) War changed British ways of life—posh people who would never have dreamed of travelling on a tram or bus before 1914, now travelled to work every day . . . paying their fares to "conductorettes." Women's fashion changed as a shortage of steel ended the wearing of tight corsets. City gents stopped wearing top hats as they were a nuisance on a bus or underground train with a low roof.

8c) Willy enjoyed felling trees at his palace at Potsdam. He was mad about stripping off the bark—which proves he was barking mad.

9b) In 1916, Patrick Gara was up before magistrates in Selby, Yorkshire, for avoiding military service. He was asked why he had not joined the army. He replied that he thought that he was safer in Selby than in the trenches! He was fined £2 and escorted to the nearest barracks. A year later, a man called Graham Whitlaw was up before the magistrates in London for not reporting for military service. His excuse was that he was a duke and a bishop

and he had been appointed Chief of the Army. He'd been appointed by King George IV (who had been dead almost 100 years). Of course Whitlaw was trying to act as if he was too mad to serve. It didn't work.

10a) Daft, but true. What use would a gun platform be in someone's back garden? You could always shell your neighbour's peas, I suppose.

Epilogue

There were lots of tragedies in the First World War. Almost every family in Britain, France, Germany and Russia lost someone. You can go to any town or village and see the names of the dead carved on stone memorials. Many of the men who joined together died together and left their home towns desolate.

But that wasn't the *real* tragedy. The cruellest thing of all was that the First World War *didn't* solve any problems and it *didn't* bring peace. It led to the Second World War and far, far more misery, death and destruction.

Those whose names are carved on the memorials believed they were fighting for peace. Many would have given their lives gladly if they knew they had died in "the war to end all wars."

What went wrong? Big mistakes and small accidents. One accident so small that no one noticed it at the time. It happened in a German dugout during the Battle of the Somme. A British shell smashed into the trench and killed most of the Germans in it. But by a hideous chance one German escaped with just a shell splinter in his face.

He lived. He lived to start another war. His name was Adolf Hitler. Lucky Hitler—unlucky world.

Sometimes history is changed by great events like the First World War—sometimes it is changed by freak accidents in a fraction of a second: the arrow that hit King Harold in the eye at the Battle of Hastings . . . the shell that *failed* to kill Hitler.

History can be horrible. But each of us should find our nearest war memorial, stand in front of it and read the names.

Then say, "Never again."

If everyone says that, and means it, then the deaths will not have been such a waste.

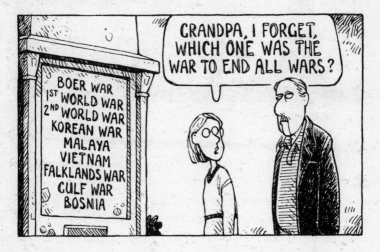

FRIGHTFUL
FIRST WORLD
WAR
GRISLY QUIZ

**Now find out if you're a
Frightful First World War expert!**

BEASTLY BATTLES

There were lots of famous fights and crazy campaigns throughout the war. See if you can figure out which of these beastly battle facts are true and which are false.

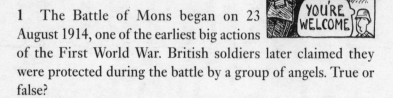

1 The Battle of Mons began on 23 August 1914, one of the earliest big actions of the First World War. British soldiers later claimed they were protected during the battle by a group of angels. True or false?

2 French soldiers were taken to the front line for the Battle of the Marne in September 1914 by taxi. True or false?

3 There were three major battles around Ypres in Belgium throughout the war. In the last battle there a young Winston Churchill—the great Second World War leader—was almost blinded in a gas attack. True or false?

4 The Battle of the Somme began on 1 July 1916, and went on until 18 November. The French and British attacked German lines. In that time the British suffered 57,470 casualties. True or false?

5 The French and British attack at Arras began on 1 October 1914. It was a failure for the Allies because they only managed to capture a single hill. True or false?

6 Verdun was the longest battle of the war, beginning in February 1916. The Germans were led by a prince. True or false?

7 The Battle of Cambrai in November 1917 was such a disaster for the British that the government ordered that church bells were not allowed to ring. True or false?

8 The Battle of Jutland in 1916 was the most famous sea battle of the war. The British won and the German fleet did not sail again for the rest of the war. True or false?

9 The Battle of Neuve-Chapelle was fought between 10–13 March 1915. More shells were fired in the first 35 minutes of this battle than in the whole of the Boer War, just 15 years earlier. True or false?

10 The Battle of the Aisne began in September 1914. It was named after a nearby town. True or false?

TERRIBLE TRENCHES QUICK QUIZ

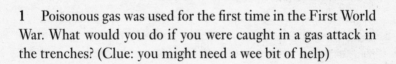

Take this quick quiz to find out if you would have survived life in the terrible trenches.

1 Poisonous gas was used for the first time in the First World War. What would you do if you were caught in a gas attack in the trenches? (Clue: you might need a wee bit of help)

2 How could you tell when an enemy bombardment was about to begin? (Clue: vile vermin)

3 Trench toilets were buckets or holes dug into the mud. With hundreds of soldiers suffering from deadly dysentery, they filled up quickly. Where could you go to poo if the foul latrines were full? (Clue: a number two in no man's land?)

4   Things could get pretty chilly in the trenches and lots of icy infantry soldiers suffered from frostbite. How did they save their frozen feet? (Clue: you'll get snow help from me!)

5   Trench foot was caused by cold, damp and unhealthy conditions (the trenches were filled with mud and water and poo and bodies). What could you do to prevent having your feet chopped off because of this disgusting disease? (Clue: grease is the word)

6   Lice loved life in the trenches. They would live on the soldiers and make a mighty meal of them. How did the men try to get rid of the lice? (Clue: flaming lice!)

7   Many soldiers tried to give themselves a "blighty" (a wound just serious enough to be sent home) to escape the terrible trenches, but what would happen if they were found out? (Clue: it was a deathly disaster)

8   If you were a sniper, what was the best way to avoid being seen by the enemy? (Clue: think about it—you'll soon twig)

9   In an emergency, what was the best way to make a splint for a soldier with broken bones? (Clue: you're gun-na have to think of something)

10   How did the army try to reduce cases of dysentery in the trenches, caused by dirty water? (Clue: water with a twist)

Nutty nicknames

Soldiers in the First World War had nicknames for everything—their weapons, ranks and rations. See if you can understand the soldiers' slang and figure out which weird words mean what.

1. Tommy	a) Senior officers
2. Brass hats	b) Experienced soldier
3. Blighty	c) Britain
4. Coffin nails	d) Cigarettes
5. Jerry	e) British soldier
6. Old sweat	f) Jam
7. Whizz bang	g) German soldier
8. Conchie	h) Tea
9. Char	i) Conscientious objector
10. Pozzy	j) Artillery shell

ANSWERS

Beastly battles

1   True. The British managed to beat back the Germans despite being outnumbered and they thought that God had sent a ghostly army of angels to help them. To this day, no one really knows the truth about the Angels of Mons. . .

2   True. France ordered every taxi cab in Paris to be available to take soldiers to the front line so they would get there in time for the big battle.

3   False. It was a young Adolf Hitler who was smothered by the ghastly gas. In the whole of the First World War, horrid Hitler was awarded six medals for bravery!

4   False. The casualty figure of nearly 58,000 was for the first day alone—1 July. This is still a record.

5   False. It was a success for the Allies because they managed to capture a single hill. That hill, known as Vimy Ridge,

captured by Canadian forces, was very important!

6   True. The Germans at the Battle of Verdun were led by Crown Prince William, son of crazy Kaiser Wilhelm.

7   False. The Battle of Cambrai was considered such a success for the British that church bells were allowed to be rung for the first time since the war began.

8   True (and false). It's true that the German fleet was so badly damaged by the British that it spent the rest of the war in dock, but no one could claim it was a great success for the British—they lost thousands of men.

9   True. Methods of warfare and weapons had changed dramatically between the end of the Boer War in 1902 and the First World War.

10 False. Like many other battles in the First World War, including the Somme and the Marne, it was named after a nearby river.

Terrible trenches quick quiz

1   Pee on your hanky and then tie it over your nose and mouth. This weird wee trick really worked—the chemicals in urine kept out the gas.

2   Watch the rats. Rats were everywhere in the stinking trenches and soldiers believed that they knew instinctively when an attack was about to happen and disappeared. If you couldn't see a rotten rat then you were probably in for a beastly bombardment.

3   A shell hole. Who needed specially dug holes when the Germans made them for you with their bombs? Just find a cosy shell hole and squat.

4   Rubbing them with snow. In fact we now know that rubbing frostbite with anything actually makes the damage worse. So

134

rubbing it with snow was not only parky and painful it was also pointless!

5   Cover your feet with grease made from whale oil. A single battalion in the trenches could use up to ten gallons of gooey grease every day!

6   They would burn them with a candle. This was a tricky business and more than one careless corporal set his clothes on fire in the process.

7   They would be shot. Yup—the usual punishment for soldiers who tried to cheat their way out of the war was to be sent for trial and killed.

8   Camouflage yourself as a tree. Sneaky snipers would slither into no man's land to get closer to the enemy. To avoid being spotted they would hide under cover of a fake tree!

9   Use your rifle. Other things could be used to help soldiers with broken bones until the medics arrived—pieces of wood, bayonets, swords—but the rifle made a good sturdy splint. Not much good if you run into the enemy while your gun's tied to your lieutenant's leg, though!

10   They added chloride of lime. This was believed to purify the water supplied—but the soldiers hated it because it made the water taste disgusting!

Nutty nicknames
1e) 2a) 3c) 4d) 5g) 6b) 7j) 8i) 9h) 10f)

INTERESTING INDEX

Where will you find "beetle-racing," "fried lice"
and "smelly whale oil" in an index? In a
Horrible Histories book, of course!

Terry Deary was born at a very early age, so long ago he can't remember. But his mother, who was there at the time, says he was born in Sunderland, north-east England, in 1946—so it's not true that he writes all *Horrible Histories* from memory. At school he was a horrible child only interested in playing football and giving teachers a hard time. His history lessons were so boring and so badly taught, that he learned to loathe the subject. *Horrible Histories* is his revenge.

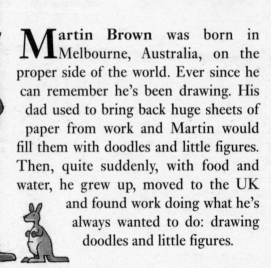

Martin Brown was born in Melbourne, Australia, on the proper side of the world. Ever since he can remember he's been drawing. His dad used to bring back huge sheets of paper from work and Martin would fill them with doodles and little figures. Then, quite suddenly, with food and water, he grew up, moved to the UK and found work doing what he's always wanted to do: drawing doodles and little figures.

Make sure you've got the whole horrible lot!

ISBN-10: 0-545-99785-2
ISBN-13: 978-0-545-99785-0

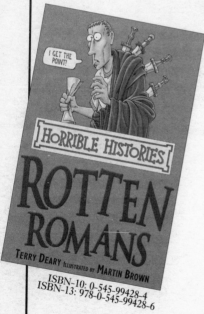

ISBN-10: 0-545-99428-4
ISBN-13: 978-0-545-99428-6

ISBN-10: 0-545-99784-4
ISBN-13: 978-0-545-99784-3

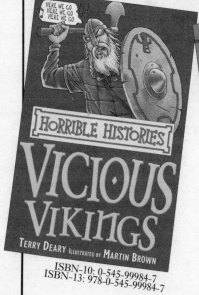

ISBN-10: 0-545-99984-7
ISBN-13: 978-0-545-99984-7

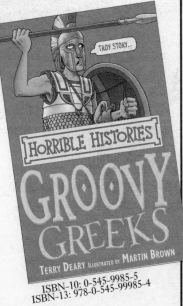

ISBN-10: 0-545-9985-5
ISBN-13: 978-0-545-99985-4

"Nice to have a woman in the house," Drew's father commented, loud enough for the neighbors in the next county to hear.

Drew cringed. Did the old man even think about how Stephanie might feel when he put her on the spot that way?

She didn't seem to have a problem with it. She chuckled and flipped the last pancake onto a plate. "I'm certainly outnumbered here, girls to boys," she said, setting the platter of pancakes in the middle of the circular oak table and tickling Matty on the ear.

The boy squealed and wiggled.

"Me, too," Jamey insisted.

Stephanie moved around the table and leaned around Drew so she could tickle both boys at once. "It's a good thing I have two hands."

Drew closed his eyes, trying not to breathe, because if he did, the oriental scent of her perfume was going to get to him. He was sure of it. He'd always been a sucker for orchids and jasmine...and now, beautiful Stephanie, whom his boys liked as much as he did.

Books by Deb Kastner

Love Inspired

A Holiday Prayer
Daddy's Home
Black Hills Bride
The Forgiving Heart
A Daddy at Heart
A Perfect Match
The Christmas Groom
Hart's Harbor
Undercover Blessings
The Heart of a Man
A Wedding in Wyoming
His Texas Bride
The Marine's Baby
A Colorado Match
*Phoebe's Groom
*The Doctor's Secret Son
*The Nanny's Twin Blessings

*Email Order Brides

DEB KASTNER

lives and writes in colorful Colorado with the Front Range of the Rocky Mountains for inspiration. She loves writing for Love Inspired Books, where she can write about her two favorite things—faith and love. Her characters range from upbeat and humorous to (her favorite) dark and broody heroes. Her plots fall anywhere in between, from a playful romp to the deeply emotional. Deb's books have been twice nominated for the *RT Book Reviews* Reviewers' Choice Award for Best Book of the Year for Love Inspired. Deb and her husband share their home with their two youngest daughters. Deb is thrilled about the newest member of the family—her first granddaughter, Isabella. What fun to be a granny! Deb loves to hear from her readers. You can contact her by email at Debwrtr@aol.com, or on her MySpace or Facebook pages.

The Nanny's
Twin Blessings

Deb Kastner

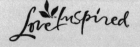

Recycling programs
for this product may
not exist in your area.

™ LOVE INSPIRED BOOKS
ISBN-13: 978-0-373-87748-5

THE NANNY'S TWIN BLESSINGS

Printed in U.S.A.

"For I know the plans I have for you," declares the Lord, "plans to prosper you and not to harm you, plans to give you hope and a future."
—*Jeremiah* 29:11

As always, to my family—
Joe, Annie, Kimberly, Katie, Isabella and Anthony.
Without your support, there wouldn't be a book.

Prologue

PARENTS OF PRESCHOOLERS ONLINE COMMUNITY
CLASSIFIED ADS

WANTED: Nanny for three-year-old twin boys. Two-month temporary live-in position includes stipend, room and board. Assistance in relocation to Serendipity, Texas, provided. Mandatory two years' experience with references. Please respond with resume and salary requirements.

Chapter One

Stephanie Cartwright would have described the Texas prairie in early spring in two words: dry and barren. Endless miles of dirt, rolling hills of dry grass and dark, skeletal weeds, stretching out as far as the eye could see.

The land was a mirror of her heart. Or maybe it was her frame of mind that was coloring the landscape in dreary shades of gray. As if that wasn't enough, she exited her subcompact rental car to find her nostrils angrily assaulted by a strange, pungent odor—no doubt the scent of cows or horses or other livestock.

Did it smell like this all the time? She hoped it was just the direction of the wind adding to the eye-watering stench in the air, because for better or for worse, Serendipity, Texas, was where she'd be living for the next couple of months. As far away from the east coast—and her ex-boyfriend—as she could get. Hidden from the world in a tiny town in the middle of nowhere.

And way, *way* out of her comfort zone.

But it wasn't as if she could turn around and go back home. There *was* no home to go back to. Trying not to breathe too deeply, she clenched her fists and fought for control as her feelings once again vacillated between devastation and anger. At any given moment since she'd boarded the plane for Texas, she had struggled with one of those emotions, sometimes both at the same time.

Her eyes widened as a large, square-headed and very intimidating dog wandered up and situated himself on the wood-planked porch steps to the house where her new employer, Drew Spencer, presumably waited.

Peachy. Another obstacle. Just what she needed….

Stephanie was a nanny. She'd expected to be greeted by children, not canines. She had little experience with animals and had never even owned a pet.

The dog shook his head and licked his chops. He appeared to be welcoming her, though she couldn't be certain. For all she knew he was putting her on the menu.

"Hello there, big guy," Stephanie crooned, speaking in the same soft, gentle tone of voice she used to calm small children. She prayed it would work. "Nice puppy."

The dog's ears pricked. His mouth curved up naturally, as if he was smiling at her, and he wagged his tail with unreserved enthusiasm. Was that a good sign?

"Don't worry. He's harmless." Warm laughter emanated from behind the screen door, startling her.

If she wasn't a twenty-three-year-old woman in perfect health, she probably would have thought she was experiencing a heart attack. Every nerve ending in her body crackled with an unexpected jolt of electricity. She hadn't realized someone was watching her, and her face flamed in embarrassment.

A man who quickly introduced himself as Drew

Spencer opened the screen and stepped out onto the porch. "Sorry about that. The four-legged Welcome Wagon that greeted you is Quincy, the over-enthusiastic pit bull. I should have put him in the house."

"He's very...friendly." Stephanie straightened her shoulders and curled her lips into what she hoped was an inviting smile.

"Very," Drew agreed, chuckling. "He may look like a tough old watchdog, but Quincy is as harmless as they come. If you were a robber he'd invite you into the house and show you where the silver was."

"I'm more interested in your gold," she teased as her gaze locked with Drew's intelligent but darkly shadowed green eyes.

Her breath caught. It was as if the scene had suddenly gone from black-and-white to a rainbow of color. To put it bluntly, the guy was one tall drink of water.

Which is to say, he was *nothing* like she'd imagined him to be.

In the emails they'd exchanged, Drew had seemed staid, rigid and academic—at least on paper. Even the times they'd spoken on the telephone, she'd thought his voice was dull and lackluster, with little emotion or variation in his tone. Somehow she'd imagined he looked the way he sounded.

The man standing in front of her, however, wasn't anything like her mental picture.

Uh-uh. Not even close.

He was wearing a pair of worn but polished brown cowboy boots, crisp blue jeans, a navy button-down dress shirt and a loosely knotted burgundy-colored necktie. He had strong-boned, even facial features, and thick brown hair lightly brushed his forehead. He looked as if he'd be as comfortable on a horse as he was in the classroom. All that was missing was the cowboy hat, and Stephanie had a good notion that he owned one.

There were no dark-rimmed, pop-bottle-thick glasses. No nerdy slouch or nutty-professor grin. Just a long, lean and fantastic-looking elementary school teacher in the guise of a cowboy.

She shook herself mentally, thoroughly appalled at where her thoughts had gone. What difference did it make whether her employer was a gorgeous cowboy or a geeky academic? She was here solely to watch over his children, not to gawk at him, and she knew how important first impressions were.

Specifically, his first impression of her.

She'd intended to appear poised and confident when she met Drew face-to-face for the first time. Not that she generally *felt* composed or self-assured—but she was good at faking it.

Widening her smile, she extended her hand. For a moment, Drew just stared at it as if he didn't know how to finish the gesture. The left corner of his mouth curved up, then down and then into a tight, straight line that matched the unyielding right side of his lips.

Stephanie nearly pulled back her arm. She couldn't tell what he was thinking. Had she botched things already?

Waves of relief washed over her when he finally reached out to shake her hand. His firm, steady grip reassured her, as did the way his mouth finally relaxed, his lips bowing upward in what could almost be considered a smile.

A tow-headed young boy peeked around Drew's leg and sized Stephanie up with a thoughtful stare. She paused, observing the child and allowing him a moment to adjust to her presence before she introduced herself to him. Presumably he was one of her two future charges, and he was a real cutie-pie, with large blue eyes and trim white-blond hair combed over to one side like a miniature Cary Grant.

Stephanie immediately relaxed. Her senses had been jarred by both the dog and the man, but kids she could handle. She was comfortable with the little ones.

She was one of the lucky ones who'd found out early what she wanted to do with her life—care for children, whether it was as a babysitter for her younger foster brothers and sisters, in her first official job as a superintendent at a bounce house or as a nanny for a high-society family. As long as there were children, she was happy.

Eventually she wanted to teach in a preschool and had already gotten her degree in early childhood education, but she had not yet pursued her teacher's certification. For now, she was content being a nanny.

"Who are you?" the three-year-old asked bluntly.

Drew coughed into his hand but she could see he was covering a smile. His eyes lightened for a moment, sparkling with barely concealed laughter. She arched an eyebrow at him, amused at how valiantly he tried to keep a straight face at the nerve of his precocious offspring.

She struggled not to giggle, herself. It was funny.

She was glad Drew hadn't corrected the boy on her behalf, as many of her foster parents over the years would have done when their children had misspoken. The child's question was direct, but it was equally as innocent.

Leave it to a three-year-old to get right to the point of the matter.

Stephanie didn't mind. She was used to the straightforward, curious nature of children. She much preferred it, in fact, versus lying, deceitful adults. At least kids were honest.

With a smile, she crouched down to the boy's level, looking him straight in the eye to let him know she was taking him—and his question—seriously.

"My name is Miss Stephanie," she answered earnestly. "And I'm happy to meet you—"

She hesitated, glancing up toward the door, seeking Drew's input on the little boy's name, since she knew she'd be caring for identical twins. Instead, the answer came from a gruff, guttural voice from somewhere behind Drew's right shoulder.

"His name is Matty." Using his cane for leverage, an older, scruffy-faced gentleman Stephanie presumed must be Drew's father inched around him. "He's the bold one. And this sweet little guy," he continued, gesturing toward the child cuddling in his arms with his face tucked shyly into the old man's chest, "is Jamey."

As far as Stephanie could see, the twins were completely identical in looks, but she had no doubt she'd be able to tell them apart once she'd spent some time with them. There were bound to be differences in personality, if not tiny distinctions in their looks.

"Hello there, Matty and Jamey," Stephanie responded as she stood upright. "How are you fellows doing today?"

Jamey curiously peeked out at Stephanie, and Matty laughed and ran around the old man's legs.

"I figure you already know that the rude fellow blocking the doorway and not inviting you inside the house is my son, Drew," the old man continued. "Although most everyone in town calls him Spence, on account of our last name." He grunted noncommittally. "And I, my dear, am Frank. Please come in."

Drew's father winked and flashed an engaging grin, then set little Jamey on his feet and ushered both boys through the door. Quincy the pit bull stood up, stretched lazily and followed the twins inside.

Drew hesitated a moment, the corners of his lips once again curving down as his brow furrowed. He shoved his hands into his pockets and shifted uncomfortably from one foot to another, looking a great deal more like the staid, solemn school teacher Stephanie had initially imagined him to be. Something was definitely bothering him, and she wondered if it had anything to do with her. Why else would he be smiling one minute and frowning the next?

Her apprehension hung almost palpably in the air, on her part, if not on his. He certainly wasn't what she'd expected. Perhaps she wasn't what he'd anticipated, either. Maybe he was wondering how to gently let her down, to send her packing again. But Drew obviously had *some* serious motivation in bringing her here to take care of his twins, something beyond what they'd discussed when she'd interviewed for the position.

She had no clue why he had decided to look so far out of town to find someone to watch his children, and it was one of the first questions she planned to ask him when the opportunity presented itself. Granted, Serendipity was tiny, but it was hard to imagine there were no adequate forms of child care Drew could call upon in a pinch. At the very least, there must be a few teenagers who would be vying to earn a little extra spending money.

So why her?

It was a fair question, and one that she eventually meant to get to the bottom of, but in the end, she realized it didn't matter to her all that much what his motivations were. The point of the matter was that she was here now, and this man had unknowingly offered her a way out of a really bad situation. He'd given her a place to hide from a spoiled, abusive boyfriend who didn't know how to take no for an answer. Drew Spencer's offer to hire her as a live-in nanny from now until the end of the school year was truly an answer to prayer—two months to heal her heart and get back on her feet, to give herself a fresh start.

It wasn't enough that her ex-boyfriend Ryan had torn her heart to shreds—he'd also ripped her home and her job right out from under her. She'd naively given up everything for him, only to find out he was playing her.

She was proud of herself for finding the self-esteem to walk away from a toxic relationship, but that didn't stop her from being a little bit anxious about the way it had ended—Ryan was used to getting his own way, and he was frighteningly possessive. He'd alienated her from everyone else in her life, wanting her all to himself—even though he never had any intention of putting a ring on her finger.

How could she help but look over her shoulder, even knowing she was far away from New Jersey? Ryan had threatened to come after her, and he had power and money behind him to do it. She hoped she'd done enough to keep herself safe.

She needed somewhere secluded and private to regroup and refocus her life, to make plans for her future, though at the moment, she had no idea what that would be—other than finding more permanent housing and a stable job.

In the meantime, Serendipity was a good place to hide.

Drew wasn't overly keen on having a nanny living in his house and getting under his feet. He was already so busy he barely had time to breathe, and he didn't need the added complication of having someone in the way, especially a beautiful woman who smelled like orchids and jasmine.

Unfortunately, he had little choice in the matter. Drew was working off the advice of his lawyer, who had *strongly* suggested he get someone to watch his boys full-time until the end of the school year, particularly since the custody mediation with his ex-wife wasn't progressing well. His lawyer had called it making a *good faith effort* to show he was taking care of the boys.

It had better be good. It was costing Drew a good part of his pension plan. And it was causing him a *great* deal of stress.

Heather had recently been making all kinds of verbal threats about taking the boys away from him, and though none of them had yet come to fruition, Drew still felt as if she was holding him hostage where the kids were concerned.

He knew full well that Heather didn't have any intention of shouldering the responsibility of raising children. She probably planned to pawn them off on her parents, or worse yet, whatever boyfriend she was living with.

Drew's gut felt as if it was filled with molten lead, as it always did when he thought about the callous way Heather had left him—and even worse, how she had abandoned the twins. He prayed he could eventually find forgiveness in his heart for her, but he was human, and forgiveness was a long way off, especially now that she was locking him in a battle for custody of the children.

For Heather, this wasn't about what was best for Matty and Jamey. She was only interested in hitting Drew where it hurt. He couldn't even imagine life without the twins. He would *have* no life without his sons.

And Heather knew it.

"Which name should I call you?"

Stephanie's golden voice slowly penetrated into his thoughts. She flashed him a dazzling smile that exposed both rows of straight, white teeth. "Do you have a preference?"

"I'm sorry?" he asked. His eyebrows rose in confusion as he was mentally jerked into the present.

"Shall I call you Drew or Spence? Your dad said the folks in town call you Spence."

"Oh, yeah. Right. No...Drew is fine."

He didn't know why he was stammering, and he certainly had no clue why he'd just given her the answer he had. Only members of his immediate family called him Drew. The words had just slipped out before he'd had a chance to think about what he was saying, but he didn't correct himself. As a live-in nanny, Stephanie was going to be a part of the family for a while, even if she was everything he *didn't* want in a nanny.

Not outwardly, anyway.

What had happened to the peculiar cross between Mary Poppins and Nanny McPhee that he'd been expecting to show up at his door? Instead, Stephanie had soft, delicate features, high cheekbones, a pretty smile, wave upon wave of sun-drenched, fair hair and warm brown eyes that a man could easily get lost in.

He didn't feel like it sometimes, but he was still a living, breathing man. He was going to trip over Stephanie's beauty every time he looked at her. He'd erroneously assumed, from her upside-down umbrella avatar on the Parents of Preschoolers classified board that she'd be...

Plain?

Homely?

Truth be told, he didn't know what he'd been expecting, only that the woman still waiting on his doorstep was not it.

Emphasis on *waiting*. On his *doorstep*. He ought to kick himself for his discourtesy.

Stepping aside, he gestured for her to go in ahead of him. He averted his gaze from her female sway, but he was unable to keep himself from inhaling the rich oriental fragrance that wafted over him as she swept by. She smelled every bit as good as she looked, which really wasn't helping matters any. He was uncomfortable enough as it was.

There was no sign of his father, but the twins were huddled around the toy box in the living room. They already had several trucks and trains on the floor and were reaching for more.

"One toy at a time, boys," Drew reminded them. "Remember our rule." His gaze shifted to Stephanie. "I tidy up this place at least five times a day, and there are still toys scattered everywhere. They haven't quite mastered the one-at-a-time rule yet, and they're easily distracted."

Stephanie chuckled lightly. "Comes with the territory. I don't mind at all. *Preschoolers* and *messy* go together like butter on toast."

"Right," he agreed, noting that her expression softened and her shoulders lost their stiffness when her attention was directed at the children.

Offering Stephanie a seat on the couch, Drew positioned himself on the antique chair near the fireplace. Seconds later, Jamey slipped onto his lap and Matty climbed up his back, wrapping his little arms around Drew's neck and practically choking him in the process.

Or was it was Stephanie's smile that was making his throat close so forcefully?

"Have you had dinner? I can make you a sandwich if you like."

"I'm fine," she insisted with the hint of a smile.

"Coffee, then?"

She shook her head, and the conversation drifted to a standstill.

Less than a minute passed before Matty's curiosity got the best of him. The small boy crawled off Drew's back and launched himself at Stephanie, who caught him with a laugh and tucked him next to her on the couch, under her arm. There was a toy airplane in reaching distance, and Stephanie grabbed it, giving it to Matty complete with a *vroom* sound.

To Drew's surprise, Jamey crawled off his lap and settled up on Stephanie's knee, his thumb tucked in his mouth, a habit Drew hadn't yet been able to break him out of.

Incredible.

Drew had never seen Jamey cozy up to a person as quickly as he had to Stephanie. It was as if she'd earned the boys' respect the very first time she smiled. She tickled the boys on the ears and they both squealed with laughter.

"These little men are absolutely darling," Stephanie said, giggling along with the twins. Her eyes were shining, lighting up her whole countenance. She was definitely in her element with the children.

"They're a handful," Drew countered teasingly, though he spoke the truth. He was unable to stop himself from grinning, despite his misgivings about the situation.

"Oh, I'm not worried about that. I love children. I'm happy to be here."

Drew could see that, and he could sense it, too. She had become immediately attached to his kids, and they clearly liked her. He would be foolish to put her off just because she didn't look like the nanny he'd pictured in his head. It was what was inside a person's soul that really counted—like seeing the way his kids had instantly warmed up to her and instinctively trusted her. That spoke volumes about her, in Drew's mind. Kids had a way of perceiving things about people that weren't so obvious when seen through an adult's eyes.

His father picked that moment to hobble across the hallway behind Stephanie. He paused and gave Drew two thumbs-up, grinning and wagging his bushy gray eyebrows for emphasis.

Apparently *he* approved of her—which was an absolutely frightening thought. Whoops. Drew hadn't thought of *that* particular ramification of hiring Stephanie. Pop wasn't viewing her as a nanny for his grandsons, but as a potential future wife for his son. Drew had seen the impish light in his father's eyes before, and it never boded well.

He couldn't imagine how ghastly it would be once his father put his head together with his best lady friend and cohort in mischief, Jo Murphy, the gregarious owner of the Cup O' Jo Café and the town's chief matchmaker.

Nanny or not, his pop and Jo Murphy would see romance where there was none. Before he knew it, they would be pestering him half to death. Stephanie, too, for that matter, and she certainly hadn't signed on for *that*.

"I hope my father won't be too problematic for you," Drew said. "The twins love the gruff old guy, but the simple fact of the matter is that he is getting up in years and he can't do everything he thinks he can. He doesn't require any special physical care or anything. For his age, he's as fit as a fiddle. But he has a tendency to involve himself in matters that don't concern him. You may want to keep your eye out for him so he doesn't cause you any trouble."

He paused and chuckled, but it was a dry, nervous sound rather than a happy one. "Have I overwhelmed you yet? Made you change your mind about working here? I'm sure you're ready to turn right around and hop on the next plane back to the east coast."

"I think I can handle your father," she assured him. "How ornery can one man be?"

"You would be surprised." Drew cocked his head and twisted his lips in amusement. "He's going to be in your way. Constantly. And he has an opinion about everything."

She shrugged. "Doesn't everybody?"

"Maybe, but my father is especially blustery when he gets into one of his moods. Which is often. Just so you know."

"Not a problem," she assured him. "I tend to get along with everybody."

Somehow, he believed she did.

"Boys," he stated firmly, addressing the twins, both of whom by that time were using Stephanie as playground equipment, swinging over her shoulders and sliding down her legs—not that she appeared to mind. The crystal-clear sound of her feminine laughter laced the air like stardust.

Drew gestured toward the hall. "Why don't you two run along now and get ready for bed? I think Pop-Pop is waiting for you. I'll be there in a minute to read another chapter of our story to you."

At least that would keep his father occupied for a while, getting the two squirming, over-excited preschoolers into pajamas and tucked into bed. Drew ruffled their fair hair and kissed each of his boys softly on the forehead before urging them to the back hallway where their room was located.

"Sorry about the interruption," Drew said once he'd herded the twins down the hall. "Bedtime is a real zoo around here."

He returned to his seat and braced his elbows on his knees, ignoring the quivering sensation in his stomach as their eyes met.

He cleared his throat, wondering how to start the conversation. There was a lot she needed to know about why she was here, issues he hadn't felt comfortable discussing over the phone, but that she ought to be aware of if she was going to be working for him.

And he had a few more questions for her, as well.

Like why she'd chosen a temporary position in Serendipity when she'd clearly had a successful career in child care on the east coast. It wasn't *What's a pretty lady like you doing in a place like this?* But it was pretty close. He wasn't sure if he should be prying, yet it seemed an obvious question.

If it was none of his business, she would no doubt tell him so. But something about her expression gave him pause to consider.

With just the two of them in the room, she appeared uneasy—like a cornered animal, with wide, wild brown eyes staring back at him. Though she was trying to hide it, she was clearly uncomfortable sitting here with him.

Maybe she was just nervous about starting a new job in a new town, but somehow he thought it was more than that. He hoped she wasn't reconsidering the position. It had been next to impossible just to find someone suitable for these circumstances the first time around. He didn't know if he would find anyone else willing to do the job.

He fidgeted in his chair, which was unusual for him. Normally, he would just blurt what he was thinking outright. He'd been told on more than one occasion that he was too blunt and outspoken. This might be a good time to work on that defect.

But how did one ease into this kind of subject?

Before he could say a word, there was a knock at the door.

Stephanie jerked in surprise, as her gaze shifted to the door.

"I'm sorry," he apologized, rising. "I wasn't expecting anyone this evening. It's probably my father's friend Jo, although she usually just lets herself in. I'll only be a moment."

Stephanie tried to smile, but the color on her face had faded into a serious shade of gray. She clasped her hands together in her lap until her knuckles were white.

"Are you all right?" he asked, concerned.

"I'm—yes," she stammered. "I'm fine."

Drew didn't think she looked fine. She looked terrified. And it had something to do with whoever was potentially knocking at his front door.

Even though he barely knew Stephanie, his deep-rooted protective instincts flared. She had nothing to fear. He wasn't going to let anyone hurt her while she was in his house, though he couldn't imagine why anyone would want to. And like he'd said, it was probably Jo Murphy, come to see his pop.

Only it wasn't Jo Murphy.

Drew opened the door to a lanky young man he'd never seen before, certainly not a resident of Serendipity.

A friend of Stephanie's? Or worse yet, an enemy?

"Andrew Reid Spencer?" the boy asked, obviously trying to sound official despite the crack in his voice.

Drew's eyebrows shot up in surprise. Why was the young man asking for him?

"Yes," he replied cautiously. "I'm Drew."

The boy shoved a manila envelope at Drew's chest and was backing up before he even spoke. Drew instinctually reached for the envelope, clutching it to his side as the young man made his pronouncement.

"You've been served."

Chapter Two

Stephanie didn't hear the actual conversation between Drew and his guest. Adrenaline made her heartbeat pulse and pound in her ears in a fierce rhythm, like a roofer hammering nails, drowning out the sound of the men's voices.

At the knock, she'd experienced a startling moment of panic where she'd actually considered hiding behind the couch. She'd been certain that the man at the door was Ryan, that he'd already tracked her down, determined to charm or intimidate her into going back with him.

Which she would never do.

She wondered how long this indeterminable fear would follow her around. Would she ever *not* jump when someone knocked on the door?

She was more relieved than she could say when she realized the visit had nothing to do with her, but she felt guilty that it was at Drew's expense—it didn't take a genius to figure out something had gone wrong in his world.

He slammed the door and returned to his chair, a

crumpled manila envelope clenched in his fist. His breath came in ragged gasps and his face was an alarming shade of crimson. Stephanie braced for the detonation she was sure was to follow, for the man was clearly a ticking time bomb.

The explosion never came. Drew yanked at the knot in his tie and stretched his neck from side to side, but he didn't yell, or sulk, or throw anything, which is what Ryan did when things didn't go his way.

Instead, Drew quietly reached into his shirt pocket for his reading glasses and removed from the envelope a crisp white set of legal documents. He released a long, unsteady breath as he silently perused the papers, the worry lines on his forehead deepening. When he was finished, he bowed his head and pinched the bridge of his nose. Stephanie thought he might be praying, but she wasn't certain. Probably staving off a headache, as well.

The pressure in the air around her seemed to intensify as her mind thought up a number of scenarios that Drew might be facing. She wanted to reach out to him but wasn't sure how. When she laid a comforting hand on his forearm, his muscles rippled with tension.

"My ex-wife is suing me for full custody of the twins." The statement was matter-of-fact, but his expression was anything but. Agony flashed through his eyes when he spoke of the woman, and Stephanie winced. She could relate to that kind of pain—of having the person you had expected to spend your life with let you down.

But there was more injury than anger in Drew's gaze. Stephanie couldn't claim to be as noble. She despised what Ryan had done to her, and she hated herself even more for having let him, for getting her priorities so mixed up she couldn't see what was happening to her until it was too late.

But for her, at least, what was done was done, and she was moving forward with her life, starting now.

For Drew, however, it looked as if his troubles were just beginning.

He cleared his throat, his lips moving silently as he searched for the right words. "Obviously, I'm pretty desperate to find adequate child care for the twins," he began, leaning his forearms on his elbows and clasping his hands together. "The boys were in day care with a local woman, but she had to move to Chicago to be near her ailing sister. Her leaving left a big gap in Serendipity, especially for me."

"I'm sorry to hear that," she replied, though in truth she wasn't exactly *sorry.* If the woman hadn't left, she wouldn't have a job. "The boys are three years old, right? Do they attend preschool yet?"

He shook his head. "Unfortunately, Serendipity doesn't have a preschool."

"Oh, my," she responded, her surprise showing in her voice. She would have thought that even as tiny a town as Serendipity would have a preschool to help the little ones with learning readiness.

"I know. It's a huge issue, right? I've been in mediation over custody of the children with my ex-wife, Heather, for some time now, and being able to send the twins to a preschool might have worked in my favor. Right now, I have temporary custody. Heather sometimes visits the kids on weekends. Right after the divorce, that was how she wanted it, but now, inexplicably, she's changed her mind."

He sighed. "I hired you in the hopes that she and the mediators would see how serious I am about taking care of the twins and would grant me primary custody without getting the court involved." He slapped the legal document with the back of his hand. "As you can see, that's not working out so well for me."

He scrubbed his free hand over his scalp, making the short ends of his hair stick up every which direction. "If my ex-wife has it her way, I won't get to see the twins at all, except for maybe supervised visits. She's claiming I'm an unfit father."

"Why did she change her mind? And why would she be so unwilling to share custody?" Granted, Stephanie had just met Drew, but she'd appreciated what she'd seen so far. No one could fake the kind of love shining from Drew's eyes when he was around his boys, or even spoke of them. He appeared to be a patient and tender father. He was even willing to hire a nanny from out of town to make sure the twins were adequately cared for full-time. If that wasn't devotion, Stephanie didn't know what was.

Besides, the boys needed their father in their lives.

"Two years ago, Heather left me and the kids because she didn't like being tied down as a wife and mother. She's a party girl, and always has been. Staying home on Friday nights just didn't suit her."

"Then why does she want custody of the boys now?"

He scoffed and shook his head. "There's the rub. I don't know. She doesn't want to be tied down with the twins, so it only makes sense that I maintain primary custody. I'm guessing she just doesn't want *me* to have them, because she wants to hurt me. I had no idea she felt so much hostility against me."

His voice was raspy with emotion, and his gaze didn't quite meet hers. "If she wins in court, the twins will be raised by various relatives and an absentee mother. I'm afraid for them. That's why I have to fight."

"Wow." Stephanie didn't even know what else to say. She'd grown up in foster care. She knew firsthand what it meant to be unloved, to be shuffled from house to house with no stability. She couldn't imagine using those two precious boys as pawns in what was essentially a vindictive game.

"According to this summons, I've got a CFI—a Child and Family Investigator—from the court coming to the house sometime in the near future to scope out the family situation. With all your credentials as a nanny for the twins, I can only hope it will help my case."

"It certainly can't hurt. I'll do whatever I can," she vowed.

"I know I have to trust God with my boys. But sometimes I find it hard to put my circumstances in God's hands. Their whole lives may be affected by what happens next."

That, Stephanie thought, was the closest he was going to get to saying he was frightened, both for himself and for his sons. And she couldn't blame him. She'd heard the stories of court cases gone wrong, where children had been hurt and even killed by misinformed decisions from the judges.

Compassion and resolve welled in her throat. She'd

only known the twins for an evening, but that didn't lessen her determination. She would help in whatever way she was able. She wasn't going to let anything happen to those boys—or Drew, either, for that matter, if it was in her power to stop it.

She'd been praying for purpose in her life. Maybe that's why God had sent her here—for a set of darling twins and their handsome, dedicated father.

Being served legal documents had shaken Drew up more than he cared to admit, and he was a little embarrassed that Stephanie had been there to witness his private humiliation. He made a quick decision to mentally shelve his emotions for now, until he had time to consider his next steps.

"I'm sorry," he apologized, suddenly noticing that Stephanie's eyes were darkened with fatigue. "I'm being insensitive. I should have postponed our conversation until tomorrow. You must be exhausted from your trip."

"I am a little tired," she admitted. "It's been a long day."

"Then let's table this discussion for now and pick it up tomorrow morning. I'll see you to your room and get your bags for you so you can settle in for the night. It's nothing fancy—just a furnished room over the garage—but it has its own entranceway so you won't be stumbling over Pop and the twins when you need some privacy."

She smothered a yawn, making Drew feel even guiltier for keeping her from her rest. Studying her face thoughtfully, he realized that her eyes were puffy and shaded by dark circles, as if she hadn't been sleeping well.

He definitely didn't want to push her when she was already exhausted, but he was still curious about her situation. It occurred to him that moving out here to be a nanny for his twins might have been a last resort for her. No one else had answered the advertisement he'd placed, and with good reason. He wasn't offering much in the way of a salary, especially for someone who'd been a successful nanny in a large east coast town. Who would want temporary employment in the middle of nowhere?

Stephanie Cartwright, apparently.

The question was, why?

"Drew!" His father's loud, gruff voice echoed down the hallway. "The boys are waiting on their story."

"Coming," Drew called back. "Give me a second. I'm sorry," he apologized to Stephanie. "Would you mind waiting a few more minutes while I tuck the boys in?"

She chuckled and gestured with her hands. "I see what you mean about your father. Go. I can wait."

"Bring Stephanie with you," the old man hollered, almost as if were eavesdropping on the two of them.

Drew tensed and turned back toward Stephanie. "Do you mind?" he asked with a quirk of his lips. "Pop's not going to stop until he gets his way."

"No problem, really," Stephanie assured him. "I'd love to spend a little more time getting to know the twins, and I'm sure they're anxious to have their daddy tuck them in."

"Probably," he agreed. Their bedtime ritual had

become one of Drew's favorite parts of the day, when his two sleepy boys were all quiet and cuddly. Tonight, however, he doubted they were either, what with all the excitement in the household. Getting them to calm down enough to go to sleep might be easier said than done.

Then again, Stephanie was a nanny. Maybe she had some fresh ideas for rustling rowdy preschoolers into bed and under the covers.

"Drew," his father called again. *Impatiently,* in typical Pop fashion. Stephanie might run for the hills yet.

"Yeah, yeah," Drew replied, winking at Stephanie. "What did I tell you?" he concluded in a mock whisper.

She giggled lightly, which erased some of the weariness from her countenance.

He felt her eyes branding into his back all the way down the hall, and unease once again bore down on his shoulders. He couldn't help but be uncomfortable. What was she thinking about?

How he'd just been served? His apparent failure as a father?

He hoped she could see beyond the legalities to his heart. Being a dad was everything to him, and he wanted to keep it that way. Having her on his side would definitely be a positive factor, especially now that this was going to court.

The moment the twins realized Stephanie had entered the room behind him, they squealed and bounced on their beds. In Drew's opinion, it didn't help matters that she jumped right into the fray, laughing along with them and stirring them up to even greater noise and excitement. The idea here was to calm them down enough to go to sleep.

"Settle down, boys," he instructed gently. "It's already past your bedtime. If you guys want me to read you a story, you need to lie down and cover up. Right now, no excuses."

"But, Daddy," Matty whined, rubbing his bright blue eyes with his little fists. "We're not tired yet."

Drew smothered a chuckle as Matty's objection was punctuated with a big yawn. The boys weren't tired—they were overtired.

"We want to stay up and play with Miss Stephie," Jamey protested.

"It's Stephanie," Drew gently corrected, ruffling Jamey's hair with his palm. "And she'll be here when you wake up tomorrow. She's your new nanny. She's here to take care of you."

Stephanie placed a hand on Drew's arm. "My name is hard to pronounce when you're just learning how to speak. Stephie is just fine."

"Steph-eee," Matty said proudly.

"Very good, Matty," Stephanie praised, causing Matty to straighten his shoulders and sit an inch taller.

Okay, that was weird—or incredible, depending on how he looked at it. She'd only spent a few minutes with the boys, and she already knew Matty from Jamey—and quite confidently, at that. How had she known which twin she was addressing?

He wasn't able to ask how she'd done it, for at that moment the boys launched off their beds onto the floor and began dancing around Stephanie.

"Boys," Drew warned, trying to sound stern. "Bedtime. I'm not going to say it again."

"Grouch," his father grumbled under his breath. Drew and Stephanie exchanged a look.

What did I tell you?

Drew didn't speak the words aloud, but he was pretty sure Stephanie correctly read his expression. Pop was going to be interesting at his best and exasperating at his worst.

Her lips twitched. He thought she might be smothering a laugh. At least she was good-natured about it.

The twins groaned in unison at his spoilsport pronouncement, but they both returned to their beds and crawled underneath the covers. He hated to be the bad guy, but someone had to take control here.

Drew set a chair between the twins' beds and pulled out the Bible storybook they were currently reading together. The book included little finger puppets which Drew manipulated as he told the stories, delighting the boys with his silly moves and goofy voices. At the very least, it usually captured their attention enough to settle them down; but tonight, to his chagrin, their primary focus seemed to be on Stephanie.

"Stephie do it," Jamey announced.

"Yeah," Matty agreed. "Let Miss Steph-eee read to us."

"What a good idea," his father added in a coarse voice. "Ladies first, and all that."

Stephanie's eyes widened at the prospect. She hesitated and cast Drew an enquiring look—ready to step in and read, but not willing to step on his toes.

It was kind of her to think of him, even though he

was clearly outnumbered. He had mixed feelings about relinquishing his nightly reading to Stephanie, even once. This was his special time with the twins, their bonding time.

But this was about what was best for the boys.

Overpowering love for his sons billowed up his chest until he thought he might burst from it. By God's grace, the twins had kept him anchored in this world when he might otherwise have drifted away. They filled his life with purpose.

He turned his face so Stephanie and the twins couldn't see what he was feeling as he faced the truth. He was in no mental condition to read out loud, and he didn't want the boys picking up on his concern. Stephanie was their new nanny. It would be good for her to start bonding with Matty and Jamey as soon as possible.

Who knew when that case worker was going to visit? His shoulders tensed and sent sharp jabs into his neck just thinking about it. The relationship between Stephanie and the boys had to look natural, without pretense.

Which actually made it pretense. He felt mortified even to think that way.

In any case, the boys were clearly anxious to enjoy her interpretation of the present story, perhaps even with the finger puppets, if she was willing.

"I guess it would be all right for Miss Stephanie to read to you," he conceded, surrendering both the chair and the book to her.

"Okay," she agreed, her dark eyes shining and a sweet smile on her face. "But only this one time. You like it best when your daddy reads to you, right?"

Both boys nodded in response to her animated question and Drew shook his head in amazement. Stephanie had somehow managed to put an enthusiastic spin on something that would otherwise have been uncomfortable and demoralizing for him.

It was almost as if she'd been able to read his thoughts and empathize with his feelings, which was an uncomfortable notion. The last thing he needed right now was a woman in his head.

"So, where are we?" Stephanie asked brightly.

Not you. *We.*

The way she instantly and effortlessly integrated herself into the family was unsettling, to say the least.

"Uh, Noah, I think," he answered, smothering the catch in his voice by feigning a cough.

Stephanie might not have noticed his forced enthusiasm, but his father raised a suspicious eyebrow. Drew pretended not to notice.

He sat on the edge of Jamey's bed and pulled the little guy into his lap, and then urged Matty to come cuddle with him, as well. Maybe this wouldn't be so bad, after all, being able to sit here with the boys in his arms.

"A long, long time ago, there was a man named Noah. God told him he had to build an ark—that's a big boat," Stephanie began, holding the book so everyone could see it.

Drew had to admit Stephanie was a good storyteller. Even his father was enthralled, hobbling over and perching on the edge of Jamey's bed next to Drew so he could watch the story in action.

Stephanie was vivacious and animated and brought

the story to life with the little finger puppets. If he was being honest, she was a far better storyteller than he. And this was clearly not her first time using finger puppets. She was a natural.

She must have often read books to the children she cared for in New Jersey, or maybe even for a library story time. He could see her doing that, captivating other little children with her storytelling as much as she was with his own kids right now.

He really didn't know that much about her, beyond what he'd read in her resume. There were a lot of blank spots in her history, more than words on paper would be able to convey. He'd have to remedy that if she was going to stay.

Wait.

What was with the *if*?

Of course she was going to stay. He had invited her. *Hired* her. No room for second thoughts now.

With effort, Drew turned his attention back to the story. Stephanie had given each boy one of the finger puppets and was drawing both of them into the action, retelling the story she'd just read to them with their own words and their own character voices.

Why hadn't he ever thought of that? The kids would retain the Biblical account much better if they were actively involved.

That sealed it—Stephanie was definitely going to be good for the boys. Maybe it was good that he *had* hired a nanny, even if it was only temporary, until the school term ended and he could be home with the boys for the summer, or at least until he'd had that court hearing at the end of May.

The twins retold the story several times, and then Stephanie tucked the puppets away and replaced the book on the bookshelf. All of the adults gathered around and listened to the boys recite their prayers as Drew tucked them in, pulling their comforters up under their chins and kissing each of the boys on the forehead.

Stephanie's face turned a pretty shade of pink when Matty named her specifically and asked God to bless her. Drew closed his eyes and prayed right along with his sons. Their family, the nanny included, needed all the prayers they could get.

Afterward, he retrieved Stephanie's bags from the rental car and made sure she was comfortable in the room above the garage. Before becoming Stephanie's quarters, the room had been his study, where he often went to read or grade papers after the boys were asleep. But when he'd decided the best thing for his family was a full-time, live-in nanny, giving her the room over the garage only made sense. He'd removed a file cabinet, relocated a couple of bookshelves and made the addition of a queen-size bed and a dresser. Voilà—comfortable living quarters.

Of course, that was from his perspective—which even he had to admit was unembellished and completely male. He had no idea what Stephanie would think of the room. He didn't know her well enough to guess, and he didn't know what kind of conditions she'd come from, what she might have to compare it with.

No doubt she'd experienced more opulence than he could ever afford. After all, her last position was for a wealthy political household in New Jersey. Did her parents have money? What kind of living had she made as a nanny? How different were city accommodations versus what he could offer her in Serendipity?

He scoffed and shook his head at his own extraneous thoughts. He was going to short-circuit himself worrying about the dozens of unanswered questions whisking around in his brain, and he had enough to be anxious about already.

Like Heather, and being served with legal papers.

Drew took a much-needed breath of fresh air on the back porch. Quincy needed his nighttime outing, anyway, so Drew figured he might as well take a few minutes to see if he could get his whirling mind to quiet down a little, but he ended up ruminating on how his life had come to this point.

His ex-wife had taken his heart and trampled on it. He'd tried to save his marriage, even seeing a counselor, but he couldn't do it alone. All his prayers and actions had been for nothing. Heather didn't want to be a wife. She'd balked at the notion of being tied down to house and home.

To his surprise and dismay, Heather hadn't even wanted to see the boys, except for the occasional weekend. And even when she'd planned to spend time with them, she'd often been late. Once she hadn't bothered to show up at all, and Drew had been left with two disappointed three-year-olds to console.

Now she suddenly wanted full custody? He'd never felt so powerless. Didn't the courts usually side with the mother?

What could he do that he wasn't already doing? Jamey and Matty were in a difficult and possibly dangerous situation, since he suspected Heather would neglect them even if she won custody, leaving them with their maternal grandparents at best, or any one of her string of boyfriends at worst. And there was nothing he could do to stop the chain of events that was unfolding.

Except the fact that he'd hired Stephanie. He prayed that having a nanny for the boys would make a difference at the court hearing. He didn't know how else to show something as intangible as love and devotion.

Shivering, he folded his arms and sighed. It wasn't the cold night air getting to him, but rather the chill inside his chest.

There was one thing he could do. On his own, he was bare and vulnerable. But he wasn't on his own. God in His Providence would take care of the twins. He had to believe that. God was in control of his future, and his sons' well-being. His children were protected in the palm of the Master's hand.

Drew bowed his head and thanked God for His many blessings. He had health and a home, and bounteous food on the table. He had family—his father, for all his gruffness, and his precious twins.

And he had Stephanie, the woman who might make the difference between his being able to secure custody of his twins or not.

God bless them all.

Chapter Three

Why did the house smell like bacon?

Drew awoke to the sizzling smell of a hot breakfast and his stomach immediately growled in protest. He hadn't had a real, home-cooked breakfast since…

Well, it had been a long time.

He shrugged on jeans and a T-shirt, not bothering to check his appearance in the mirror. His curiosity about what was happening in the kitchen trumped the urge to take extra time to spruce up before presenting himself to the world—or rather, to Stephanie.

Drew walked bare-footed into the kitchen, where he discovered Stephanie at the stove flipping pancakes, while Pop and the twins waited impatiently at the table, forks in their hands and expectant looks on their faces. Someone had set a basket of fresh strawberries on the table and both of the boys sported telltale red-stained faces.

"Good morning, Drew," Stephanie greeted as he entered the room and tousled his twins' hair.

"Morning," he echoed absently as he tried to take in the full extent of what was happening.

Stephanie was dressed in gray sweatpants and a loose-fitting pink T-shirt and had her sun-gold hair swept back in a ponytail. Even in casual clothing, she was strikingly beautiful, especially because she appeared at ease and in her element with giggling children in the room.

At home. In his house.

In the week since she'd arrived to supervise his sons, the whole house seemed to be more orderly and less stressful. She was paradoxically full of energy and yet able to create a calm, tranquil atmosphere in the house when need be. The boys loved her, and he had no qualms about having the twins stay in her care while he taught at the elementary school. He might not have known Stephanie for long, but he trusted her.

She'd apparently scoped out his pantry at some point during the week. Not only had she found all the ingredients to make breakfast, but she was wearing his *Don't Mind the Fire: Everything is Under Control* apron that he used when he grilled outside.

"Pull up a seat," Stephanie continued cheerfully. "Your pancakes are almost ready. I hope you're hungry. I made a lot of them." Her voice was as bright as sunrise on a spring day, which only served to rattle Drew's nerves even more. Ugh. He wasn't a morning person on the best of days, and this was not his best day.

"Look, Daddy. It's a kitty." Matty pointed to his plate. Sure enough, there was a pancake shaped in the form of the little boy's favorite animal.

"Really cool, buddy," he said. Fairly creative, he had to admit. Breakfast art. "I don't think I've ever seen an animal pancake before."

"Me, too. Me, too. Stephie made it," Jamey informed him, pumping his little arms in excitement and pointing at his own plate. "I got a mouse."

Stephanie's sparkling brown eyes met Drew's as she chuckled and glanced over her shoulder. "I gave it my best try, anyway. A kitty's tail is a little bit more difficult than mouse ears, and I'm not an artist on my best day."

"You don't hear anyone complaining," his pop said, in an unusually chipper voice. Stephanie's presence had seemed even to have worked on the grumpy old man.

Drew directed his gaze to his father's plate, amusedly wondering if Stephanie had made Pop an animal pancake. Like maybe a porcupine. But he seemed to be happy devouring his silver-dollar halfstack.

"What is all this?" he asked, wondering if he sounded as disconcerted as he felt. It was as if he was a modern-day man stepping into a 1950s appliance advertisement.

Fortunately, Stephanie didn't seem to notice his agitation. She just smiled and gestured to the skillets on the burners of the stove.

"It's just what it looks like. The twins said they were hungry for breakfast, and I thought I might as well cook for everybody. It's not any harder to whip up a meal for the whole family than it is just for the boys. I hope you don't mind. I asked your father if it would be okay and he said it would be fine."

He shrugged and shook his head. "No problem."

Truthfully, he didn't know how he felt about Stephanie taking over the kitchen. She fit into his family like fingers in a glove, and he wasn't sure he was comfortable with that. It was too cozy. Too personal.

Like the sweet family gatherings he'd always hoped for and pictured in his mind but had never quite had. Reality was blinding. And now Stephanie was bridging that gap with her smile and a batch of pancakes. With what appeared to be effortless grace, she flowed into the current of their family, seamlessly blending with them as if she'd been there all along.

"I take requests," she joked, waving her spatula around like a drum major marking time with a baton. "No promises, but I'll give it my best shot. An animal? Your favorite sport?"

"Plain pancakes are fine. What Pop's got on his plate looks great." He felt awkward being waited on in his own kitchen by a woman he'd invited to his house. She wasn't exactly his guest, but he hadn't hired her to cook and clean, either. He hoped she knew that.

"A full stack for you," she amended. "You're still a growing boy."

"I'm going to be, if I start eating a full-size breakfast every day."

"It's important to start the morning with a good, nutritious meal, don't you think? It gives you energy and sets the tone for the day."

Stephanie was certainly setting the tone *this* morning. Clear skies, sunny and warm. What a counterbalance to Drew's current partly-cloudy-with-a-chance-of-rain attitude.

"If we're talking about needing some energy, I'm going to require a solid jolt of caffeine," Drew added, smothering a yawn.

"I think we can include a cup of coffee or two with your meal, as long as you eat everything else on your plate and drink a tall glass of orange juice." She set a steaming mug of coffee before him and he took a long, fortifying sip.

"Because it's nutritious," Drew repeated, mimicking Stephanie without mocking her.

She slid him a smile that affected him more than he would have liked.

"Tritious," Jamey repeated, shoving a large strawberry toward Drew's mouth.

"That's right, Jamey," Stephanie encouraged, sounding just as proud of the young boy as Drew was, even though she had no vested interest in his children beyond being their nanny.

Drew barely dodged the squished-up fruit Jamey was aiming at his face and regarded the boy thoughtfully. Jamey was his shy one. It took a while for the boy to open up, and he didn't usually speak around people that he didn't know, especially adults.

But Stephanie was different. Jamey already trusted her, and Drew had to admit, if only to himself, that he could see why. She already knew which twin was which and was able to address each of them by name. Most people couldn't tell the boys apart, even after they'd been together for a while.

And her ease with the boys wasn't the only conquest she'd made. She'd even won over his ornery, cantankerous father, which was no easy feat.

"*New*-tri-shush," Matty corrected, even though the word was new to him.

Stephanie set a plate piled high with pancakes, bacon

and eggs in front of Drew. For some reason seeing this well-rounded meal right in front of him convicted him of his own lapse in parental aptitude.

Nutrition hadn't exactly been the word of the day where Drew and the kids were concerned, especially recently. An image of the blueberry toaster pastries and quickly peeled bananas that he usually served on busy school-day mornings flashed through his head, followed by a gut-tightening wave of guilt.

When had convenience food become the extent of their morning routine?

He had to hand it to Stephanie—this was the first really *nutritious* breakfast the twins had had in ages. He, too, for that matter. Pancakes, scrambled eggs, crispy bacon and a large pitcher of orange juice. His mouth was watering already.

"Nice to have a woman in the house," his father commented gruffly, loud enough for the neighbors in the next county to hear. He grunted and shoved another large forkful of eggs into his mouth. "Yes, ma'am, this is the bee's knees."

"Why, thank you, Frank." Grinning, she flipped the last pancake onto a plate. "I'm certainly outnumbered here, guys to girls. Even Quincy is a boy." She set the platter of remaining pancakes in the middle of the circular oak table and tickled Matty on the ear.

The boy squealed and wiggled in his chair.

"Me, too! Me, too!" Jamey insisted. Those seemed to be his favorite two words lately.

Stephanie chuckled and moved around the table, leaning over Drew's shoulder so she could tickle both boys at once. "It's a good thing I have two hands."

Drew closed his eyes, trying not to breathe, because if he did, the warm, spicy fragrance of her perfume was going to get to him. He'd always been a sucker for orchids and jasmine. Maybe it was the appeal of the foreign scent to his down-home-country nose.

Whatever it was, he didn't need the distraction, and he was relieved when she moved away and went back to the stove to remove the last few pieces of bacon she'd been frying.

"How do you know which boy is which?" he asked, desperately trying to stay cool and collected, at least on the outside. "Most people have difficulty telling the twins apart. Did Pop help you figure it out?"

"Didn't need to," his father replied, before Stephanie could say a word. "She had it right from the get-go."

"I've never had a problem with twins," she answered, leaning her hip against the counter. "Matty has a little dimple on his chin," she said, gesturing toward the boy in question, "and Jamey here has just the hint of a cowlick on his forehead." She leaned forward and ruffled Jamey's hair.

"Incredible," Drew murmured under his breath. He was impressed. Stephanie certainly had a keen eye for children. *His children*.

"So for lunch, I was thinking we could take in a burger at Cup O' Jo as a special treat to the boys."

In truth, this wasn't so much about the boys. This was about getting over the hurdle of Stephanie meeting Jo Murphy, who owned the café. His strategy was to get to Jo first and try to convince her *not* to play matchmaker.

Which probably wouldn't work, but he had to try, anyway.

"Cup O' Jo?" Stephanie queried. "Is that a coffee house?"

Drew chuckled. "It's *the* coffee house. You've never had coffee until you've tried a Cup O' Jo." He chuckled at his own joke. "They have hot coffee, iced-coffee and everything in between."

Not that he'd had many fancy gourmet coffees in his lifetime to compare it to. He wasn't very adventurous when it came to trying new foods and drinks. He preferred the tried and true. Steak and potatoes. Black and bold. It suited him.

"My mouth is watering already," Stephanie assured him. "Caramel frappés are my favorite."

"And Jo's niece-in-law Phoebe makes the best cherry pie in Texas," his father added, smacking his lips. "Maybe in the whole U.S. of A. We've got us a world-class pastry chef right here in Serendipity."

For once, his father wasn't exaggerating. Phoebe really *was* a world-class pastry chef. How she'd ended up in Serendipity and married to Jo's nephew Chance was beyond Drew's comprehension.

Strangers seldom came to the small town, and even more infrequently stayed. Family roots in Serendipity grew as long and thick as an old cottonwood tree. Few were pulled up, and even fewer were planted. As in Stephanie's case, visitors usually had a specific reason for visiting and left soon afterward.

"It's Saturday, so we aren't going to see the usual lunch crowd," he continued. "But there's still bound to be a few regulars catching a meal there. And, of course, you'll meet many of the town folk at church tomorrow."

Her eyebrows rose, but she didn't say a word.

He hesitated and cleared his throat, realizing he hadn't even asked her about her religious preferences before blurting out that last statement. Now he'd put her on the spot.

"Er—I mean, if you'd like to go to church, that is. I didn't mean to presume. What I intended to say was that most of our neighbors attend services on Sunday. It would be a good chance for you to meet everyone, and for people to get to know you, as well."

"Of course," Stephanie agreed, with a smile that put him at ease and stirred him up at the same time. "I'd like to go with you tomorrow. Thank you for asking."

Feeling more on edge than she cared to admit, Stephanie reached for the nearest breakfast plates, all of which were satisfyingly empty, and began stacking them into a sink full of warm, soapy water. The Spencer family seemed to have liked the meal as much as she'd enjoyed cooking it.

The one thing she'd been worried about was how Drew would react to her taking over his kitchen, but so far he hadn't said anything negative about it. In fact, he was as vocal as Frank and the twins in praising her cooking skills and appreciating her efforts.

She didn't even want to think about how things might have gone if for some reason Drew had taken offense to her actions, if he'd become angry at her poking around his pantry without her asking him first.

She'd always been that way—caring what other

people thought of her, wanting to keep the peace. Her desire to please others came from a deep-rooted need in her childhood. Foster children—especially older ones—were easily overlooked, even in the best-meaning of families. Many of her peers in the juvenile system had acted out as a way to get attention—taken drugs, joined gangs, got in fights, committed crimes.

Stephanie had taken another route to getting noticed—trying to please everyone all the time. Getting straight A's in high school when she was really a B student at heart. Keeping her bedroom immaculate when her nature was to be more cluttered and disorganized.

Being the perfect girlfriend long after all of the signs pointed to a disaster-ridden relationship.

What had she been thinking? It was thoroughly humiliating, that she'd been so desperate for a family of her own that she'd only seen Ryan's charm and the wealth. She'd convinced herself to overlook the glaring inconsistencies in Ryan's words versus his actions, blinded herself to who he really was just because he was a handsome, rich man who could have his choice of women.

He'd chosen her, and she'd thought it meant something. She thought he would propose to her. She thought they were in love, so she'd made excuses for him when he lashed out in anger, when he bruised her body as well as her pride.

But she was a victim no longer. Ryan couldn't hurt her anymore. She just had to ignore the cloud of trepidation still hanging over her head until it went away on its own.

"I didn't hire you to cook and clean for us, you know."

Drew's warm voice came from behind her, disturbingly close to her left ear, and she jumped in surprise. "You're a nanny, not a maid."

"Oh, that's quite all right," Stephanie assured him. "I don't mind at all. I enjoy doing a few tasks around the house while I work. I can keep a steady eye on the boys and tidy up a bit at the same time. Multitasking is my specialty."

"Then let me help you, at least," he said, slipping in next to her by the sink and taking the plate she was rinsing out of her hands. "You gather the dishes from the table, and I'll rinse them and stack them in the dishwasher."

"Sounds like a plan." She was glad to be able to move away from him to scoop the silverware from the table. Everything about Drew oozed masculinity, from the strength of his hands to the way his biceps pulled against the sleeve of his T-shirt. Her shoulder would fit right under his, were he to reach out to her. When he'd stepped up next to her, she'd immediately inhaled his brisk scent—an intoxicating combination of soap and man.

How could she even notice Drew that way? She *definitely* didn't want to go there. She was not in any big hurry to get her heart broken again. Besides, Drew was her employer.

In her head, it was easy to tick reason after reason why she shouldn't see him that way, but that didn't stop the awareness flowing through her when he stood at her side.

She supposed it proved she was still alive, at least. There was a time after her breakup with Ryan where she'd seriously wondered if she would survive. And now she was here, with a job and sustenance and a place to lay her head. God was good.

"You had a funny look on your face when I first opened the door last week," Drew said conversationally. "What were you thinking—apart from wondering if my dog was going to eat you, that is?"

She drew in a surprised breath. "You mean, about you? Honestly? I didn't expect you to be a…well, a cowboy, for lack of a better term."

"Ha!" he chortled. "And I didn't expect you to be…" His face turned an odd crimson color and his lips curved first into a frown and then into a grim line. "Well, it doesn't really matter what I thought. Do you like baseball?"

Now *that* was an abrupt change in conversation if she'd ever heard one.

What *had* he thought of her? Somehow she didn't think she was going to find out any time soon.

"That depends," she answered, tilting her head up to meet his gaze. "Watching baseball or playing it?"

He arched an eyebrow. "Both, I suppose."

"I'm not big on watching baseball on television, although I don't mind catching a game if someone else is watching it. I've seen a few Yankees games live. That was fun. I especially liked the hot dogs."

"That's the twins' favorite part of live baseball, too," Drew said with a chuckle.

"See? We have a lot in common already."

"And playing? How are you at hitting a curve ball?"

That, Stephanie thought, depended entirely on what kind of curve ball was being thrown. The ones life had been pitching her lately had been beaning her in the head. But she supposed he was asking about the real kind, the one with a literal ball. "If you want to challenge me to play, I'm down with it—and I'll warn you right now, I'm the woman to beat."

"Intriguing. I'm going to put your words to the test, you know. The twins are on a T-ball team, and they'll want you to practice with them. They'll probably want you to come cheer them on at their games, too."

"I would love to," Stephanie answered sincerely. In her experience, being a nanny and being a cheerleader often went hand in hand. Anything she could do to instill in her charges the self-esteem she lacked as a child was worthwhile in her book.

"Most Saturdays I take them out to practice in the park," Drew continued. "I'm not sure we'll get to it today, but maybe next weekend we can bat a few balls."

At the word *park,* Quincy whined and pawed at Drew's leg. He laughed and scratched the dog behind his ears. "You can play, too, Quincy."

She smirked. "Your dog plays baseball?"

"He makes a formidable outfielder. He'll retrieve the baseball no matter where it goes and bring it back to us. That way we don't have to run around and pick them up."

"I can't wait to see it."

Chapter Four

Drew leaned back in his chair, folded his arms and watched the new nanny sharing lunch with his children. He'd already wolfed down his own burger and was sitting with an empty plate in front of him.

He'd never expected that there would ever be a time in his life where it would be in his best interest to hire someone out of the family to care for his kids. Not in Serendipity. It just wasn't done that way here—not to mention he'd thought he'd be a married man for the rest of his life and have a wife at his side to help care for the children. But things being what they were, he had to admit he was impressed with Stephanie, even if he'd had to dip into his meager retirement account to pay for her.

Anything to keep his kids.

Boisterous, red-headed Jo Murphy, the owner of the café, sashayed up to them with refills on all their drinks. As usual, she was right on top of things, anticipating needs and meeting them before a word could be spoken.

"You almost spilled my coffee," his father complained as Jo refilled his cup.

"Oh, hush, you," Jo said, swatting at him with her free hand. "I did not, and you know it. I've poured more cups of coffee than you've taken naps," she teased merrily, "and that's saying something."

Both of them shared a laugh, their gazes locked on each other. Drew wanted to roll his eyes. It was always like this with his father and Jo.

As far as he was concerned, they ought to just admit they had feelings for each other and tie the knot, but he doubted that would ever happen. They had this odd, mutual sparring war going on between them, but it was comfortable, and he supposed it was okay for them to keep it that way.

Stephanie was looking at the old couple speculatively. Drew was sure she could see what was obviously going on. The secretive smile on her face gave her away.

After a moment she turned her attention back to the boys. Matty and Jamey were definitely benefiting from her attention. She'd convinced them to eat sliced apples with their burgers instead of their usual French fries, simply by indicating that that was what she was ordering, too. Even though she'd only recently come into the boys' lives, they appeared anxious to emulate and impress her.

"Eat your hamburger, sweetie," Stephanie encouraged Matty, who, as usual, was mostly just pushing his food around on his plate and turning his sandwich into a big, sloppy mess.

To Drew's surprise, Matty did as he was told.

The first time. No counting down. No scolding.

Stephanie simply spoke and Matty listened. She seemed to have an instinctive understanding of how to get his sons to cooperate.

Or, to be more precise, Matty *half* cooperated. He took the burger part of the hamburger and shoved the whole thing into his mouth.

Stephanie laughed. "Not all at once, sweetheart. You don't want to choke on it."

"You really have a way with children." His compliment was sincere and for once he didn't trip over his tongue.

"You ought to see me with babies," she responded glibly, and then blanched, her eyes widening. "I—I mean, wh-what I meant to say is that I've had a lot of experience with young children," she stammered. "Most of it isn't on my resume."

"Firstborn of a large family?" Drew guessed, pushing aside his plate so he could rest his arms on the table.

He'd been an only child himself, so he had been clueless about how to care for babies when the twins had come along. It had all been trial and error with him, from the bottles to the diapers.

"Families, plural," Stephanie corrected, pressing her lips together. "I was a foster child, a genuine product of the system." She glanced at the boys to make sure they were busy eating and not listening to the adult conversation. "I was in six foster homes before I hit my eighteenth birthday."

"I'm sorry." He didn't know what else to say. It had obviously taken its toll on her, and he guessed her foster years hadn't been good ones.

"No need. I managed all right. At first I resented it when I got stuck babysitting the little kids in the family I was staying with, but somewhere along the way I realized I actually *liked* taking care of children. I studied hard in high school and worked as a nanny while I pursued my bachelor's degree in early childhood education." She took a breath, trying to smile, though it didn't reach her eyes. "And there you have my entire life in a nutshell."

He cocked his head and raised an eyebrow. "Somehow, I don't think that's all there is to the story. I imagine there is much about you I have yet to learn."

As soon as he said the words he knew they hadn't come out the least bit like how an employer should talk to an employee. He'd been trying to make her feel better, and he was being borderline flirtatious. Guessing from the attractive pink shade slashed across her cheeks, she'd thought the same thing.

In Drew's mind, that left Stephanie with two options. Flirt back, or shut him down.

Her gaze dropped to the table and the crimson staining her cheeks phased into a cherry red. "Nothing I want to talk about. Not yet."

Remorse hit him hard and fast. He hadn't meant to put her on the spot. He'd only been joking. Or, at least, half joking. He really did want to get to know her better.

What was she hiding? Was it cause for concern that a woman with her credentials and background would apply for a relatively low-paying position in a small town in the middle of nowhere?

He was sure she had her reasons, but they were none of his business. He decided right then and there that he was going to keep his curiosity to himself—and try not to put his foot in his mouth again.

None of this was permanent. It was just a means to an end. Stephanie was a godsend, and his lawyer seemed to think her presence might mean the difference between him being able to keep custody of his boys or them going to live with their unstable mother.

"Okay, boys," Stephanie said brightly, as if nothing were wrong and he hadn't just stuck his nose where it didn't belong. She laid a hand on Jamey's shoulder. "I don't know about you, but I'm stuffed. What do you say we get up and walk off some of the delicious food we ate?"

She was referring to returning home on foot, just as they'd gotten there. Serendipity was such a small town that it only had one main street with a three-way intersection at the middle worthy only of a stop sign. There wasn't a single stop light in all of the town.

The Spencers lived close enough to make the trek into town on foot, even the preschoolers. Drew walked to work most days, unless the weather was particularly hot or cold.

Three women a little younger than Drew entered the café, chattering and giggling loudly amongst themselves. He'd gone to high school with these ladies, and they were some of the friendliest people he'd ever known. They'd be thrilled to meet Stephanie, and he hoped she might cultivate some friendships in town, as well.

He would have called the ladies over to introduce them to Stephanie, but he knew he needn't bother. They would approach just as soon as they'd seen that there was a visitor in town, without him having to do anything special to attract their attention.

And he was right. Within moments of entering the café, Samantha Howell, whose parents owned the local grocery, glanced in their direction and her eyes lit up with interest.

"A diet cola for me," she called back over her shoulder as she made a beeline for the new figure in town. Drew smothered a grin. He didn't know who, exactly, was going to do the ordering, because as soon as the other ladies—Alexis Granger and Mary Travis—saw where Samantha was heading, they forgot about their drinks and followed their friend to Drew's table.

"Hey, Spence," Samantha greeted warmly. "You didn't mention any relatives coming to town to visit."

Ha! He grinned despite himself. Samantha was fishing—and none too subtly, either. He found it amusing just to let them dangle for a moment, even if he was appalled by the direction in which the conversation was obviously headed. Because as soon as they knew Stephanie wasn't a relative....

"Sam, Alexis, Mary," he said, pointing to each woman in turn. "Meet Stephanie Cartwright. She's the twins' new nanny. She only arrived in town about a week ago."

"O-o-oh," Alexis purred, lengthening the syllable. "And how did we not hear about this? Where are you staying, Stephanie?"

"With Drew," she replied with a friendly smile. "I'm watching the twins full-time, and I've taken up residence at his house."

Drew nearly cringed when he saw the spark of interest in his friends' eyes. They didn't say it aloud—for a change—but he knew exactly what they were thinking.

"In an apartment above my garage," he jumped in, amending Stephanie's statement, not that it would do any good now that certain ideas had been planted in the women's heads.

Small town. Beautiful woman. Single dad. They could connect the dots, even if the picture they created was completely off the mark.

Now it was *his* face turning red.

"I didn't even know you had an apartment over your garage," Alexis commented. "How many times have I been to your house now? And I had no clue."

"It was my study," Drew explained, exasperated. "And it's just temporary," he felt inclined to add. "To help my boys make a smooth transition, you know?"

He didn't have to say what kind of transition they were making. Everyone in town knew of the demise of his marriage.

And he didn't mention the Child and Family Services Investigator or the court date. His business was his business. He sometimes spoke to Jo Murphy, who was like a mother to him, but otherwise he preferred to keep his private life to himself. Jo was ordinarily the root of the gossip tree, but she also knew when to keep silent.

The women chatting at his table? Not so much.

Affectionately known about town as the Little Chicks, they would have the news of Stephanie's arrival spread throughout the town before the day was done. Which was both good and bad.

Good, in that Stephanie would likely be approached

by many curious friends and neighbors at church tomorrow, her Christian brothers and sisters who would be there to support her if she needed it.

Bad, because now it was highly likely folks were going to get the wrong impression before even meeting her. The young ladies meant well and they were genuine in their friendship, but they hadn't earned their high school moniker Little Chicks for nothing. In this instance, their "cheeping" would be heard loud and clear from one end of the town to the other. Drew doubted it would take as much as a whole day for the news to spread about Stephanie's arrival.

Which meant going to church might turn out to be diving into a feeding frenzy, with Stephanie as the bait. People would not only want to meet Stephanie, but they would want to see her with Drew—to get the *real* story on why she was in town. Everyone would have a theory, and some of them wouldn't be pretty.

He shouldn't have expected any less. His ex-wife, Heather, had grown up in Serendipity. She and Drew had attended school together, although she'd been much more popular than he'd ever been. He was studious and academic, while in high school she had been the tri-county rodeo princess four years running.

People remembered her, and they remembered Drew's tumultuous relationship with her. A few even knew the truth about why the marriage had ended. But for those who didn't, he wasn't ready to besmirch her name with the gritty details of their breakup, even if she deserved it.

He doubted this hiring-a-nanny-from-out-of-town thing was going to slide through, however. It was just a little too out of the ordinary. People in Serendipity looked out after their own, and Heather had been one of their own, even though she'd moved away from the town after the divorce.

Drew was a third-generation Serendipity native. To hire Stephanie was like waving a red flag to tell everyone that something was out of sorts.

"They seemed nice," Stephanie commented as Alexis, Samantha and Mary picked up their diet colas and went on their way.

"That's a polite way of saying it. They're very— unreserved. Probably the most forward and social of the folks you'll encounter here, though most everyone is friendly to a fault. We affectionately refer to them as the Little Chicks."

"Because?" Golden eyebrows arched over her warm, brown eyes. Their gazes met, and his breath hitched tight in his throat.

Drew coughed into his hand to dislodge the uncomfortable feeling, but it stubbornly remained. "When they get together, they become so animated it starts to sound like chirping. The football team came up with that moniker for them in high school, and to their misfortune, it just stuck. Permanently."

"Hmm," Stephanie replied thoughtfully, her gaze seeking the door where the ladies had just left. "Well, as long as they don't mind, I guess."

Drew was taken aback by the comment. He sat back in the booth and rubbed his chin pensively.

"Honestly, I hadn't thought about it that way," he admitted with a rueful shrug, feeling a little callous that the thought *hadn't* ever crossed his mind. "But they're all good with it, at least as far as I know. They got a lot of attention in high school being the giggly girls they were, and the three of them are best friends to this day, so something good must have come out of it."

Stephanie's gaze dropped to her plate. She picked up an apple slice and bit the end off of it.

"In high school, I was the studious girl with few real friends, the one who often sat alone at the lunch table and actually did her algebra homework."

Drew couldn't believe that, not for a second. It wasn't just that she was beautiful, although there was certainly that, high school being the fickle place that it was. Had she been an ugly duckling who'd later developed into a swan?

Even if that were true, there was so much more to Stephanie than her looks, so much she had to offer. She was beautiful on the inside, as well as the outside. She was generous, and warm and caring. She was a little shy, maybe, but he couldn't imagine that friends wouldn't flock to her.

She offered him a weak smile and shrugged.

"Be careful, boys," she said, laying a gentle hand on Matty's shoulder.

Jamey and Matty had taken out their little Matchbox cars and were making roads between their plates and glasses, complete with the sounds of racing and swerving.

"Mind Stephanie," he agreed. "You don't want to accidentally spill your milk."

Stephanie stacked the plates and arranged the silverware and the glasses for easy pickup. "The service here is exceptional. We never had to ask for a refill or an extra condiment or anything. Jo anticipated our every need."

Drew's lips curved upward. "Small town."

She leaned forward and caught his eye. "During the time we've been in the restaurant, Jo has greeted every single person in the room by name."

Drew chuckled. "That's not all she knows—she's into everybody's business—in great detail. And she's not afraid to ask customers about their personal lives. But she's the most kindhearted person in the world and she is like a second mother to much of the town."

Stephanie reached for her purse and laid a generous tip on the table.

Drew protested with a shake of his head, but Stephanie insisted. "You paid for the meal. Leaving the tip is the least I can do."

It wasn't as if this was a date. The furthest thing from it, in fact. He flexed his fists and breathed deeply.

Call him old-fashioned, but it still grated against his consciousness to let a woman pay for anything when he was out for a meal with her. Stephanie was a strong, independent woman, and he respected that. But still. It might be his male pride flaring, but Stephanie was a lady and he was going to treat her like one.

She paused, almost as if she suspected he would protest.

When he didn't, she smiled. "Are we good?"

He shrugged and nodded briefly. "Sure. We're good."

But when Stephanie turned to herd the children to the washroom to clean up, he swiped the tip from the table and returned it to the pocket of her purse, replacing it with his own money.

A man had to live up to his standards, after all.

Stephanie was slightly nervous and very excited about going to services at a church where she didn't know anyone.

For one thing, although she considered herself a Christian, she had hardly ever been inside a church, much less attended a church service—at least in the traditional sense. She'd been to a few weddings and funerals, but that was the extent of it.

At first it was because her foster family wouldn't allow her to get away. She'd only been to camp meetings with her friends during the summer break.

She'd accepted Christ at one of their altar calls, but had never followed up the way she should have. She got caught up in college and Ryan, and…well, if she was being honest, there *weren't* any good excuses for why she hadn't joined a church once she had turned eighteen and was out on her own.

She just hadn't.

She was curious about what a small-town church service was like. She pictured it being cozy and welcoming, rather than closed and cliquish. The people she'd met in Serendipity so far had been gracious and friendly.

But even so, Drew had built it up to the point where it was an enormous hurdle in her mind. The idea of meeting practically an entire town all at once was a little intimidating, especially for her. She wasn't the most outgoing person in the world. She was a natural with kids, but adults, not so much. That Drew would be at her side reassured her a little, but she was still nervous.

She needn't have worried. The moment she and Drew walked through the doors of the church with Frank and the twins, she heard her name being called.

"Stephanie," Mary called, gesturing for her to join their group. "We're so glad you could make it."

"Go," Drew said. He'd had his hand on the small of her back to guide her in the door, and now he gently pushed her forward. "I'll get the boys to their Sunday school class."

Stephanie timidly entered the women's circle. "I'm happy to be here," she said, and meant it. Even though the vestibule of the church was far more crowded than she had imagined it would be, her nerves seemed to have fled as soon as she'd come into contact with the three genial women. Somehow they seemed like old friends.

"We need to make a plan," said Alexis. "How many people have you met so far, Stephanie?"

"A handful, counting you ladies."

"All right, then. I say we start at the front door and work the room clockwise." Alexis glanced at her watch. "There's twenty minutes before the service starts. If we keep the introductions short, we ought to be able to make a full circle by then."

Stephanie's nerves jolted back to life. "Everyone?" she croaked through dry lips.

"I think we're overwhelming her," Mary said, pressing a hand to Stephanie's shoulder. "Maybe we should start with a few people and go from there."

Alexis looked disappointed, but Samantha smiled and nodded.

"Take it easy on me, girls," Stephanie said, holding up her hands palms outward.

"Of course," Samantha agreed, and then pointed to a nearby table that was loaded with finger foods. "There's Pastor Shawn swiping a powdered donut while no one is looking. He probably thinks he needs a good sugar high during his sermon."

"Perfect. Let's start with him," Alexis exclaimed.

Stephanie wasn't certain she wanted to start with the pastor of the church, but the three women expertly guided her through the maze of people to the table where Pastor Shawn stood, quietly munching on his treat. He was quite a bit younger than Stephanie would have expected a pastor to be, and handsome in his own way—if one was supposed to call a pastor handsome. He looked as if he might have come from a military background, with flat-top, short cut blond hair that reminded her of a Marine.

"Pastor," Alexis said, giving him a friendly hug as they approached. "This is Stephanie Cartwright. Drew Spencer hired her as a nanny for his kids."

"I'm sure you'll be a great help to them," he answered, extending his hand to Stephanie with a genuine smile. "I'm Pastor Shawn O'Riley. If you need anything, don't hesitate to ask."

"Thank you. I will."

"How long have you been a nanny? Do you enjoy your work?"

"Yes, sir, very much. I got my Bachelor of Science degree in early childhood education. I worked my way through school as a nanny, and continued in the profession even after I graduated from college. Eventually I'd like to teach preschool, but I'm perfectly content at the moment watching over Drew's adorable little twins."

The gleam of an idea appeared Pastor Shawn's blue eyes. "Maybe you can teach preschool here in Serendipity."

Stephanie tilted her head in surprise. "I thought there wasn't a preschool."

Pastor Shawn shrugged nonchalantly, but there was something in his gaze that seemed serious. "Not yet. Maybe you could change that. Never forget that you have something unique to offer—here in the town, and to the world."

"Have you ever taught Sunday school before?" Alexis queried. "Mary is the volunteer in charge of rounding up teachers, and we're always short. What do you say to teaching the three- and four-year-olds, Stephanie?"

She shook her head. "I'm only going to be here for a couple of months. It's a temporary position, just until—" She was going to say until Drew cleared up the custody issue, but she wasn't sure he wanted people knowing about that. "Until the end of the school year," she said instead.

"Do what you can when you can. You are exactly where God has called you to be," Pastor Shawn said. "That's the title of my sermon today. Well, not exactly. I'm paraphrasing."

"Even though I'm not staying in town?" Stephanie wasn't sure she should be questioning the pastor about the sermon before he'd even preached it, but she was definitely interested in the answer.

"God's placed you right here, right now, for a purpose. It's your job to figure out what that purpose is, and then to act on it."

Samantha rolled her eyes. "Pastor Shawn always makes it sound so simple. If it were that easy, there'd be a lot more harmony in the world."

"Amen to that," Pastor Shawn agreed, reaching for another donut and popping it into his mouth. "Well, I'd best be going. I need to robe up before the service."

"Okay. Where to now?" Alexis wondered aloud. "Pastor Shawn took up an awful lot of our time."

Stephanie was still trying to digest what the pastor had told her. She'd been so busy looking over her shoulder into her past that she hadn't been living in the present. She realized that it was high time she did.

"Are you ready to go into the sanctuary?" It wasn't a female voice who asked that question. It was male. And it was Drew.

"Oh. We didn't have time to introduce her to everyone yet." Alexis sounded dejected.

"You ladies can continue your little tour after church, in the fellowship hall," Drew said with an amused chuckle.

"I'll catch you later," she told the Little Chicks as Drew took her elbow and guided her toward the sanctuary.

Frank was already seated on the far right rear section marked for handicapped people. Sure, Frank walked with a limp, but Stephanie hardly considered him handicapped. With his cane, he could probably beat her in a footrace if he put his mind to it.

Not surprisingly, Jo was sitting with him, her head close to his as she whispered something in her ear. They sure did make a cute couple.

Drew led her to the second row to the left and gestured for her to go in before him. Immediately, he knelt down and bowed his head, his lips moving silently as he prayed.

For a moment, Stephanie simply sat on the pew by his side, watching him and wondering what he was praying for.

It felt a little awkward for her to kneel down beside him, since this was her first real experience with church, but she ignored her discomfort as she folded her hands in front of her and opened her heart in prayer.

After speaking to Pastor Shawn, she had a lot to pray about. Living in the present, having a purpose. It was all pretty overwhelming. How was she supposed to find out why God had brought her to Serendipity and what she was supposed to do here?

Peace flowed through her as she continued to kneel in prayer. She might not know all the answers, but she was exactly where she needed to be to ask the One who did.

Chapter Five

By the time Stephanie had been with the Spencers for three weeks, they'd established a fairly predictable routine. Stephanie had never been happier taking care of children as she was with Matty and Jamey. The Spencers included her in everything from family devotions to board games. Sometimes she almost forgot she wasn't family.

Drew didn't treat her like hired help. He regarded her as an equal, with respect and courtesy. He was a gentleman from the tip of his hat to the heel of his cowboy boots, and his reading glasses and necktie in between. He didn't look down on her, as Ryan had.

Ryan came from a rich family and thought everyone was below him, her included. And she'd let him treat her that way. He'd insisted she quit her job, not because it was beneath her, but because it was beneath *him*.

And then, as it turned out, *marriage* was beneath him—at least, marriage to her. He'd wanted the milk without the cow, and that was something she could never do. So she'd left. Or maybe she had run away.

She didn't like to think of the past, and purposefully

pushed her memories back whenever they surfaced. She refused to live in fear. As Pastor Shawn had reminded her, she couldn't serve God by living in the past. She needed to embrace the now, and that was exactly what she intended to do.

Though she'd settled comfortably into the household, she hadn't yet had an official tour of the town. When she commented about it, Drew promised to show her the sights on Saturday. She found herself looking forward to the outing—as much to spend time with Drew as to see the town close up.

Thus far, she'd only visited the church on one corner of Main Street, and Cup O' Jo on the other. She thought it would be fun to walk the length of the town and see what all of the other old buildings looked like. Drew had promised the twins they'd play baseball in the park afterward, so everyone was happy.

Once they reached the square at the center of the town, Stephanie paused, taking a moment just to enjoy Serendipity's unique ambiance. The town had been built in the late 1800s, and she imagined it looked nearly the same as it had back then.

As they wandered down the town's solitary main street, Cup O' Jo Café, Emerson's Hardware and Sam's Grocery caught her eye. Nearly every shop, all built with rugged clapboard, had a personal name attached to its shingle. The air smelled slightly of what she thought must be horses—and maybe cows—but oddly, it was no longer an unpleasant odor for her, and it wasn't as if she could see any livestock around, although she'd seen more than a few animals while making the short trek into town.

Of course, there was the quaint, small white chapel at the end of the way, with its red doors and a pointed steeple with a bell and its ability to hold far more people than it looked capable of. She wondered if they ever rang that bell for Christmases or weddings.

Their feet echoed on the wood-planked sidewalk as they continued down the street. The three old men in bib overalls congregated in front of Emerson's hardware store waved as they passed, and a few children of various ages ran through the streets playing a game of hide-and-seek, but for the most part there wasn't much action, especially for a Saturday afternoon. Stephanie could not believe how quiet it all was.

"There's not much to show you," Drew said, sounding as if he was apologizing for the town—or rather, the lack of one. "In Serendipity, pretty much what you see is what you get."

"I like what I see," she assured him.

She wouldn't admit that her statement encompassed the good-looking man walking next to her who was wearing boots and a cowboy hat and looking very pleased by her comment about his town. His kids were cute. And the way he devoted himself to them, being an attentive father, was very attractive, perhaps because she was a nanny and making sure children were well cared for was her living.

So maybe she did like what she saw. She supposed she could add that small addendum—to herself.

"I haven't noticed any schools around," she remarked as they strolled along the wooden sidewalk. "Where is the elementary school where you work?"

"The town is kind of shaped like a T," Drew explained, pointing to the only side street off the main thoroughfare. "Main Street here is our major cruising district," he joked, "but you'll find the police and fire stations down that way, along with a small library and two school buildings. We have one for the elementary kids, and then the middle and high schoolers share a building. There's a football field between them, but for the most part, our kids' sports teams use the community center to practice and play."

"That sounds a little cramped."

Drew chuckled. "Sometimes. But you've got to remember we're only talking about a population of eight-hundred-some-odd people. I imagine the class sizes where you're from are a bit larger than here in Serendipity."

"Much larger. Thirty-five to forty students per classroom."

"Wow. I have eleven."

"Eleven what?"

"Students in my fifth-grade class," he clarified.

"Seriously?" Stephanie was starting to picture an old one-room schoolhouse with Drew teaching up front, a ruler in his hand and a cowboy hat on his head. "Even my online college classes had more students than that."

"What we lack in numbers we make up in sincerity," he informed her, feigning an affronted sniff. "Virtually every adult in town graduated from Serendipity High School—home of the Panthers—and they all have a vested interest in both our competitive sports teams and our musicians. We also have a formidable debate team," he teased with a wink.

"Oh, now you're talking," Stephanie responded,

maybe a little too enthusiastically. "I was on the debate team in high school."

"Really?" He sounded as if he didn't believe her.

She tilted up her chin, not that the gesture made much of a difference, since he was so much taller than she. "I'll have you know that not only was I *on* the debate team, but I was team captain two years running."

If she sounded animated when she spoke of high school debate, it was with good reason. She had hoped touring with the debate team would help her break out of her painfully shy shell, and it had. She'd made new friends and had even found a date to her senior prom through debate.

"Are you trying to tell me that arguing is your forte?" Drew smothered a grin by coughing into his fist.

"Not arguing. Logic," she replied tartly. Which was true, even if *none* of her recent actions contained the least bit of logic.

"The words *logic* and *woman* do not belong in the same sentence," he informed her, trying to keep a straight face. Instead, he ended up outright laughing—so much so that it took him a moment to regroup. "But seriously," he continued, swiping his fingers over his eyes as his lips continued to twitch, "if you want to volunteer to coach debate while you're here, I'm sure the high school team would welcome your expertise."

Her eyes widened. "Are you serious? Just like that?"

"Just like that. Why are you surprised?"

"Having the credentials to work with children, especially in a school setting, is more complicated in New Jersey. I'm a nanny, not an educator."

"I thought nannies *were* educators. It seems to me you've already taught my boys a lot and you've only had them for a few weeks."

"Well, thank you, I think. But teaching preschoolers and teaching high schoolers is hardly comparable."

He lifted an eyebrow. "No? You'd be surprised. You'll have less trouble with the preschoolers."

She chuckled. "Probably. I'd like to give back to the community while I'm here, but I think I'm better suited for something like the preschool Sunday school class than a high school debate team."

"I'm sure Pastor Shawn will be happy to hear that. It's going to be a striking loss for our debate team, though."

Her gaze snapped to his. "I said *like* Sunday school. Don't go telling Pastor Shawn I've discovered my calling."

His eyebrows rose, and he cocked his head. "Haven't you?"

Without answering, Stephanie broke her gaze away from his and reined the boys in so they wouldn't dart out into the street after a couple older children who chose that moment to run past them. She hadn't seen a single car go by, but it still made her nervous.

Drew gestured with his chin. "It's okay. You can let the boys go."

"Into the *street?*"

He chuckled. "Sometimes I forget you come from somewhere where there are cars on the road."

"And—what? You all ride horses?" she teased.

"Well, yes, ma'am, we do," Drew said in a comical accent that was nothing like his genuine soft-spoken drawl. "See right there? We've got a hitching post and a watering trough and everything—right in front of the bar."

The *bar* he was so playfully indicating was Jo's café, but to Stephanie's surprise, there really *was* an old hitching post and watering trough in front of it, which she hadn't noticed before, maybe because it blended in so well with the town's old-West flavor.

"Well, I'll be," she murmured under her breath.

"Yeah. See? I told you so."

Jamey came around from behind her and vaulted upward into her arms. The move caught her off guard, but she managed to catch him underneath the shoulder blades and swing him around in a circle.

"I won't doubt you again," she promised.

Matty squealed and lunged forward, his hands in the air. "Me too, me too, me too!"

Stephanie obliged the small, wiggling boy, laughing along with him as she swung him around in the air.

"Is it always so quiet around here?" she asked, gesturing to include all of Main Street.

Drew held his hands out for Matty, who crawled from Stephanie's arms into his, while Jamey attached himself to Stephanie's leg and didn't look as if he was going to let go anytime soon.

"We haven't reached the park yet. That's where all the action is on Saturday afternoons. And you've already experienced Sundays at the church."

Oh, yes. She had. After that first week, she'd resolved to attend every Sunday service with Drew. The last week's sermon was as interesting and relevant to Stephanie as the first week's had been, and she was excited to go again tomorrow and hear what new insights Pastor Shawn had for his congregation.

"And let's not forget the parties. Serendipity throws whopping shindigs. Generally for anything and everything they can find to celebrate."

Stephanie wasn't the party type, but she thought she might like to go if Drew was with her. She knew lots of the town people now. She already considered the Little Chicks dear friends.

"Maybe I can attend one before I have to leave town."

His eyebrows rose and his gaze turned pensive. "I'd like that. I mean, I think you'd like it. May Day is coming up. Some of the ladies from the church organize a fairly large social event every year. Flowers and Maypoles and tons of food. They even crown one lucky lady May Queen." He made a face. "Except for the food, it's not really my cup of tea, but I'd be happy to take you, if you want."

Before Stephanie could answer him, Matty and Jamey sprinted off down the street. Stephanie quickened her pace to catch up with them.

"Not so fast, boys," Drew called, but the boys didn't appear to hear him. Stephanie's breath caught when the boys rounded the corner and darted out of sight.

"Not to worry," Drew insisted, laying a hand on her arm. "The park is just around the corner. They'll be crawling around on one of the jungle gyms by the time we get there."

"I'd still feel better if I could see them."

Moments later they rounded the corner and reached the park themselves. Stephanie had to admit she was impressed. As Drew had said, there was a large green-belt that might have covered the expanse of a city block, had they been in a city.

Serendipity might be small in size, but it was big in heart. The playground equipment looked as if it had been pieced together—a little wood here, a little plastic there. A few steel pipes and girders. There was no real architectural plan that Stephanie could see. It wasn't *pretty*. But it was definitely made with love. The important thing where children were concerned was that it was safe and functional, and that there was a lot of it.

This park fulfilled all three of those requirements.

And it was a good thing, because there were a lot of kids. Skipping, swinging, playing, laughing children swarming over the playground equipment like ants.

Drew hadn't been kidding when he'd said this was how Serendipity townsfolk spent their Saturday afternoons—congregated at the park. Kids of all ages squirreled over the playground equipment while adults assembled in small groups where they could speak with one another and still keep one watchful eye on the kids.

And he'd been right about the twins, as well. Matty and Jamey had already each climbed aboard one of a circle of spring-loaded "horses" painted in primary colors. The boys' little arms and legs pumped furiously as they rocked their steeds.

Neighbors and friends smiled and waved as they approached. Several people called greetings specifically to her. It was amazing how fast she'd become enmeshed into this community. She felt more at home here than she had anywhere else she'd ever lived. She had to remind herself that this was only temporary, that she wouldn't be staying for long.

A woman carrying an infant in a lime-green sling was the first to draw near. Stephanie recognized the duo as Cup O' Jo's official baker, Phoebe Hawkins, and her baby, Aaron. Drew greeted Phoebe with a kiss on the cheek and then excused himself to speak to a friend.

Stephanie hadn't had much of an opportunity to speak with Phoebe before now, but it didn't bother her that Drew had left her alone to speak with the woman. She'd heard a lot about Phoebe from Frank. Phoebe had been a world-class pastry chef, but had somehow managed to end up married to a local man—Chance Hawkins, Jo's nephew.

"It's nice to see a new face in town," Phoebe said with a welcoming smile.

"Um…thank you?" What was the correct response for that?

Phoebe laughed, a light, cheerful sound without the least bit of censure or guile.

"By that I mean to say, until you showed up in town *I* was considered the last *new face* in town, and I've been here almost two years. You've been taking the heat off of me." Her pretty mouth curved into a frown as she surveyed Stephanie's dismayed expression. "Oh, don't let me frighten you. People around here are the greatest."

"I know. Just a couple of weeks in church and I already feel like I'm part of the community."

"The townspeople have a way about them, don't they? I don't think I've ever come across friendlier people. I spent years traveling the world learning to cook, but no place compares to Serendipity.

"I heard you're taking care of Drew Spencer's twins," Phoebe commented, gently bouncing the baby boy in her arms. Stephanie wondered how the whole town seemed to know about her, even though she had yet to meet everyone. The town gossip tree seemed to be especially sturdy in Serendipity.

"You're not a relative, are you? Please tell me you're not Drew's cousin or something." Phoebe cast Drew an appreciative glance that seemed to say, *"I'm happily married, so everyone should be as happy as I am—and Drew's perfect for you,"* and then turned her gaze back on Stephanie.

"I'm not a relative," Stephanie verified. She wasn't completely ignorant of what Phoebe was thinking, and she decided she ought to stop that train before it started. It wasn't the first time she'd felt that vibe from someone in the town—the Little Chicks all seemed to be pushing her toward Drew, and even Frank made a couple of remarks that suggested he thought she'd be better suited as Drew's wife than as his twins' nanny.

"There's nothing romantic about the reason I'm here," she continued quickly. "I'm the nanny, and nothing more—and it's a temporary position, at that. For some reason more than one person in this town seems to think I'm here to marry him, not take care of his kids."

"I know, right? Like a mail-order bride or something." Phoebe rolled her eyes. "Right idea. Wrong century."

Phoebe put her at ease, and Stephanie chuckled. "He

needed someone college-educated and here I am. I'm only here until the end of the school term, when he'll be able to watch the boys himself."

"Temporary, huh? Believe me, I'm the last person on the planet who would want to put pressure on you—I've been right where you're standing. But I'm warning you right now that the rest of the people in this town aren't going to leave you alone." She gazed meaningfully at Stephanie. "You and Drew are too easy a mark for folks to pass on. They don't have much live entertainment around here, so they make it up."

"Lovely," Stephanie murmured, only half joking. She glanced at Drew. He had his back to her and was speaking to a couple of men that looked to be around his age. She had to admit Drew was an attractive man—tall, broad-shouldered, even-featured. She could see how someone might make the mistake of thinking she was interested in him in a romantic way. Who wouldn't find the single dad attractive?

But she wasn't here for a relationship, and he certainly wasn't in the market for one. She had to wonder how *he* was going to feel about all this potential matchmaking? The pressure would be intense, especially because these were his friends and neighbors, people he'd known all his life. He was clearly still recovering from a nasty divorce. The last thing he needed was the community pushing a romantic involvement between him and his temporary employee.

"Is there anything I can do about it?" She didn't realize she'd asked the question aloud until Phoebe chuckled and shook her head.

"I can only tell you what happened to me. Let's just

say I lost that particular war." She kissed her baby on his dark-tufted head, her gaze filled with adoration. Aaron responded by gurgling and pumping his long legs, his breath coming in short pants as he stared back at her. He was clearly excited to have his mama's attention, and she cooed back at him.

He was an adorable baby, and Stephanie had to cross her arms against the compelling urge to reach for him. It was as instinctive to her as breathing.

Phoebe must have sensed her feelings, for she pulled little Aaron from the sling and offered him to Stephanie. "It seems like this little bruiser grows bigger every day. He's getting heavy for me. You want to hold him for a minute?"

"Oh. Yes, please. He's just gorgeous." Stephanie appreciated Phoebe's kindness more than she would ever know. She held the squirming bundle of joy close to her heart and burrowed her cheek next to his, breathing in his baby scent. There was nothing like it in the world.

Someday, God-willing, she would hold a baby of her own. Several, if she had her way.

"I wish I could tell you that you were going to get away from Serendipity without losing your heart, but I'm afraid I'm living proof of it working the other way around."

"So figuratively, at least, you lost the fight? It doesn't look like you mind too terribly much."

Phoebe laughed. "Oh, no. Not at all. Quite the opposite, actually. I hadn't the least intention of starting a relationship when I came to Serendipity. Like you, I had a temporary position. I was just looking for a break from my crazy schedule back home for a while." She sighed with contentment. "Instead, I found a home here. I fell completely and madly in love with Chance. One minute we were working together, and the next we're married with two children—Aaron and Lucy, his daughter from his first marriage."

"That won't happen to me," Stephanie assured her. "Like I said, I'm only passing through town." For a moment, she wondered what it would be like to stay in Serendipity, to make it her permanent home.

The idea took a moment to settle, but it quickly took roost. What *would* it be like to live in a place like Serendipity, where everyone knew her, where friends and neighbors really cared?

Did she have something special to offer in return, as Pastor Shawn had said?

Was it possible, as the pastor had suggested, that she could make her dream into a reality and start a preschool in the town? Even the thought of it nearly overwhelmed her. She was finding it difficult to catch a breath. But she couldn't simply set the notion aside, no matter how hard she tried.

Phoebe flashed her a knowing glance, as if she had discerned information Stephanie was not privy to. "That's what I said, too. I'm living proof that love can creep up on you when you least expect it. And Serendipity—it grows on you. If you're not careful, you'll be woven into the fabric of the town so tightly that you can't be cut away from it. I'm just warning you."

"Warning her about what?" Drew asked, rejoining the ladies.

Phoebe looked amused, but to Stephanie's relief, she

deflected Drew's question. "I was just telling Stephanie here how Serendipity tends to grow on you."

"Does it, now?" Drew drawled, his gaze narrowing as it moved between the two women.

"Are you taking her to the May Day picnic next Saturday, Spence?" Phoebe asked, her voice bubbly with excitement.

Really? Stephanie cringed. She thought Phoebe was going to be on her side, but it looked as if she was already trying to set the two of them up. Phoebe had certainly made it sound as if she was pushing Drew to ask her out on a date.

Drew sighed, sounding taxed. He must have caught on to the sudden influx of underhanded matchmaking ploys, as well. He was clearly stressed about something.

"Of course. I started to explain about the party, but then we got to chasing the boys and our conversation got derailed somewhere along the way. So what do you think, Steph?"

Her heart started pounding erratically, which was ridiculous, since he *wasn't* asking her out on a date. If he had been, she would have had to say no. But since he was only asking her as a friend and an employee, she felt obligated to accept.

Obligated. And she was just going to keep telling herself that until she believed it.

"Yes. I'd enjoy that. Are you going to be there, Phoebe?"

"Oh, definitely. The whole family will be there. The whole *town.* Even more people than Sunday's regular church crowd. If you haven't been introduced to everybody in Serendipity, you'll be able to meet them next Saturday at the May Day picnic."

Drew looped a half Windsor through his necktie and adjusted it without looking in the mirror. As was his habit, he wore a tie to school every day. He might be a small-town teacher, but he took his job seriously—maybe too seriously—and always tried to represent the children in his care to the best of his ability. That included the way he dressed—slacks, an oxford shirt and a necktie.

Even on a Monday morning, when he was exhausted. He hadn't been sleeping well lately. Knowing a case worker was going to show up at his door any day now.

When he entered the kitchen, Stephanie was already there, serving up scrambled eggs and toast to his father and the boys. She had his *Everything is Under Control* apron wrapped around her tiny waist again, but this time he wasn't as jarred by the sensation of seeing her dressed in his apron as he had been that first time.

In fact, she looked as if she belonged in his kitchen, and he was comfortable having her there. And it wasn't some kind of misogynistic male chauvinism making him feel that way.

It was the look on his boys' faces that sold him. Even his father wasn't complaining for a change. She really did have everything under control.

"Eggs and toast, coming right up," she said, *way* too brightly for seven o'clock in the morning. He'd never get used to living with a cheerful morning person.

Not that he was going to need to.

"Thanks, but I don't have time to catch breakfast this

morning," he said, waving away the plate heaped with steaming eggs that she offered him. He glanced at his watch and frowned. "I'm already late. I have two new bulletin boards to set up before class."

"You can't leave without eating. It's my secret recipe, guaranteed to put a smile on your face."

While the eggs looked and smelled tempting, *she* was the one putting a smile on his face. His breath caught in his throat when their eyes met. She challenged him with her warm brown gaze. It was almost enough to make him back down.

"Yummy," Matty agreed. Jamey just kept eating.

"How long will it take you to eat—all of two minutes? I've got a meeting this morning with the Little Chicks to help plan games for the kids for the May Day picnic, and you don't see me running off without eating."

She pleaded with her eyes just as much as with her smile, blinking just rapidly enough to cause his heartbeat to rise in synch with her eyelashes. It was *totally* not fair for her to use her feminine wiles that way.

"Give the woman a break and eat the food," his father growled.

Drew looked from one to the other of them and sighed. "Oh, all right," he finally conceded, only because he knew he could eat the meal and be on his way faster than he could get out of the house arguing about it. He took the plate Stephanie offered and sat down at the head of the table. "I'll eat, if it'll make you feel better."

"It'll make *you* feel better," she insisted. "How you fellows got along before I arrived is a mystery to me."

She slid into the chair next to Drew and picked up her fork.

"Bananas and toaster pastries," his father grumbled.

Drew hoped he could avoid a close scrutiny of his pre-Stephanie nutritional principles. He'd learned a lot since she'd started joining the family for meals.

"I was hoping I'd have the opportunity to speak to you about the educational system in Serendipity. Since you're a teacher, I thought you might be able to shed light on a few questions I have," she said with a soft sigh. "But I guess I can wait until you get home from work."

One look at the disappointed expression on her face and Drew decided his bulletin boards could wait.

"Ask away," he said, shoveling a forkful of fluffy scrambled eggs into his mouth. He was startled by how good it tasted. What had she put into the eggs that made them so good?

"What I'm most curious about is why there is no pre-school in Serendipity. Doesn't the town see a need for early childhood education and pre-kindergarten reading readiness?"

He paused and wiped his lips with his napkin. "The children in our school district perform well above the national average on state exams, so it's never been what folks would consider a huge detriment not to have a pre-school for the children. Most of the kids get some help at home. But even so, I personally think a preschool would be a real blessing to the community, and I've lobbied with the town council for just that very thing for years."

"That surprises me." She paused, and then her eyes

widened as she realized how her comment had sounded. "Not that you are aware how essential a preschool is," she amended, "but that there isn't one. It seemed to me that there were quite a few preschool-aged children at the park the other day."

Drew nodded. "There are. And now that my own boys are preschool-aged, I realize more than ever what a gap there is in the formal learning structure. But right now it's all we can do to keep the elementary program running well. There's just not enough funding available, so according to the town council, the preschool will have to wait."

He shook his head. "There always seems to be something on their list that appears to be more critical, at least in the short term. I'm not judging them. The town council is made up of gracious volunteers, and I wouldn't want the job myself. They have a tough time deciding how to keep Serendipity up and running."

"That's too bad." Stephanie tilted her head and pursed her lips, her expression speculative.

He wondered what was going through her mind, and then decided he didn't really want to know. The less involved he was with this woman, the better. He was already getting in too deep as it was. More and more he found himself thinking about her when he least expected it—and that was a distraction he did *not* need right now.

Besides, she appeared to snap out of whatever was bothering her quickly enough. When she smiled, it was with her eyes as well as her lips. She made what was almost a purring sound from the back of her throat and stood, moving to the sink and rinsing off her plate.

"Well, at least I'm around for the time being, for the twins, anyway. Readiness is as natural a part of a preschooler's daily life as breathing. You just have to pay attention so you can take advantage of those opportunities."

Drew sighed. "That's a great disadvantage of being a single parent. What with my work I sometimes don't feel like I'm around enough. I can't take advantage of all those teachable moments."

"Don't worry about the twins," Pop reminded him. "Stephanie's not the only one who does teachable moments. I'm here twenty-four/seven, and I'm perfectly capable of caring for those boys. I love them. And I expect I have a thing or two to teach them, too."

Drew knew that particular bullet was aimed right at his head. His father still hadn't forgiven him for hiring a nanny from the outside when the older man lived at the house, even if his dad liked Stephanie for dozens of other reasons, most of which Drew didn't want to think about.

"I know you love them, Pop. I have other reasons for having Stephanie with us."

His father grunted and spread his newspaper. "Well, you kids do whatever you want. I have a date today."

"A date?" Drew's eyebrows rose. "With who?"

Pop lowered his paper enough to pin Drew with a scowl. "Like you don't know."

"Jo Murphy?"

"Hmmph," was his father's only answer.

Stephanie chuckled.

"Since when did you start calling an outing with Jo a date?" Drew demanded, unwilling to let this go.

"You have a problem with that?"

"Well, no." He didn't have the least bit of a problem with Jo Murphy. He loved her like a second mother.

"It's not a *date* date," his father insisted, backtracking. "Best you keep your nose out of my business."

"I think it's lovely," Stephanie crooned.

She would.

Drew remembered that he was late and started shoveling food into his mouth as quickly as possible, barely chewing between bites. Matty and Jamey stopped eating to watch their father's foray into bad table manners.

He swallowed and cleared his throat. "Sorry," he apologized contritely. "I'm being rude."

His father grunted his agreement, but Stephanie just shrugged, her mouth tugging upward in amusement.

"It's just that—I really am in a hurry. Boys, stop gawking at me and start eating." He was in his own kitchen, in his own house, explaining his actions as if *he* was the preschooler.

He pushed his plate away, despite the fact that he'd only eaten half the eggs and only one slice of toast. He was flustered and disconcerted and he was going to be his own man—even if that meant going hungry.

Chapter Six

Wednesday evening found Drew and Stephanie doing housework. He'd received a call from his lawyer that the Child and Family Investigator would be coming by sometime in the next couple of weeks. He'd tried not to show how distressed he was, but Stephanie had grown to know his moods too well.

She also knew he didn't like to talk about his feelings. Instead, she had graciously suggested they thoroughly clean the house so he would feel a little more confident about the case worker's visit.

He'd never known a woman as kind and sensitive as Stephanie. She knew just what to say and do—not only with him, but with the kids. It concerned him a little bit that the whole family was beginning to rely on Stephanie for more than just simple child care during the weekdays. She'd become a staple of their household. He didn't want to think about how upset the twins would be when she left.

And he most certainly didn't want to think about how *he* was going to feel when she left.

He finished mopping behind the refrigerator, huffing and puffing as he carefully slid the large appliance back to its original position. Wiping the sweat off his forehead with his shoulder, he leaned his forearm on the end of the mop and surveyed his work.

The worn white vinyl kitchen floor showed years of wear. He couldn't get some of the scuff marks and scratches out no matter how hard he applied himself. Using information he'd gathered on the internet, he'd stripped the buildup with vinegar and then covered the area with a thick coating of shiny floor cleaner, but he wasn't happy with the results. Now he was wondering if perhaps he hadn't used the most reliable sources. Information gleaned from the internet was hit or miss at best.

Stephanie peeked her head around the corner where the kitchen met the living dining room. "How is the kitchen coming along?" she asked brightly, but didn't give him the opportunity to respond. "Your floor looks nice. I dusted all the furniture and pictures and polished all the wood with some wax I found in the closet. Now the whole house smells like lemons."

She'd pulled her hair back into a ponytail, making her look even younger and fresher than she usually did. It was a stunning reminder of how different they were— Drew was older and wiser, neither of which necessarily was a good thing.

Used goods, so to speak. And she deserved better than that.

She'd clearly been applying herself to her labors, for her face was flushed with exertion and a few tendrils of wispy hair had escaped her elastic and were curling against her hairline, wreathing her face in gold.

She'd never looked more attractive. Or more completely off limits.

It escaped him why he had to keep reminding himself over and over again why he *shouldn't* be noticing her as a woman. Clearly, he wasn't nearly as strong-minded as he'd imagined himself to be. Put a pretty lady under his nose and she might as well be leading him by it—like a bull with a ring through his snout.

"Thank you for helping me out. I feel better now knowing that at least the case worker is going to find a clean, organized house when she comes."

"Don't ever be afraid to ask if you need an extra hand with something. I like to be useful. It makes me crazy to sit around and do nothing." She shrugged. "Since your dad and Jo have the boys locked in a serious game of Candyland, I really don't have anything better to do, anyway. You're rescuing me from dying of chronic boredom."

She gave him an encouraging smile that flickered into a flame in his stomach and lit his insides with warmth.

"I'd be nervous, too, if it was me and my children under the microscope," she murmured, reaching for his hand. "But don't worry. I'm sure the case worker will be more interested in how attentive you are as a father to the boys—and you *are* a great father, by the way—than by whether there are any dust bunnies hidden in the corner. Which, for the record," she continued, teasingly waving her dust cloth under his chin like a flag, "there aren't."

Even under the stress he was feeling, she managed to make him smile, which was just one more reason of many to like her. He was pretty sure he'd smiled more in the past few weeks than he had the entire year before that. After Heather had left him, he wasn't sure he'd ever smile again, and now look at him—grinning like a fool.

Maybe he was a fool. But it felt good, anyway.

"I had the rugs cleaned a couple of months ago, which got out most of the big stains. If we run a vacuum over the carpet and wash the living room windows, I think we'll be good for the night."

"Great. Where can I find your vacuum? I'll get that, and then after you finish the kitchen, you can take care of washing the windows. I don't do windows," she joked, using the old cliché.

Drew chuckled and gestured toward the floor he'd been mopping. "Yeah, this vinyl is pretty much hopeless. At least I think I can get the windows clean, if I apply a little elbow grease. Like the rest of the house, I'm ashamed to say it's been a while since they've had a thorough cleaning. I feel overwhelmed just keeping up with work and the boys. Cleaning house somehow seems pretty far down the list."

"Understandable."

At least she didn't chide him. "The vacuum is in the hall closet, buried somewhere behind our winter coats. If you dig deep enough you should be able to find it with no problem."

"I'm on it." Stephanie disappeared around the corner and Drew turned back to his work, applying yet another coat of vinyl cleaner on the floor for good measure. If a little product made it shiny, a lot ought to make it gleam, right?

Stephanie must have found the vacuum without incident, for a few minutes later he heard the telltale hum of the motor. The kitchen floor was as good as it was going to get. He might as well go do something truly productive. He grabbed a bottle of glass cleaner and a roll of paper towels and joined Stephanie in the living room.

She was laughing at something, her beautiful brown eyes shimmering with delight. He quickly saw why. She was playing with the dog.

Quincy had never been a big fan of vacuums. In fact, he was a big chicken when it came to being around any loud devices. He usually tucked his tail and ran and hid underneath one of the beds.

But today he'd apparently decided the vacuum cleaner was attacking Stephanie, and he was having none of it. Quincy valiantly charged at the machine, lunging and nipping at it to keep it away from his beloved mistress, who, over the course of the past few weeks, had become the dog's favorite person on the planet.

It had become a game between the two of them—Stephanie pushing the vacuum out and Quincy chasing it back in again. The woman was clearly having at least as much fun with it as the dog was. Her laughter was contagious.

"I see you have a new BFF," Drew said with a chuckle as soon as Stephanie shut off the machine. "Quincy was certainly ready to take on the vacuum cleaner for you. Normally he's terrified of vacuums, just so you know how special you are."

Drew's throat closed as he said the words and he swallowed. Hard.

"My knight in furry armor." She crouched and wrapped her arm over the dog's neck, scratching his broad chest with her fingers. "Who could resist a face like this?" Laughing, she planted a kiss on the dog's forehead.

"I can tell you like dogs. And you appear to have the same amazing affect over them as you do on children."

"I've never owned a dog," she said with a tinge of sadness.

"No?" He was surprised, since she was so good and natural with Quincy.

"I lived in a series of foster homes growing up, and then in the dormitories while I was in college. I could have had a small dog at my apartment after I'd graduated, but Ryan—my ex-boyfriend—didn't like animals."

Ex-boyfriend. He heard the catch in her voice and saw her wince, almost as if she were being struck by an invisible hand. Was this Ryan the reason she'd left New Jersey and come to Serendipity?

Drew already didn't like the guy. Whoever this ex-boyfriend of hers was, he'd clearly hurt Stephanie, which didn't set well with Drew.

And what kind of a man didn't like animals, anyway?

"Maybe someday, though," she continued wistfully. "I'd love to have a dog, if I ever settle down permanently."

He could easily see her settling down, with a house and a dog and children of her own. If he didn't know anything else about her, he knew this—that she would be an excellent mother someday, caring and compassionate and dedicated, just as she was with his boys.

"To tell you the truth, I've been praying about maybe staying in Serendipity."

His heart jolted into his throat. How could a man be alarmed and relieved at the same time? And yet that was exactly how he felt.

What was she saying? That she wanted a more permanent job offer?

He turned away from her, not wanting to meet her gaze until his emotions were under control. He didn't want her to see how confused he was.

He couldn't give her a job even if he wanted to, and he admitted there was a large part of him that *did* want her to stay with him. And, of course, the boys wanted her to stay.

But he was already making a painful dent in his retirement account just to have her here now. He couldn't extend her stay indefinitely, no matter how well she got on with the twins.

But there was far more to it than that—something much harder for him to admit. If she stayed then he was going to have to confront his attraction to her, feelings he'd rather avoid if at all possible. He didn't want to have to admit he was falling for her.

Even to himself.

Well, *that* wasn't the reaction Stephanie had imagined she would receive. Not from Drew. Up until this point, he'd been very supportive of her. She hadn't expected him to turn away from her.

His less-than-stellar response to her idea of staying in town put an instant damper on her mood. Talk about a killjoy.

She didn't know what she expected. Maybe just that he would think it was a worthwhile idea to consider, or that he was happy that she might be staying.

She frowned. It was just an idea, not yet even fully conceived. She didn't need his permission, or his support, to stay in town, but deep in her heart she'd hoped for both. She'd met a lot of people here in Serendipity, many of whom she now considered her friends, but there was no one she felt as close to as she did to Drew.

He was her employer and the twins' loving and committed father, but she'd anticipated that he was much more than that. She'd thought—hoped—he was her friend.

There were times when he'd even been flirtatious with her. Deep inside she'd wished perhaps—

But, no. She wouldn't allow herself to go there, even in her mind. Obviously she was setting herself up to have her heart ripped in two again, and how stupid was that? If she'd learned anything from last time, it was that she shouldn't give her heart lightly.

"What do you mean you want to stay?" Drew asked bluntly. He was being his usual self—solemn and straightforward about everything. The image of the staid academic entered her mind. He might look like a cowboy, but clearly he was an uptight school teacher at heart. It would have been laughable if it wasn't so serious.

Unfortunately, it was serious. This was her life she was talking about, and whether he encouraged her in her decisions or not, she wanted him to know all the facts.

"It's just something I've been tossing around," she began. "I've been speaking with Pastor Shawn. He's encouraged me to get involved here in town. I'm helping Mary with the Sunday school kids at church this weekend, and I've helped with the planning for the May Day picnic. I've made a lot of friends here, and quite frankly, I don't have anything or anyone to go back to on the east coast. No house, no job. Nothing."

His gaze turned compassionate as he searched for the right words. "I remember you saying you were a foster child, so you have no family, right?" His eyes and the gentle tone of his voice didn't match the furrow in his brow, which marred his otherwise handsome face. "Friends?"

"A few." No one close. No one she could turn to in a crisis, which she'd only discovered when she'd become suddenly homeless and not a single one of her *friends* had a spare room to offer her. There was no one who cared enough to reach out to her and lend a hand.

The truth was that Ryan had forced her to alienate all of her friends, and all of his friends took his side when she broke things off him.

"I don't want to be on that coast, never mind in the state," she admitted, feeling the heat of shame rush to her cheeks, leaving her hands and her feet cold—and her heart like ice. "Back in New Jersey, my ex-boyfriend Ryan is a member of the old-money Forsythe clan. They have the ability to throw their weight around and make my life pretty miserable." Ryan would throw *his* weight around, probably literally, but she wasn't sure she wanted to say that yet. "I'd certainly have difficulty trying to get another job within their sphere of influence, which extends pretty far."

"I get what you're saying," he stated thoughtfully. "And I'm sorry things worked out for you that way. I really am. But I have to wonder how Serendipity is going to be any better for you in the long run. There are other places you could go. Wouldn't you be better off in a larger city?"

When she sighed, he reached for her hand, covering her cold fingers with his warm ones.

"I'm not trying to rain on your parade," he continued. "I know I think too black-and-white sometimes. I'm just trying to be practical. There aren't any families with substantial amounts of money around here, not anything remotely like they'd need to hire a full-time nanny. There are no millionaires or oil barons among this crop of simple folks."

"I realize that," she admitted.

"Frankly, it'll be difficult to find a job in your field, or even close to your field. You could do day care, maybe, if you can get a mortgage on a large house."

She shook her head. "I don't have that kind of money. Not nearly enough to put a down payment on a house, even in Serendipity."

"You're creative. I'm sure you'll come up with a solution to your problems."

His encouragement warmed her heart. "There must be some way for me to get by," she murmured, more to herself than to Drew. "I'm willing to work hard."

"Yeah, I know you are," he agreed. "But doing what? Working as a waitress at Cup O' Jo?"

"I don't know. Maybe. Like I said, at this point it's only conjecture. But there's more."

He raised his eyebrows and nodded for her to continue.

"I would like to start a preschool here," she admitted softly. "I see the need, and I think I have the skill set to fill it."

"If anyone can do it, you could."

She sucked in a breath. He had shocked her again, this time by his encouragement.

"I have a bachelor's degree. I should have no trouble getting teaching credentials in Texas. I have some administrative experience from when I worked as a supervisor for a bounce house as a teen. And if anything good came out of my relationship with Ryan, it is that I've seen how rich people raise money. I know how to generate community awareness. I've been to quite a few charity fundraisers. I think if we ask the right people, we can get the money we need to start the school."

"Wow. You've put a lot of thought into this."

"And prayer. More than you know. I'm only in the beginning stages of my planning. There's still a lot to do, working out the logistics and so on, but I wanted to tell you now, so you can pray with me." She sighed softly. "I've never really sought the Lord's guidance for my life before. This is all very new to me."

He didn't say anything. He just stared at her, his expression unreadable.

"What?" she asked when she couldn't stand the silence any longer. "You think I'm an idiot with a whacked-out scheme, don't you?"

"No," he responded so quickly that she knew he was telling her the truth. "I think you're incredible."

Did he really mean that?

She searched his eyes, which had darkened to a deep jade. He was so close she could feel his warm breath on her cheek. His fingers brushed the sensitive spot at the nape of her neck.

She reached up and brushed her palm along his jaw.

"Thank you for believing in me," she whispered.

And then she kissed him.

Chapter Seven

"I guess my son is a little bit brighter than I thought he was," came a low, gruff voice from somewhere out of the scope of Drew's present realm, which consisted only of Stephanie. Her lips. Her exotic scent. The sweet softness of her skin as he cupped her face in his palm. His heartbeat was hammering so hard in his ears that he almost didn't hear his father speak. It was no surprise to him that he was a little slow on the uptake.

Stephanie, however, wasn't. She bolted out of his arms and across to the other side of the sofa as if he'd electrocuted her. She covered her cherry-red cheeks with both hands and groaned.

Not that he was any happier about the situation than she was. He wanted to pull her back in his arms, which would be the absolute worst thing he could do at the moment.

This was a worst case scenario, and he was pretty sure Stephanie knew that, too. He had absolutely *not* wanted to be interrupted in a private moment that he would rather no one except he and Stephanie know about.

"Not a word, Pop. Not one word," he warned, knowing full well his threat wouldn't stop the old man from saying exactly what he thought of the situation.

He caught his father's gaze and silently pleaded with him. *Please don't embarrass Stephanie.*

Drew didn't care about himself. He was used to the old man's blunt speaking. But Stephanie's face had gone from bright red to an alarming white, and she looked as if she'd like to shrink into the plush fabric of the burgundy-colored sofa and disappear.

And it was all his fault. Drew shouldered one-hundred percent of the responsibility for getting caught in this situation. She might have initiated their kiss, but if she hadn't, he knew he would have.

The spark between the two of them was set to blaze no matter who struck the match. And he should have known better. Instead of sharing a special moment just between the two of them, they'd now announced whatever fledgling feelings they might have for each other to the two biggest gossips in the town, and all without saying a word.

So much for older and wiser. He wasn't some slap-happy youth riding on too many hormones. He was a single father with two boys he would always put first—*always*—but especially now, with court-appointed social workers breathing down his throat.

He couldn't and shouldn't *date,* and he wasn't ready to court a woman. It was *because* he cared for Stephanie that he had to nip this relationship in the bud. She might think staying in Serendipity was good, for now. And he had no doubt she was completely sincere in her aspirations to build a preschool in town.

But dreams had a funny way of being crushed by life. He had ten years on her—ten years of learning the bitter truth about reaching for the stars.

Falling back to earth hurt. A lot.

He wanted to spare her and protect her from that pain. And, while he was at it, he ought to protect her from his father's teasing.

Unfortunately, the most obvious way he could think of doing that was going to hurt her feelings—for now. But in the long run, she'd thank him for it.

"Did you finally come to your senses, boy?" his father asked, groaning as he gingerly lowered himself into the forest-green armchair and stretched out his feet onto the matching ottoman. "All I have to say is—good for you. It's about time you came around."

Drew frowned, knowing that was not even *close* to all his father had to say on the matter.

"Don't be ashamed, dear," Jo said, settling in on the couch next to Stephanie and patting the younger woman's knee. "I can see that you're blushing, but you needn't worry. We've all been hoping and praying that you two would get together."

Drew didn't know who the *we all* was, and he figured he probably didn't want to know. He had to stop this train—fast. Pumped with adrenaline, he verbally stomped on the brake as hard as he could. "You're mistaken, Jo. We're not together."

Jo just chuckled. "No, of course not, dear. Your father and I just imagined what we saw when we walked into this room a minute ago."

"What you saw didn't mean anything. We just shared a kiss. Don't read anything into that that's not there."

He saw Stephanie flinch, and he knew he had wounded her with his blunt and purposefully callous words, but he didn't know how else to handle the situation. She probably thought he was a royal jerk—and he was. But she could not possibly imagine the things that would happen to her if he did not end this right now.

Pop and Jo wouldn't waste a second before telling everyone in town that Drew and Stephanie were a couple. News would spread like a wildfire and then Stephanie would have no relief from the pestering. Jo served meals at the café. It wasn't difficult for Drew to imagine her bringing this juicy new morsel of relationship gossip into the conversation at every single table she waited.

And if the folks in town thought they were a couple— watch out. As well-intentioned as they might be, they would be endlessly throwing the two of them together. If Stephanie really did stay in Serendipity, she'd end up being miserable, and it would all be his fault.

"Stephanie is only contracted to stay until the end of the school year," he stated firmly, "or until I've retained custody of the boys. Whichever comes first."

He didn't say that she might stay in town indefinitely. Now didn't seem the right time to bring that up.

"Right," Stephanie agreed softly. To her credit, she straightened her posture and her expression. "Don't forget, I'm just an employee. Drew is my boss."

Jo laughed briskly. "That doesn't mean a thing, sweetie. Not in Serendipity. Besides, it sure didn't look like an employer/employee relationship when we walked in. Bosses and employees have been getting married practically since Noah landed the ark."

"Married?" he exclaimed, with probably more emotion than he'd shown in a good while. "It was a mistake, and it will never happen again." Drew wondered how he sounded. Probably not very convincing—he wasn't all that confident it was a one-time thing himself. He wasn't even sure he wanted it to be.

When he was around Stephanie, his head never moved as fast as his heart. The yearning to pull her into his arms and keep her by his side was incredibly strong. But chemistry was impulsive, and he was not an impulsive man. The last time he'd followed his heart had ended in disaster, save for the two beautiful boys who had come out of the relationship.

He could not do it again. And he would keep telling himself that until he believed it.

Someone had delivered an anonymous basket of flowers to the Spencers' door step this morning, reminding everyone that this was May Day, Serendipity's celebration of spring.

It didn't feel like spring to Stephanie. Not if Drew didn't want her here, which he'd been pretty clear about. Not in his house, and not in Serendipity. He was sending her packing at his earliest convenience.

Okay, so he hadn't said quite that much. He'd said that their kiss meant nothing and that she was only his temporary employee. As far as Stephanie was concerned, that amounted to the same thing.

She pulled her hair back into a loose ponytail and applied a bit of eyeliner and a light coat of mascara, mostly to try to hide how puffy her eyes looked again this morning. It had been three days since Drew had openly stated that their attraction to one another was a mistake, and she was still struggling with her emotions.

She was determined to be strong and composed during the days, with Drew and the boys always around, not to mention the many other people about town that she had met. She didn't want anyone to know her heart was breaking. She felt like an idiot for letting herself become vulnerable to a man again.

She'd thought Drew was different, but he'd just done what Ryan had done—stomped on her heart, and her pride.

But no way was she going to let *him* know how deeply he'd affected her, so she pulled her emotions inward and presented a smiling face to the world.

Nighttime was a different story. In those moments between sleep and wakefulness when she was all alone, the pain of rejection and of unrequited feelings would bubble up inside her. Sometimes she was just too tired to tamp her emotions back down and she ended up shedding a few tears. All she could do was hope that in the morning, her makeup would cover all the signs of her midnight distress.

She supposed it was nice to *know* she was being rejected outright, and not have to guess at it.

But she didn't regret kissing him, even if he hadn't experienced the kind of bolt-of-lightning revelation she had had when their lips met.

For her, it was a game-changer.

All that stuff she'd said about staying in town and starting a preschool was true. But now she realized there was more to the equation. Much more.

She was falling in love with Drew.

If he had been willing to admit he had feelings for her, or if nothing had happened between them in the first place, then she could easily see herself staying in town.

But if Drew didn't want her in Serendipity, that was a different story. Maybe she was simply too emotionally battered to fight any more, but she didn't think she had the strength to move on without literally *moving on*.

Only she was having a hard time picturing herself living anywhere except Serendipity. But it was equally as difficult to picture herself somewhere without Drew and the twins.

Stephanie picked up the duster she'd left on a shelf in the hall closet and moved toward the mantel of the fireplace in the living room, dusting over it the same way she'd done every day since she and Drew had been caught in a compromising position by Jo and his father. Not that there was anything left with dust on it. She just needed something to do, a way to keep busy to keep from going crazy with her thoughts.

Today was May Day, and she was supposed to be looking forward to a fun Serendipity picnic. Instead, she dreaded it. It was like stabbing an already open wound to watch the happy people of Serendipity enjoying themselves while she wasn't even sure where her life was going in the next thirty days.

If she didn't have to go, she probably wouldn't, but she'd been put in charge of running the preschool and toddler games, so she had to be there. Besides, Matty and Jamey would be disappointed if their Miss Stephie didn't attend the festivities with them.

The boys were in the corner entertaining themselves

by emptying the entire toy box, spreading toys from one end of the living room to the other. She usually tried to enforce Drew's one-at-a-time rule, but today she didn't care if the boys made a mess. It would give her something to clean up, and it was keeping the twins happy.

Since they'd be gone most of the day, Drew was the kitchen, trying to get his weekend grading done before they had to leave. Hence another reason to dust—to stay out of his way. They hadn't really spoken about what had happened, and after a few days, Stephanie assumed he didn't want to talk.

As for herself, she was too afraid of blurting out her feelings if she was provoked. And since she knew that nearly anything would provoke her—a grimace, a smile, silence, the word *hi*—she thought it was better just not to take the risk of being around him.

Frowning at her own weakness, she turned back to her dusting—and her thoughts.

Why couldn't Drew at least admit there was an attraction between them, even if he didn't want to pursue it any further? They were adults. They should be able to talk about it.

But he'd called their moment together *nothing*.

And she should be able to deal with that.

So why couldn't she?

Because, she finally managed to acknowledge to herself, Drew meant something special to her. She was only now beginning to realize just how much.

The feelings she'd thought she had toward Ryan now seemed the essence of weakness and immaturity. Her ex had taken advantage of the fact that she struggled with her self-esteem. He'd seen the way she tried to please everyone and he'd used that to his advantage. He'd used *her*.

And despite the fact that he'd been studiously avoiding her all week, deep down she knew that Drew was everything that Ryan wasn't. He might not want to talk about what happened between them. He might be blunt, and sometimes not cushion his words. Yet for all that he was respectful and deeply caring in his own way.

Like so many of the folks she'd met in Serendipity, he was a committed Christian who worked out his faith in his life rather than merely giving lip-service to it. He was a phenomenal father—he'd walk over broken glass for his kids, and then turn around and walk back again. And despite the good-natured bickering between the two men, Drew clearly loved his father—enough to bring him to live in his home when he could no longer care for himself on his own.

And one other thing…he was a great kisser. Strong, yet gentle, just like everything else about him.

No two ways about it—Stephanie was falling for him. And, for reasons he wouldn't go into, he didn't feel the same way about her.

So the question yet remained…could she stay in Serendipity, where she'd be constantly running into him? Could she hazard the possibility of having to watch him fall in love with another woman, maybe even marry her and bring her home to be the mother to his kids?

She'd been asking herself the same questions all week, trying to picture herself living somewhere else other than Serendipity, or more specifically, at the Spencers. She'd never before been invited into real, active family life. Her past employers had never welcomed her into their lives—she had been nothing more than a servant, and she had been treated like one. Even her foster families had kept her on the fringes of their daily lives, never really warming up to her and letting her in.

Living with the Spencers had given her a taste of what it meant to care for other people, and have them care for her. What it meant to be a family. It wouldn't be easy to walk away.

She tried to picture her Saturday mornings alone reading a newspaper rather than sharing in the intimate devotions and prayer time that she now shared with the family over the breakfast table, hearing Drew gently leading his little ones through the Scriptures. It was difficult to imagine not being around to read the boys a book at night, which had become a mainstay in the Spencer household ever since she'd arrived. Even Drew had said how much he enjoyed listening to her create voices for all the characters she was reading about.

She supposed she could read a bedtime story to the children of another family, but the thought of that nearly broke her heart. She had fallen in love with the rowdy, tow-headed boys, and even cranky old Frank held a place dear to her heart.

But all of that meant nothing without Drew.

The doorbell pealed and Stephanie brushed stray tendrils of hair off her face with the back of her hand. She assumed it was Jo here to visit Frank, though usually the woman let herself in with no more than an obligatory knock.

Stephanie checked her watch. It was only midmorning. Jo was usually busy at the café at this time of day, cleaning up after the breakfast crowd, especially on Saturday. And today was May Day. She'd be scurrying around trying to organize the dozens of dishes Cup O' Jo would supply for the picnic.

It didn't appear that Drew heard the door, or else he was expecting her to get it. He was probably grading papers or planning lessons for the upcoming week. He tended to be really focused when he was working, to the point of shutting everything else out.

No matter. It wasn't as if she was super busy and couldn't be interrupted. In fact, she welcomed the disruption of her depressing train of thought.

She pulled the door open without looking to see who it was. "Come on in. Coffee's on."

"Thank you so much," said an unfamiliar female voice in a moderated but scratchy low tone. "Coffee would be nice. One cream, two sugars. What can I say? I like mine sweet."

A tall, thin woman Stephanie guessed to be about fifty years old stepped into the house as if she owned it. For all that she was no-nonsense in her attitude and her expression, her clothes were at the height of fashion and she had a blue streak colored into the one of the underneath layers of her highlighted brown hair. The streak was nearly invisible until she brushed her hair back behind her ear—which she did, probably unconsciously, a few moments after she'd entered the house.

Stephanie was positive she hadn't seen this woman around town, which could only mean one thing.

She was the Child and Family Investigator.

Chapter Eight

"Is Drew Spencer here, please?" the woman queried in a businesslike tone. "I've been sent by the court to speak with him."

What was Drew's case worker doing here—on a Saturday, and apparently unannounced? Stephanie was certain Drew would have mentioned it if he thought she'd be coming around.

Stephanie looked at the duster in her hand, her ratty blue T-shirt, gray sweatpants and purple toe socks, and then—last but definitely not least—the toys the twins had strewn from one end of the living room to the other. There was no possible way to hide any of that.

She groaned inwardly, hoping her distress didn't show on her face. Never let the enemy see you sweat, and all that.

At least she'd put Quincy in the backyard. Otherwise the case worker might have had the kind of welcome she herself had had the first time she'd visited the Spencers. That particular meeting might not have gone as well with this woman as it had with her. Who knew if the investigator liked dogs or not?

This was Drew's worst nightmare come to life. He'd talked about being caught off guard, and this situation definitely qualified as that.

"Uh," she murmured, buying a moment to think, "please have a seat on the sofa while I run to the kitchen and get you that coffee." She gestured toward the couch and spurred herself into action. She needed to warn Drew before he accidentally waltzed into the living room and had a heart attack.

Drew looked up from his papers as Stephanie skidded into the room, sliding on her socks. Drew had overdone it just a little bit with the vinyl cleaner and the floor was out-and-out slippery. She was aiming for the cupboard where the coffee mugs were housed, and she grasped the counter for support, adrenaline causing her breath to be quick and uneven as she turned to face him.

He was as casually dressed as Stephanie had ever seen him—jeans and a tattered, grease-stained white T-shirt that looked as if he'd been working under the hood of a car with it. His feet were bare. There was a day's worth of stubble on his chin, which was actually quite attractive, if she'd had time to admire it. He was usually so conscientious about being clean-shaven. His hair looked as if he'd been scrubbing his fingers through it, which he probably had been, since he was clearly deep in thought. When he looked up, his reading glasses magnified the brilliant green of his eyes.

"What's up?" he asked, tapping his pen on the table. "You look like something scared the life out of you. Did you find a spider on the windowsill or something?"

A *spider?* First of all, she was absolutely fine dealing with bugs. And secondly, the woman currently sitting in the living room was much, *much* worse than the average, run-of-the-mill insect.

She pressed her knuckles onto the table and leaned toward him. "Okay, I don't want you to panic, but—"

"What is it?" he broke in, standing abruptly to his feet. "Is it one of the boys?"

She put a hand to his chest to restrain him from darting out into the living room before she finished her explanation.

"No, it's not one of the boys," she assured him.

He sighed and slid back into his chair. "Good. You really had me worried there for a second."

"It's your case worker."

"What?" Again, he stood abruptly to his feet, this time nearly knocking over the glass of orange juice he'd been drinking. "Here? Now?"

"Unfortunately, yes." As calmly as she could under the circumstances, she took a mug from the cupboard and filled it with steaming coffee, then put a dollop of cream and two healthy spoonfuls of sugar in it. It probably wouldn't help, but perhaps she could sweeten the woman. "That's who was at the door a minute ago."

"We don't even have time to pray," he said, blowing out a frustrated breath and running his palm back over his hair. "We're not ready. I'm not dressed for it."

Stephanie had lived in plenty of large, metropolitan areas, where most of her guy friends put a lot into how they looked, but for Drew, it was different, more organic. His trademark shirt and tie, unusual for the town's blue jean dress code, set him apart, said a lot about him as a man. She knew it would really bother him to appear in his present attire.

Not to mention his entire future with his kids was at stake.

And she wasn't in any better condition. She sighed, looking down at her own super-casual outfit. What a disaster.

"Well, she's already seen me, so there's no help for that. I've been made. But I can serve her the coffee and give you a moment to clean up."

He hugged her so tight it knocked the wind out of her, and then pecked her squarely on the mouth. "You're the best, Steph."

And then he was gone, dashing out the back door of the kitchen, which led…outside. She wasn't sure exactly what his plan was, but now that she thought about it, the only entrance to the hallway, and thus his bedroom, was through the living room, which is where the case worker was presently located.

Drew would just have to come back in the way he'd left and deal with the reality that the case worker was going to catch him in jeans and a T-shirt, sans shoes.

"Sorry for the wait. Here's your coffee," she said as she reentered the living room, realizing that she still didn't know the woman's name.

Instead of taking the seat on the couch she'd been offered, the court investigator was down on the floor playing choo-choo train with the twins—short skirt, high heels and all.

Stephanie breathed a sigh of relief. Any woman who would take the very probable chance of getting a run in her black stockings just to play toys with a couple of preschoolers couldn't be all bad.

At the sound of Stephanie's voice, the woman smiled and stood to her feet, looking amazingly graceful as she moved. She made Stephanie feel like all thumbs.

"Thank you," she said, taking the coffee Stephanie offered her and finding a seat on the sofa, only to exclaim and jump up again, reaching behind her for the sharp-spined green plastic stegosaurus that had fallen in-between the cushions.

"Oh, my!" Stephanie exclaimed, reaching for the errant toy. "I'm so, so sorry. This place isn't usually so untidy. Boys, pick up your toys, right away."

She hoped the twins couldn't hear the sheer panic in her tone. She hoped the *case worker* hadn't heard the panic in her tone.

"Don't apologize for the toys," the woman said. "I don't usually make it a practice of stopping by unannounced, especially on a weekend. I just happened to be driving through Serendipity today."

She paused, and Stephanie couldn't help but raise an eyebrow at that unlikely scenario.

"I know, right? I was on my way home from another appointment, a special case—farther out even than this town. Since I was close, I thought I would save myself the trouble of having to drive back out here another day." She shrugged. "It was a last-minute decision, or else I would have phoned. I hope I'm not inconveniencing you too much. And I'm Eileen, by the way."

"I'm Stephanie Cartwright, the boys' nanny. My little charges here are Matty and Jamey Spencer." Thankfully, Jamey wasn't acting quite as shy as he usually did, and was staring at Eileen with open curiosity. Matty was his usual boisterous self, which, she supposed, was good. She probably shouldn't be trying to analyze the boys' reactions the way Eileen would see them, but she couldn't seem to help herself. "Their father, Drew—"

She was going to say *will be along any second now,* but he stepped out of the back hallway and cut her off.

"Is right here. Eileen, I'm so sorry to have kept you waiting."

Stephanie had to consciously stop herself from gaping. Drew had appeared looking—and smelling—fresh out of the shower. He had slipped into a green oxford shirt, black slacks and his cowboy boots, with a necktie and a sports jacket for good measure.

He glanced at Stephanie and his eyebrows furrowed for just a moment as they shared an unspoken *close call.* She smiled and brushed her fingers across her cheek, reminding him that *he* should be smiling, because otherwise she thought he might forget. He pasted a smile on his face and gave her an almost imperceptible nod, then took a seat on the antique chair near the sofa.

"I was just telling your nanny here that I happened to be passing through town today," Eileen explained. "I hope it's okay that I stopped by on a Saturday."

"No. Yes. Of course. That's fine," Drew stammered.

Stephanie prayed as hard as she ever had. She didn't know how interested God was in minute details, but if He was, she hoped He'd help Drew take a breath and calm down.

"You have a lovely home here, and I'm very impressed with your boys," Eileen commented. "I had a few minutes to interact with them while Stephanie was getting coffee."

"Thank you. I—"

Drew looked toward the twins. His eyes widened and he swallowed. Twice. Then he yanked on the knot of his necktie as if he was choking—definitely not a good sign. "What happened in here?" he squeaked.

Stephanie jumped in before Drew had the opportunity to completely lose his composure. "If I were to guess, I'd have to say Hurricane Jamey and Matty the tornado." She turned toward Eileen, feeling as if she needed to explain. "This is entirely my fault. I should have had them putting one toy away before they took another one out."

Drew's rules—the way he wanted things done. If she'd listened to him, the house would be a shining example of family harmony right now and not an accident within a catastrophe.

Not to mention how that made *her* look, as a so-called professional—as if she hadn't been paying attention to what the boys were doing and didn't know how to keep order. What kind of nanny was she, anyway?

"Please don't apologize," Eileen said for the second time. "Believe it or not, it's nice to see a nice, normal family for a change, in all their chaos and madness. Many times people are so nervous about me coming around that they present to me picture-perfect households with cardboard-cutout pictures of family life."

Eileen chuckled and gestured with her hands. "Families are messy. From what I can tell, your boys are very well-adjusted. There's a lot of joy to be found in a box full of toys—or should I say, an *empty* box."

Eileen's laughter appeared genuine enough, Stephanie thought, and the shine in her gaze encompassed all of them. *Don't overanalyze the situation,* she mentally coached herself. She found herself reading something into Eileen's every word and gesture, but it was incredibly hard not to, what with Drew's family life—his sons' futures—hanging in the balance.

"So I understand you are a fifth-grade teacher," Eileen stated, turning to Drew.

"That's correct," he affirmed.

"Tell me a little about the work you do."

As Eileen pulled Drew into conversation, Stephanie took the opportunity to gather the boys around her.

"What do you say we put some of these toys away?" she asked in a secretive voice that got both the twins' attention.

She dropped to her hands and knees and gathered some blocks in her arms. In her experience, children responded better to joining into an activity than in being told what to do and left to their own devices. And at the moment, giving her mind and her hands something to do seemed like a pretty good idea.

"Matty, you get the dinosaurs," Stephanie whispered, allowing the boys to enjoy the conspiratorial atmosphere, even if that same air was making her a little bit nervous. "Jamey, please pick up the cars. I'll put away the rest of the blocks, and that should about do it."

"Cars," Jamey repeated, and then picked one up and thrust it up under her chin. "Green."

Succinct and to the point, like his father. No mincing words.

"That's right, Jamey. It's green. What color is this one over here?" She pointed to a red car.

"U-u-m," Jamey said, frowning in concentration. "It's…orange!"

"Close, sweetheart." Stephanie wasn't sure whether Jamey's mistake was in recognizing the shade, or rather because his favorite color was orange.

She surreptitiously glanced at the case worker to see if she was watching her interaction with the children—which was completely appalling, once she thought about it. She didn't want this to become some kind of drama with the kids playing parts.

It wasn't as if she was staging a program for Eileen to see—at least she hoped she wasn't. Case worker or no case worker, this was about the boys. Colors and numbers were games they played every day, preschool readiness in the form of fun and laughter.

"Okay, Jamey," she said with an encouraging smile, holding up the tiny car. "Try again."

"It's red," Matty exclaimed, not waiting to be invited into their little game. Matty had already mastered his colors and was working on numbers and counting.

"That's right, little dude," she affirmed, not wanting to shut the exuberant preschooler down in his tracks. "Can you find me five dinosaurs to count?"

Matty nodded and began lining up his dinosaur crew on the rug beside her. Stephanie turned back to Jamey and picked up another car.

"Blue," answered Jamey, before she could ask the question.

"Woohoo, buddy! Way to go. And look at Matty with his dinosaurs. You guys did great." She high-fived Jamey and then Matty, giving each of them a special moment of attention.

"Pound it," Jamey exclaimed, offering her his knuckle. Laughing, Stephanie *pounded* it. She learned something new every day, and the importance of pounding it after high-fiving had been one of the first things Matty and Jamey had taught her.

Eileen was chuckling, as well, so apparently she'd been watching their interchange, or, at least, the last part of it.

That said, she wasn't taking any notes. Stephanie was shocked. The woman hadn't even brought in a briefcase or portfolio. For some reason Stephanie had expected her to be scribbling her thoughts about them on one of those long yellow legal pads like lawyers used.

Instead, Eileen was just observing. How could she possibly make an accurate report without taking notes? How would she remember what she saw? Was it possible she'd get her details mixed up? She said she'd seen another family earlier in the morning.

Stephanie didn't know, and she couldn't ask. All she could do was hug the kids tight, wait and pray that the court would rule in Drew's favor.

Chapter Nine

Forty-five minutes. Forty-five minutes of sheer agony and torture. At least, that was how Drew saw it. The knot in his gut hadn't loosened at all, even though Eileen was now headed to her car and was preparing to leave. He stood at the door and watched until she had pulled away and her vehicle was no longer visible. Only then did the tension in his shoulders and neck begin to ease.

"So what happens now?" Stephanie asked softly, stepping up beside him and resting her hand on his elbow. She, too, was staring out the door and down the road.

"According to my lawyer, we wait."

"For how long? Do they mail you something, or do you have to go to court to find out what the case worker thought?"

"My lawyer will receive a report of the case worker's *findings,* and will email it to me. Then, if necessary, we'll start planning a strategy for the courtroom."

He growled in frustration and scrubbed his eyes with his fingertips, resentment swelling like thunderclouds in his *head*. He was incensed that this situation was so completely out of his control. He'd worked overtime to be ready for the case worker and he'd still been caught off guard.

"I *hate* this," he rumbled. "I hate that I have to *plan a strategy* in order to keep custody of my sons. This is not the way it's supposed to be."

"No, it's not," she agreed. "And then having some case worker—a complete stranger—come to your house to sit and stare at you and ask a whole bunch of questions was pretty unnerving, I have to say."

He turned toward her, basking in her warm brown gaze, which told him better than any words she could say that she really did understand and sympathize with his situation. She was probably the only one who could. She'd been right there beside him throughout this crazy day.

He framed her face with one hand and brushed his thumb across the velvet softness of her cheek. He wanted to kiss her again. Desperately. Was there any better way to show his appreciation, which he could never put into words?

Bad idea.

He dropped his hand to his side, using every bit of the willpower he possessed to step away from her. She was like flame to a moth. He was going to get burned if he wasn't careful. Or worse yet, he would hurt her.

"You were absolutely fabulous today," he told her, his voice unusually husky.

She looked dazed, and he couldn't tell what she was thinking. He cleared his throat.

"I don't believe I would have made it out of there in one piece if it hadn't been for your quick thinking."

"Thank you, but I don't know about that."

He leaned his shoulder against the door frame and folded his arms against his chest, mostly to keep himself from reaching out to her again. "Believe me, you were outstanding."

"I do have one question—how did you get from the backyard into your bedroom?"

His lips twisted in amusement. "If you have to know, I climbed through my window," he informed her.

"You—"

She burst out laughing, putting a hand to her neck and throwing her head back merrily. "Now *that* I would have liked to have seen."

"It was quite undignified, and I'm glad there was no one there to witness it."

"You cleaned up pretty good. I think you made a decent impression with Eileen," she said, fanning herself with her hand to tamper her amusement.

"You think?" The cords of muscle in his neck tightened. With all the fun he'd been having bantering with Stephanie, he'd forgotten his predicament. It had only been a moment, but for that short amount of time, he'd let go of his fear.

He honestly didn't have a clue how things had gone with Eileen, only that all his preparation—cleaning the house from top to bottom and making sure all the kids' toys were organized and put away—had been for nothing. And the interview itself was nothing like he'd expected it to be.

But he had to let it go, or it was going to eat him

alive. Good or bad, the experience was over and there was nothing left for him to do about it.

Except, as he'd told Stephanie, *wait and pray*.

Stephanie didn't think that even the May Day picnic would be able to take her mind off the harrowing morning she'd had, but she found it was actually nice to be around neighbors who did not want to talk about anything more pressing than how thankful they were that the day of the picnic turned out to be sunny.

She hoped Drew would also be able to relax a little bit, but she could see the lines furrowing his brow from where she was sitting, a good twenty feet away from him. He was smiling and she heard him laugh from time to time, but she knew him well enough now to be able to see how he was really feeling, even when he was trying to present something different to the world.

She wondered if he could see the same in her.

Someone had erected a Maypole in the center of the park, and many of the older kids were winding and unwinding the colorful ribbons that flowed from the top of the pole.

Maybe a little preschool action would get her out of her own funk. She opened the box at her side. It was a fishing tackle box, full of makeup.

"Who wants their face painted?" she called loudly. Immediately several children, Matty and Jamey included, were running toward her and shouting. Now *this* was what living was all about. Maybe that's what Pastor Shawn meant when he said to find your purpose and then act on it.

She had a heart for these precious preschoolers. She

just had to figure out a way to make what was in her head work out on paper, and then in brick and mortar, and whiteboards and storybooks.

For a good hour, she painted butterflies and cat whiskers onto little children's faces. Mary came to help her, and soon they'd managed to paint the face of every child who wanted it.

Alexis and Samantha were busy leading the older children in sack races and three-legged races. Stephanie had heard of such things, but the reality was so much better. And then when some of the adults took the places of the children, the scene actually stoked her to laughter.

Where else but in Serendipity would grown men tie their legs together and hop around hooting and hollering like little kids? She couldn't remember enjoying a festivity more in her life, in spite of the fact that she'd had such a stressful morning, or maybe because of it.

People had been sampling many of the food dishes all through the afternoon, but now it was time for everyone to settle down on their blankets and eat a full meal. Frank joined Jo at a table set up for the older folks, and Drew and Stephanie and the twins shared a blanket spread across the manicured lawn.

Pastor Shawn gave a blessing, and then everyone dug in. Stephanie had brought fried chicken and brownies. Jo had explained how she needn't bring a whole meal for the family, just something to share. The women had set up one of their traditional thirty-yard spreads, a length of folding tables that really did measure thirty yards. Stephanie was amazed by the fact that the whole thing was covered with various types of dishes, everything from salad to dessert.

Stephanie was relieved that she and Drew seemed to have lost some of the tension from earlier. She didn't know whether it was from going through the stress of the investigator visiting, or whether it was that the boys were with them, but she was glad she and Drew were back to small talk, at least.

She was just finishing up a piece of Phoebe's famous cherry pies when Pastor Shawn stood up to make another announcement.

"Now as most of you know," he said in his preacher's voice, which easily carried across the park, "we have one more tradition here at our Serendipity May Day celebration. Alexis, will you please come do the honors?"

Stephanie's most outgoing new friend took Pastor Shawn's place, with Samantha by her side. Samantha's arms were behind her back, and Stephanie assumed they were about to hand out some kind of prize for the games today.

"Every year the ladies of the church elect a very special woman to be named May Queen. This honor belongs to a person who graces us with new hope to our community, the way spring brings new hope to summer."

Alexis paused for effect. "Today, I'm pleased to announce that our new May Queen is…Stephanie Cartwright!"

Stephanie's mouth dropped open. Her shocked gaze flew to Drew's, but he didn't look all that surprised. In fact, he was the first to applaud. Everyone else was quick to join in as Samantha retrieved a floral wreath from behind her back and proceeded to crown Stephanie with it.

She didn't know what to say. Tears streamed from her eyes. She certainly wouldn't have expected herself to be in the running for May Queen. This was a community award, wasn't it?

As she looked around at the people she now considered her friends and neighbors, she realized it *was* a community award.

And she was a part of that community.

Since it was late on a Saturday night and the kids were tucked soundly in bed, Stephanie was working on the particulars of opening her new preschool. She'd eaten dinner with the Spencers and read the boys a couple of books at bedtime, but now she was alone in her apartment, very much enjoying being up to her ears in the beginning stages of her dream.

Painting faces on all those precious kids during the May Day celebration two weeks ago had made her more excited than ever to make that dream a reality. She could feel it, so deep inside her heart that her pulse virtually sang from it.

She'd shifted that dream into overdrive since May Day, working on the various details of her preschool every chance she got, often late into the night.

Legal forms and notebooks full of preliminary research stood in precariously leaning piles on her desk and around her laptop computer. She'd left curriculum catalogs spread along the foot of her bed—quite messy for someone who had once forced herself to be a chronically neat person.

It felt good to let go of others' perfect expectations of her and just be *herself,* rather than constantly worrying that she was letting someone down.

She realized that she probably should be actively seeking some other type of temporary employment in Serendipity, not to mention a place to live, but she just couldn't bring herself to put any real effort into it.

But she knew her current arrangement wouldn't last. The case worker had come and gone, and school would be out for the summer in a couple of weeks. Drew hadn't yet heard the outcome of the investigator's report, but that was bound to happen any day, at which point a court date would be set. He knew she was planning to stay in Serendipity, so even if he needed her to testify in court, he'd know where to find her. There'd be no reason to remain with the Spencers once school was out for the summer.

Which meant Drew would soon be broaching the subject of her leaving. She was surprised that he hadn't already. She supposed she could speak up herself, but quite frankly, she didn't want to.

Why would she, when she was so content?

She absolutely adored Matty and Jamey. There were no other children on earth who had ever touched her heart the way they had. If she hadn't had enough of a reason to want to start a preschool here in Serendipity before, she had it now—for the boys.

Frank kept her on her toes and laughing, especially when Jo was around. As far as Stephanie was concerned, those two needed to stop their bickering long enough to find their way to the altar and get hitched. If ever there was a couple who belonged together, it was Frank and Jo.

And as for her feelings for Drew—they hadn't changed, except to grow stronger. Sometimes she'd catch him looking at her and think he might be softening toward her, but then he'd back off and turn all reserved again.

Which left the two of them at an impasse.

She scoffed to herself and straightened the nearest stack of papers. Mulling over her feelings for Drew wasn't going to do her any good. As it was, her thoughts were interrupted by the man himself knocking at the door.

"Come on in," she called, swinging her chair around to face the door. "It's open."

"You're starting to sound like a local. I'm sure you locked your doors in New Jersey."

She tilted her head up to him, her gaze burning into his. She just wished he could try to understand how she felt. *Fitting in* was something she'd never had before.

But how could he understand? He'd grown up in a loving family and within the close-knit Serendipity community. He had no idea what it was like to grow up feeling absolutely alone in the world.

She decided it was time to bring up the subject they'd both apparently been avoiding.

"I don't suppose Serendipity has a newspaper? I need to pick one up so I can take a gander at the current want-ad section."

"We had a paper at one point. It went out of business a few years ago. Anyway, there weren't any want-ads in it. At least not the kind you're looking for."

"Not for an apartment *or* a job? Surely employment positions have to open up from time to time somewhere in Serendipity. I'm not too picky. Will work for food."

Drew shook his head. "Most of those kinds of transactions are word-of-mouth around here. No sense spending money for an ad in the newspaper when you can advertise in church for free. Besides, you have a place to live."

Taken aback, her eyes widened. "I do?"

"Well, hello—where do you think you've been sleeping these past few weeks?"

"Yes, but my contract with you is almost over. I'm sure you'll hear from the case worker soon, and unless she needs to visit again, my role in that drama is finished. I'm happy to stand up as a witness for you in court, but you don't need me still living here for that. Not once the school term has ended."

He lowered his head and quirked his lips. "Like you said, your contract isn't up. Yet. So don't be too hasty getting a new job. Like the Bible says, don't worry about tomorrow, it'll take care of itself."

"I don't think I've ever heard that verse before. Pastor Shawn's wonderful sermons have inspired me to start reading the Bible, but I haven't gotten very far. It's a lot to take in, with so-and-so begetting so-and-so and so on."

Drew grinned and leaned his broad shoulder against the door frame. "Started in Genesis, did you?"

Stephanie's eyes widened. "Isn't that where you're supposed to start a book? At the beginning?"

"Well, sure, but the Bible isn't just any book. Not to go into any deep theological discussions or anything, but I find it's helpful to read parts of the Old Testament and the New Testament at the same time. I have a schedule that helps me read through the whole Bible in a year. I could make a copy of it for you, if you'd like."

Stephanie nodded, her heart welling at the way he showed he cared, even when he was trying to stay distant from her. "That would be nice. Thank you."

Thank you didn't seem to be good enough. She was so grateful that God had led her to work for Drew, a man whose faith showed clearly in his daily life and his spoken word. Drew had helped her in so many ways, and not just to get away from a bad situation in New Jersey. She'd never be able to express her appreciation to him.

He shifted, hooking his thumbs into the front pockets of his jeans. "I'll be sure and get that for you. In the meantime, you might want to start reading the Book of Matthew. You'll find that verse we were just talking about not too many chapters in."

His blue jeans and dark gray T-shirt were a welcome change, though she was used to seeing him without shoes—they were the first thing to go once Drew stepped into the house after work. The man leaning on her door frame in casual clothes, his hair rumpled and a dark shadow of whiskers across his jaw, wasn't remotely like the nerdy academic she'd imagined before she'd come to Serendipity.

She liked the shirt-and-tie Drew, but she thought she almost liked the casual Drew better. He looked as if he was ready to mount a horse and ride off into the sunset—except maybe for his lack of boots.

"Horse?" Coming slowly back to earth, *horse* was the only word Stephanie heard Drew say.

"I beg your pardon? Something about a horse?"

"Well, sure. If you're going to stay in Serendipity, you have to learn how to ride a horse."

"Hmm," she said, suspicious of his motives. "So I can tie my old nag to the hitching post in front of Cup O' Jo?"

He chuckled. "Something like that. You up for it? Tomorrow? We can either take the kids with us, or else it can be just you and me."

Something about the way he said *just you and me* made her stomach flutter. Was she getting mixed signals from him, or was it all in her imagination?

Was there hope, or was she just setting herself up for another bad fall?

Chapter Ten

Drew settled himself down on the front porch steps and leaned his palms back against the wood planks. Matty and Jamey were wrestling around in the dirt in front of the house. Pop had gone to get Jo so they could watch the boys while Drew and Stephanie went riding, but the old couple hadn't yet returned. The boys were wiggly and rambunctious at the best of times. Drew couldn't be expected to keep them corralled indefinitely. They were kids, and kids wanted to play.

"I really didn't know what to wear to go horseback riding," Stephanie said, skipping down the stairs of her apartment. "I don't have cowboy boots, so I guess sneakers are going to have to do, yes?"

"Ah. No. Sshh!" Drew protested, but it was too late. The twins had heard the words *horseback riding*. He had forgotten to tell Stephanie that he hadn't mentioned to the twins where they were going. The boys loved horseback riding and he didn't want to disappoint them.

Now, it looked as if he wouldn't have to. The twins were already jumping up and down and cheering about going on *their horseys*. And while Drew might have been tempted to weather the storm and leave them with Pop and Jo, anyway, he knew Stephanie had too soft a heart not to take the boys with them.

And here he'd really been looking forward to having some time alone with her.

"Oh, hey, little dudes," she said, reaching down to hug both of them at the same time. "I didn't realize you guys were going with us."

"Yeah," Drew said, groaning. "Neither did I."

Stephanie was already rounding the boys up and herding them inside. She certainly had an amazing way with them. And it wasn't just the boys. She'd reached each and every member of his family. With her pancake breakfasts. Her cheerful morning personality. The way she threw herself so completely and with such joyful abandonment into any project she wanted to accomplish, from dusting the mantel to playing board games with the boys.

He owed her a lot—far more than he was able to pay her in a salary. Which was a stress in itself. He'd almost reached the end of the meager savings he'd set aside for that purpose. If he had more—

If he had more—what? He would ask her to stay on as the nanny? He shook his head. That didn't seem quite right.

"I have a great idea!" Stephanie exclaimed, snapping Drew out of his thoughts. He had to smile when she became animated about something. The woman had boundless energy, and such an upbeat personality that a man would have to be made out of stone not to respond to her.

"What do you say we invite Pop-Pop and Auntie Jo

along for our ride?" she asked the twins. Jo was the designated aunt to every one of the town's children, Drew's own boys being no exception.

He groaned again. When he'd first suggested this little outing, he'd been anticipating a more intimate situation, just him and Stephanie.

Alone.

Not that he begrudged his sons tagging along. He would never do that, and he knew Stephanie wouldn't, either.

But Pop and Jo?

Talk about a way to ruin a date—or whatever it was. Those two would undoubtedly talk nonstop throughout the whole ride—bicker, actually, knowing the two of them. Putting Pop and Jo in the same county was one state too close. He loved the older folks, but—

"Hey, are you okay? You have an odd look on your face, like you ate something that didn't agree with you." Stephanie ushered the boys inside the house, encouraging them to go put on their *cowboy clothes*. "Do you still want to go horseback riding today?"

"No, no. I'm fine. And obviously the boys are excited."

"I hear a *but* in there."

"But inviting Pop and Jo? Really?"

"That's the best part!" When she smiled, her whole countenance lit up. He was almost inclined to agree with her, just to keep seeing that look on her face.

He shook his head and chuckled. "You can't honestly believe that."

"Oh, dear," she exclaimed, a frown worrying her

lips. "Your father isn't in any condition to ride a horse, what with his bum leg and all, is he?"

"Ha!" Drew burst out. "Don't let *him* hear you say that. The old man's been riding longer than he's been walking. He's better on horseback than he is with his cane—although he may be just as dangerous."

"Oh. Good, then."

"I'm still unclear how adding Pop and Jo to our little excursion can be considered the *best* part."

Her sly grin explained more than her words ever could, and Drew broke out in another round of laughter. "Matchmaking. Turnabout is fair play."

"I have no idea what that means," she informed him, although he suspected that she did. There was no way she could possibly have missed all the times Pop and Jo had pushed them together, trying to merge them into a couple. The persnickety old folks weren't exactly the most subtle individuals on the planet.

"Don't you?" he prodded.

She pretended like she didn't hear him and continued her own train of thought. "If ever two people should be together, it's Jo and your father."

"That's a scary thought."

Again, she ignored the sarcasm in his comment. "We just have to figure out a way to make them admit they care for each other. That ought to be simple, right?"

He crossed his arms. "If you say so. Personally, I think you'd have better luck tying two cats together by their tails. You'd probably get scratched less, too."

"You have no faith in the power of love."

"Hmph." His arms were already folded, so he crossed one ankle in front of the other. If he could have crossed anything else, he would have. This whole *power of love* conversation was frightening the socks off of him, and it wasn't just because they were discussing getting his Pop and Jo together on a permanent basis, as terrifying as that thought might be.

He scuffed the tip of one boot against one of the porch's rough wood planks and then lifted his tan Stetson, brushed back his hair with his fingers and planted the hat back on again, this time low over his brow.

"Are you ready to ride, or what?"

Stephanie wasn't anywhere near ready to ride a horse. She'd never been close to one of the creatures in her life. She wouldn't have ever imagined that she would come to enjoy the pungent odor of horseflesh and hay that assailed her nostrils as she entered the dimly lit stable, but she'd come to associate the smell with Serendipity. As her love for the town grew, her appreciation for the scent of livestock grew, as well. But that's where her pleasure ended and her panic began.

She hadn't realized that horses were so large in person. She'd only ever seen them on television, and they didn't look quite so large with actors riding them.

She couldn't even see over the shoulder of the enormous mare Drew had given her to ride. It reminded her more of an elephant than an equine. Was he seriously expecting her to mount this thing?

He had to be joking. He'd given her the biggest, tallest horse in the stable.

Frank and Jo were already mounted on their own trusty steeds, and Drew was helping the boys onto their horses, as well. The older couple had been thrilled to be invited along on the family outing. Drew's phone call had caught them before they left Cup O' Jo, so they met Drew, Stephanie and the boys at the town stable, where Drew rented out horses for them for the day.

Stephanie set her jaw. If Frank and Jo could get on their horses, so could she, she thought, determined not to make a fool of herself. She stared at the stirrup as if it was a mountain she must scale.

How was she supposed to get her leg extended enough to lace her foot through one stirrup, much less find the momentum to swing her other leg up and over?

She'd seen it done in the movies, and the actors always made it look easy. There must be a trick to it, and she would just have to figure out what it was.

She grabbed the stirrup in both hands and lifted her left foot, hopping around on her right one until she was finally able to thread the left through the leather.

She was certain she was going to break something— probably her neck. The saddle horn looked like her best chance for leverage, so as soon as she was sure she could maintain her balance for a moment, she grasped for the top of the saddle, breathing a sigh of relief when her fist closed tightly around the protruding leather.

Success. Now it was just a matter of getting enough of a start to be able to pull herself up and over.

She took a deep breath and counted down.

Three. Two. One.

Before she could so much as hop, skip or jump, she found herself floating in midair, with no stirrup or saddle horn in her reach to help her balance, only a pair of strong hands at her waist. A moment later, she found herself upright on the saddle, her legs dangling off either side. The horse shifted underneath her and she squealed and lunged for the mare's mane, but she needn't have bothered, for Drew hadn't yet released his hold on her waist. It was both reassuring and unnerving at the same time, having him holding her this way.

"Slide your other foot into the stirrup, grip with your knees and lean back on your heels for balance," he instructed briskly, sounding a little amused.

She wasn't surprised. She must have looked like an utter fool trying to mount the horse on her own. She realized she probably should have waited for his help to begin with, but she still had a little pride, although she suspected that by the end of the day, she wouldn't have enough vanity left to fill a tea cup.

She was vitally aware that Drew was still touching her, making sure she stayed upright in the saddle while she found her equilibrium. She thought she had her balance, but she appreciated his gentlemanly kindness and attentiveness just the same. It was nice of him not to allow her to take a very unladylike nosedive.

Perhaps she was enjoying his attention a little more than she ought to be. She had to remind herself that they were trying to play matchmaker for Frank and Jo—not each other. It was easy to get sidetracked with him looking up at her that way. She glared down at him, but she couldn't find it in her to put any real feeling behind it.

"You could have at least warned me before you launched me up like a rocket," she grumbled good-naturedly. "You took ten years off of my life just now."

"You looked like you needed a little help," he drawled.

"A *little?* You select the biggest horse in the barn for me and you think I need a *little* help? What am I missing here?"

"I picked Juliet because she's the gentlest horse in the herd. She wouldn't go much beyond a trot if there was a nest of hornets on her tail. You're perfectly safe with her."

"Well, that's a relief." She couldn't help the note of friendly sarcasm that accompanied her statement.

"Are you two going to sit here blabbing all day or are we going to have us a trail ride?" Frank demanded, pulling his appaloosa alongside Stephanie's bay.

"I've still got to saddle up Romeo," Drew informed him. "You guys go ahead and lead the horses out to the corral. I'll be along shortly."

Jo, who was leading the twins' horses by their halters, reined her horse toward the stable door. "Get a move on, old man," she shouted over her shoulder. "Drew can tack up faster than you can get your old nag out this door."

Frank grunted and nudged his horse into a walk. "Always tellin' me what to do," he groused at no one in particular as he followed Jo and the boys out.

Stephanie watched them leave without as much as flinching a muscle. She was afraid even to breathe, as she had no idea what types of movements might possibly startle her horse. Drew had placed Juliet's reins into her hand before he'd disappeared into one of the stalls, but he'd left out some vital pieces of information. She had a few questions about this riding business, things she needed to know *before* she shifted this horse into gear.

Like how to steer. And more importantly, how to
stop. She had a sudden vision of Juliet running at break-
neck speed through an overgrown field—with Stephanie hanging on for dear life.

A trip to the emergency room might be a fine way to
bring Frank and Jo together, but it wasn't Stephanie's
idea of a good time.

"Hey, sweetheart," said Drew, leading his horse out
of one of the far stalls. He walked his now-saddled
black toward her. "Why aren't you out with the rest of
the family?"

Her heart lurched into some sort of up-tempo Latin
beat at the casual way he included her in his family
unit, though she knew he was probably talking off the
top of his head and didn't mean anything by his words.
She'd been tagging along with them for several weeks
now, so she supposed it only seemed natural.

But *sweetheart?* Was that off-the-cuff, as well?

"Um, let me see here," she answered blithely. "Maybe
because I haven't the slightest idea what I'm doing.
I've never even been near a horse before, never mind
attempted to try to ride one. Where is the ignition,
again?"

Laughing, Drew mounted and pulled his horse in
front of her. "Don't worry about that. Just sit back and
enjoy the ride. Juliet will follow Romeo anywhere."

Drew clicked his tongue and Romeo danced to the
side and then moved forward. Stephanie waited for her
own mount to follow, but Juliet just snorted and tossed
her head, refusing to move an inch.

"Drew," she called quickly, before he, too, disappeared from view. "This isn't working."

Drew pulled back, glanced behind him and laughed. "Loosen up a bit on the reins, sweetheart. You've got a good *whoa* going on there."

"Oh." It took her a moment just to recover from his easy grin and the way he'd called her *sweetheart* again as if it was the most natural thing in the world. If this was going to be a habit with him, she thought she liked it. He had her world in a tailspin. But right now she needed to concentrate on following his advice.

He leaned back in the saddle, tipped back his hat and winked at her. She decided she definitely liked the casual Drew, the one in jeans and a cowboy hat and old, scuffed riding boots.

Her left hand was fisted over the reins, and she could immediately see what Drew was trying to tell her. The lines were tight from Juliet's mouth to her fist. Taking a deep breath, she released the death grip she'd been holding on the saddle horn and used her right hand to loosen the reins through her fingers, hoping they wouldn't slip from her hands.

"That's better," Drew encouraged. "Now nudge her with your heel."

Stephanie hardly touched her foot to Juliet's side. "Giddy-up, horsey," she quipped, feeling ridiculous.

Drew pulled his horse around in a circle so their mounts were side-to-side.

"She has to feel it," he explained. "Like this." He leaned over and grabbed her ankle, and then dug it into the horse's side with surprising force.

Stephanie gasped, certain that Juliet was going to bolt. Instead, the mare just whickered and plodded forward at a pace even Stephanie could handle.

"There you go. See?" Drew was very encouraging, considering she put the R in rookie when it came to horseback riding. "You're riding a horse."

"Not as well as your three-year-olds," she replied tartly, but she sat a little taller in the saddle just the same, and lessened her hold on the saddle horn—at least marginally.

Drew pulled his mount ahead of her, and this time Juliet did, indeed, follow Romeo, outside the stable door and into the corral where the others were waiting.

"Thought you guys might have gotten lost," Frank grumbled. "Or stopped for a little kissy-face."

"Frank!" Jo scolded.

"Pop!" Drew protested at the same time.

Stephanie just blushed.

With a rumbling, self-satisfied chuckle, Frank urged his mount forward, leading all of them out of the corral and down a well-worn grassy path. The boys followed, and then Jo, Drew and finally, Stephanie.

She didn't mind bringing in the rear. For one thing, no one could see her awkwardness in the saddle. And for another, it gave her a good excuse to watch Drew from behind.

And what a view it was. Just as she'd suspected the first time she'd seen him, he cut a fine figure on a horse—tall and lean and broad-shouldered.

While she was already starting to feel saddle sore, Drew moved as one with his mount. Unlike Stephanie's horse, Drew's black was skittish and full of power, yet Drew held him completely under control, the animal's power leashed by man. It was as if Romeo was an extension of him, and it was a beautiful thing to watch.

He was a beautiful thing to watch.

She was falling for him. Hard. It wasn't as if she could deny her feelings anymore, and she wasn't sure she wanted to. It was far more than just their intense initial attraction, or the potent, almost palpable chemistry between them.

She was intrigued by every single thing about him. The way he always dressed up to go out, yet went barefoot inside his house. The way he chewed on the arm of his reading glasses when he was deep in thought. The tender way he brushed his sons' hair off their foreheads when he put them to bed at night. The kiss they'd shared, a magnetic and wonderful moment she would never forget.

She no longer believed he thought what had happened between them was *nothing*. Privately, she believed he'd been trying to protect her with his unusual and unendorsed chivalry.

She knew he was fresh from a painful divorce. His child custody issue was the biggest thing on his mind— and rightly so. She wouldn't expect any less from a man so completely committed to being a good father for his twins.

But when all was said and done, after Drew was able to walk away with a clear conscience and could look toward his future, she was still going to be around. If God was willing, Drew Spencer and his wonderful family would always be a part of her life.

And if God especially blessed her, a big part.

"Can we run the horses, Daddy?" Matty asked excitedly as they all drew up in a field.

"We want to run," Jamey echoed.

Oh, no. Stephanie definitely did *not* want to run, or gallop, or whatever it was called on a horse. And hopefully, neither did Juliet.

"Please, no," she said aloud, speaking both to Drew and to her horse.

Drew guided Romeo around in a small circle and grinned. His smile alone was enough to warm her heart, stoking it into a tender glowing flame. "Are you sure you don't want to try a trot? It's a lot of fun."

She knew he was teasing her rather than pressuring her, so she shook her head and laughed. "Thank you, no. Count me out. Juliet and I will be just fine staying right here to wait for you."

"I do believe I'll hang back and keep Stephanie company," Jo said, her usually exuberant voice sounding strained, at least to Stephanie's ears. Frank must have heard it, as well, for he pulled around and trotted his horse to Jo's side, a deep frown lining his face.

"Are you okay, honey?" he inquired in a voice that was surprisingly gentle, especially for Frank. "You sound like you've got a thorn in your shoe."

Well, that sounded more like the old man she knew.

"What I have," Jo informed him, stretching forward in the saddle, "is a bogus hip. And at the moment, that lousy piece of metal is giving me all sorts of grief."

Stephanie hadn't realized that Jo had had a hip replacement. What was the woman doing up on a horse? That had to be painful.

"You're a stubborn woman," Frank said, sliding off his mount and limping to the side of Jo's horse, lifting one stirrup to adjust the girth on her saddle. Stephanie privately thought that in a fair race, Frank was equally as stubborn, which was what made it so fun to watch the two of them going at it full steam.

"I'm just sore. And who wouldn't be, at this age? An old woman has the right to grumble now and again."

"Not in front of me, you don't," Frank retorted. "My poor ears can't handle that sort of thing. You'll give me a headache."

Which, translated, Stephanie thought, meant he'd really been worried that Jo might be hurt. But, of course, he'd never admit it.

"I'm fine," she insisted. "I just need a moment to catch my breath."

"Before we even started, I asked you if you were up for riding today," Frank accused, narrowing his eyes on Jo. "You said you were. I don't know what you were thinking, woman. You shouldn't have come. You're going to really hurt yourself one of these days and I may not be there to help you."

Jo glared at him. "Don't you even think about telling me what I can and can't do, Frank Spencer. Not now, and not ever. I've been riding horses all my life. No stupid hip replacement surgery is going to keep me from doing what I love, and neither is some obstinate old man."

"When the good Lord was handing out common sense, woman, you must have been standing behind the door."

Jo laughed. Stephanie was amazed at how they got along with each other, saying things no one else would dare.

"And you were running the other way," she countered.

"I could have run back again just as fast. I'll have you know I was the master of the hundred-yard dash in my time."

"Sure. At field day in elementary school."

Stephanie's attention began to drift. She knew there would be no stopping the two older folks once they got going, and they were on a roll now. Besides, she wanted to see what Drew was doing.

She turned in her saddle and looked behind her, no longer completely terrified that her horse would bolt as soon as she shifted her weight.

Drew had taken the boys a little way off and was allowing them to *run*. Actually he had them at a slow trot, but the twins were still bouncing around in the saddle. So much so that, if it was anyone else but Drew watching them, Stephanie would have been afraid one of the boys might take a tumble and hurt themselves. But she had complete confidence in Drew, and the utmost faith that he knew exactly what he was doing, both with the horses and with his sons. The twins were perfectly safe in his capable hands.

Drew glanced up and she waved. When he tipped his hat in response, her heart fluttered and it took a moment for her to catch her breath.

She'd never felt like this with Ryan, even before he'd turned abusive. He was always pushing her, too hard and too fast, and she'd unconsciously held back.

Now she knew why.

Drew followed the boys back over to where she waited with her mount, and she assumed they would all be ready to head back home, but Frank and Jo didn't seem to notice Drew's return, or if they did, they ignored it. The two older folks were deep in conversation, their mounts side by side. Frank was leaning his hand on the back of Jo's saddle as he spoke closely into her ear.

Drew reined in close to Stephanie and smiled as he realized the direction her gaze was directed. "How goes the matchmaking?"

"Uh," she responded blankly. She'd been concentrating most of her resources on learning to ride and staying in the saddle. And what was left of her attention kept drifting to Drew. She'd completely forgotten her ulterior motive for going on this horseback outing had originally been to force Frank and Jo together as a couple and compel them to admit their feelings for each other.

Fortunately, they seemed to be doing just fine coupling off on their own, although in their typical back and forth way.

Stephanie wasn't sure they'd ever truly admit to having feelings for each other.

"I'm afraid I'm failing in that regard," she admitted. "I don't think we're any closer to seeing a wedding in their future than we ever were."

"Don't feel bad. You wouldn't be the first to be unsuccessful in that endeavor. Maybe those two simply aren't meant to be together. They both live with family. Maybe it's better that way. Family won't kick them out when they get annoying."

"And yet it's clear they care for each other," Stephanie added thoughtfully. "You should have heard how concerned your father was when he thought Jo might be hurt. It was really touching."

"Touching?" Drew parroted, chuckling and patting Romeo on the neck. "I don't know about that."

"Daddy, Daddy," Matty exclaimed as he bounced forward on his horse. "Pop-Pop and Auntie Jo are holding hands."

The way the little boy said it made Stephanie laugh. *Holding hands* may as well have been *flying to the moon to eat green cheese.* Completely impossible and equally as unappealing in the eyes of a three-year-old boy.

Matty was loud in his exuberance and excited by his finding—loud enough for Frank and Jo to hear what was being said. Frank spurred his horse a comfortable distance away from Jo, but not before Stephanie had switched her gaze their direction and had seen the truth.

Frank and Jo really *had been* holding hands.

Interesting.

Drew must have seen it, too, because he began sputtering and gasping, trying to harness his amusement. "Shush now, Matty. It's not polite to talk about what other people are doing."

"They love each other," Jamey insisted, pulling back too hard on his horse's reins and causing his sorrel to toss her head.

Matty was exuberant in his haste to one-up his twin brother and make his final observation.

"They should get married."

Chapter Eleven

Pop and Jo had gone ahead with the kids, leaving Drew and Stephanie alone to walk their horses back to the stable.

"It's really nice out here," Stephanie remarked, gesturing at the rolling meadow before them. "There's something wonderfully stark and majestic about Texas. The spring wildflowers peeking through the dry grass are absolutely lovely."

The wildflowers weren't the only gorgeous thing in this field, but all he said was, "Texas is a beautiful place."

In truth, he had nothing to compare it to. He was Texas born and bred, and proud of it. He'd even attended college within the Lone Star State. He'd never seen a reason to go any farther.

"I'll be honest with you.... I didn't notice the beauty of Serendipity when I first drove in." She looked sheepish for a moment. "To me it looked dry and barren. Of course, I hadn't been out of the metropolitan areas much back on the east coast. Now that I've been here awhile, I think I would balk if I went back to all the black asphalt the city has to offer."

"I know what you mean." He tipped his hat back with his palm and studied her, thinking about how she'd blossomed under country life. She was just blooming—her cheeks a healthy rose and pure delight in her eyes. She didn't even notice his gaze on her because she was too busy enjoying the nature around her. She brought a new kind of beauty to Texas—not just in her outward features, but in her heart.

She glanced at him and the color in her face heightened. "Well," she said softly, "as lovely as this is, we probably ought to be heading back. I'd hate for the twins to tire Jo and Frank out too much. Jo's been a trouper, but I think the horseback ride might have been too much for her. If you ask me, she looked peaked there toward the end."

See, now here was why Drew was so attracted to her. She always put the needs of others before her own.

Sometimes too much, in his opinion. She was probably right about the boys tiring the old folks out, but was it completely selfish of him to want a little more time with her?

Alone?

Or maybe that was the real issue. Maybe she was uncomfortable being alone with him. Which wasn't surprising, he supposed. He knew he'd hurt her pretty badly by denying there was anything between them. Now that he was considering if there *could* be, he wondered if it was too late.

"I'm sure Pop has everything handled," Drew assured her. "He's really good with the kids. And for all his griping, Jo is super important to him. He won't let her overdo it."

"Do you think your pop is maybe softening toward the idea of something more serious with Jo?"

"Maybe."

"It's all on your father's shoulders, you know. If it was up to Jo, she would have had him standing at the end of the aisle a long time ago, tuxedo and everything. She's in love with him, you know."

Her expression took on the dreamy quality that Drew noticed most women had about them whenever they talked about engagements and weddings. Usually he would have balked and spurred his horse for the hills, no matter whose wedding they were talking about.

What had changed?

"I think he might feel the same way about her." It half frightened Drew to think about his father being serious about a woman. It *completely* frightened him that *he* might be getting serious about a woman.

About Stephanie.

As they turned their mounts for home, they rode together side by side, enjoying an easy conversation about nothing in particular. As daunting as his emotions were, he waited to feel uncomfortable. He *wanted* to feel uncomfortable.

But it didn't happen. He was suddenly extremely grateful that Stephanie hadn't listened to his nonsense about leaving Serendipity. She belonged here every bit as much as he did. His heart was singing. He could breathe again. For the first time in forever, he felt alive.

* * *

The next Saturday, Drew and Stephanie were enjoying a lazy afternoon sitting out on the porch, speaking in hushed tones from time to time, but mostly just enjoying the fresh air and the late-spring weather.

Stephanie was working on some paperwork, something to do with the preschool, he imagined. He was ostensibly grading papers, but he kept glancing over at Stephanie. He wanted to say something to change the dynamic between them, but how did a man apologize for the callous way he denied their relationship to others?

He'd just returned to his grade book when Matty charged out the front door screaming at the top of his lungs, tears flowing down his face.

"Help Jamey! Help Jamey!" He kept repeating the same phrase over and over.

Stephanie immediately crouched to his level and opened her arms to him. "What's wrong, honey? Where is your brother?"

"In there. In there. He can't breathe," the distressed little boy sobbed. "He's choking."

Drew's pulse jolted to life and painful shots of adrenaline surged through him. He was right at Stephanie's heel as she scooped Matty into her arms and darted for the living room. Panic lengthened his steps and his heart roared in his ears. He prayed as he went, even before he knew what, if anything, was wrong.

God knew, and that was what was important. Drew felt more inadequate than confident in his job as a parent, especially as a single parent. Confusion and disorder were the words of the day with his two unruly preschoolers. There always seemed to be one crisis or another rearing up around the house.

He knew he shouldn't be worried. It was probably nothing—a simple cough or a sneeze, or even Jamey playing a trick with his brother. But something in Matty's demeanor set off alarms in Drew's head. He instinctively sensed that this time it was something different. Something serious.

Should he call 911?

In a matter of seconds, a dozen scenarios crossed Drew's anxious mind. He'd heard of children swallowing toys or suffocating themselves with plastic bags. He prayed through his worried thoughts, but that didn't lessen the sheer terror of the possibility that his son was hurt.

Lord, protect Jamey.

Drew had always been careful not to let the twins play with toys that weren't specifically made for their age range, and he was absolutely certain there was no plastic of any kind lurking around at their level.

Drew rounded the corner into the living room just after Stephanie. Jamey was hunched over on his knees on the floor, nearly motionless, one hand at his throat, the other across his midsection.

He was definitely choking, but Drew had never before witnessed anything like what he was seeing now. He'd expected Jamey to be hacking and coughing and rolling over and pounding at his chest.

The reality was infinitely more terrifying.

Jamey wasn't making a sound. He opened and closed his mouth convulsively, but there was no gasping, no wheezing. Not so much as a squeak.

And he was turning blue. Not the heated red of adrenaline-fueled panic, but a frightening purple-blue from a lack of oxygen.

Drew fumbled for the cell phone in his pants pocket, knowing even as his fingers closed around it that it would take too long for the paramedics to show up at the house.

Jamey couldn't breathe. He needed help now. He was already starting to waver and sag toward the floor, his usually bright blue eyes glazing over.

"Jamey? Can you hear me, son?" Drew rushed toward Jamey and dropped to his knees in front of the boy. He held his own breath, waiting for a response.

Anything to give him hope.

But the boy didn't react to Drew's words. It didn't even seem as if he was aware Drew was there. He was quickly losing consciousness, and Drew didn't know what to do about it.

His heart screamed in his head as he reached for Jamey and waited for the emergency operator to pick up. He hoped they'd be able to talk him through whatever measures were needed to get the boy breathing again.

What was the best course of action? Should he try and do some kind of modified Heimlich maneuver? Should he turn the boy upside down? Pound him on his little back?

Would that make things worse or better? What about CPR? Or was that only for when a baby's heart stopped?

Drew didn't know. He didn't have any answers, and he certainly didn't want to do the wrong thing and make it worse. It ripped him apart to feel so helpless, and yet he couldn't act for fear of making a mistake.

"Here," Stephanie said, her voice surprisingly calm and collected as she thrust Matty into his arms. "Take Matty."

Her gaze willed him to hold it together. The intensity in her eyes gave him a new sense of hope and strength. "Stay on the line until you get an operator and do what you can to send those paramedics out here as soon as possible."

Just like that, Stephanie took control of the situation. She knelt down behind Jamey, wrapped one arm diagonally across his chest to support him and placed the other one at his back. There was no pause, no hesitation, as she leaned him forward and pounded him firmly between his shoulder blades with the heel of her hand.

Drew winced with every one of the five firm strokes he counted, but he trusted Stephanie's instincts. She'd been trained in first aid. He hadn't. And now he wished he was.

Why hadn't he thought about this before? What if Stephanie wasn't here to perform the maneuver?

He'd be useless and panicking. That's what.

"Come on, little guy," Stephanie urged. "Breathe for me."

She placed her fist under his ribcage and gave five quick thrusts.

Still nothing.

"Stephanie?" Drew croaked out.

Why wasn't it working?

Stephanie didn't appear to hear him, but Drew didn't

repeat her name. As much as he needed answers, he understood why she didn't respond. Her entire focus was on Jamey, and that's where Drew wanted it to be. She had returned to thumping him slowly and rhythmically on his back.

"Come on, little man. Cough it up." Her encouragement sounded upbeat to Drew's ears. He was panicking to the point of hysteria, but she appeared in control of the situation, or at least as much as a person could be.

Please, God, let it work.

Suddenly Jamey heaved violently and a small green square launched from his throat onto the carpet several feet away.

The boy rolled into Stephanie's embrace and wailed in fright.

Drew had never heard such a welcome sound.

"Thank you, God. Thank you, God. Thank you, God," he murmured over and over again.

He rushed forward and swept Jamey into his arms, closing his eyes to pinch back tears and reveling in the feel of the boy's arms wrapped so tightly around his neck that his own air was cut off. He kissed Jamey's face and his shoulders and his hair until the boy was squirming to be released.

Reluctantly, he set his son on his feet. The boy rushed to his twin and the two of them immediately started playing with their preschool-aged train set, the one with big wooden wheels and a caboose.

It was as if nothing had happened—as if Jamey had forgotten his traumatic experience already. By the time the paramedics arrived, he'd probably have moved on to yet another toy, with the joyous, limited attention span of a three-year-old boy.

Drew shook his head in amazement. Children were so resilient. Much more so than he was. This was one day he wouldn't forget. *Ever.* He hoped he never had to experience that level of sheer terror again in his life.

He'd learned a valuable lesson today. He could have lost his son because of his ignorance. He planned to sign up for the very next child CPR class available, even if he had to drive for an hour to find one.

If it hadn't been for Stephanie...

He was so thankful for her presence here today that he knew he'd never be able to find the words to express it. He'd been so caught up in the fact that Jamey was breathing again that he hadn't noticed Stephanie's response. She was still sitting on the floor, her hands braced on her knees and an incomprehensible look on her face, somewhere between relief and queasiness.

"There aren't words," he started, but then stammered to a halt. There really *weren't* words that could convey what he felt, how grateful he was that she'd been here at the house.

That she'd saved his son.

She shook her head and wouldn't meet his eyes. "I'm glad he's okay."

"He's *alive*," he amended, emotion swirling through him and tightening his throat. "Because of you. And don't say it was nothing. It's *everything.* My sons mean everything to me."

He moved to her side and reached for her. Her fingers were quivering, and she was clearly trying to catch her breath.

Drew was confused by the sudden change in her demeanor. Only moments before, she'd been so calm and collected. So in control.

Now she appeared vulnerable. Fragile.

"Sorry," she apologized briefly. "I think my nerves just kicked in."

Drew didn't consider his actions—he just wrapped his arms around her waist and tucked her in close to his chest. The spice of her perfume didn't smell so foreign anymore. It was uniquely Stephanie. He closed his eyes and, in a moment's diversion, lost himself in the scent.

In her.

She shivered. He rubbed a hand along her back, making the same comforting noises he did with his sons when they needed soothing. And then he heard her sniffle. He leaned back, seeing the tears in her eyes.

"It's all good," he said, his voice low and husky. He brushed his thumb across her wet cheeks, drying her tears. "I don't think Jamey is any worse for the wear."

"Thank God," she replied. "But what if it hadn't worked? What if he'd—"

She didn't have to finish the sentence.

Drew swallowed around the lump in his throat. "But it did work. And Jamey is fine, thanks to you. Look at him playing in the corner. He's happy."

"Yes, he is," Stephanie agreed softly. "And so am I."

His heart welled as he met her gaze. "Really?"

"Really."

Stephanie crouched and reached for the slimy green square projectile that had clogged Jamey's throat. The paramedics had arrived within minutes of Drew's call in to them, and the whole house was alive with noise and confusion.

Wet. Sticky. Gooey.

Hard candy?

How had Jamey gotten a hold of hard candy?

"What's all the racket?" Frank Spencer demanded gruffly as he limped into the room, a scowl burrowing his brow. "Can't an old man get a decent nap around here?"

Stephanie was surprised Frank hadn't heard Matty's terrified cries. Apparently he'd been awakened by the sirens, or else by the ruckus of the paramedics entering the house.

Two men briefly introduced to Stephanie as Zach Bowden and Ben Atwood had rushed to the living room to check Jamey out. He appeared to have recovered from the incident without harm, but the paramedics wanted to be certain before they headed back to the station.

"Not now, Pop," Drew warned, his attention only marginally on his father. He was sitting crouched on his knees, holding Jamey on his lap as Zach examined the boy's lungs with a stethoscope.

"What's wrong with Jamey?" Frank demanded. When Drew didn't answer, the old man turned to Stephanie.

"Would you like to explain to me why we have paramedics in our living room?"

"I'm wondering the same thing," came a high, warblelike voice from the door. Jo rapped twice on the open door. It was a formality, since everyone already knew she was there because she'd spoken first. She confidently entered the house of her own accord before anyone invited her in.

"I was on my way to the café when I saw the ambulance pass by. You may be the lawyer, Frank, but I'm the official ambulance chaser." She chuckled at her own joke.

Frank didn't look amused.

Drew welcomed the new company with a brisk nod. "Hey, Jo. We had a little mishap with Jamey."

A *little?* Stephanie's heart had stopped beating for a full minute while she'd worked on Jamey. She'd never been so frightened in her life. That hardly qualified as trivial, though she knew Drew didn't mean it that way. She knew from the look on his face that he'd been even more terrified than she was.

"Zach? Ben?" Frank would not be put aside. He pounded his cane on the hardwood floor like a judge with a gavel. "What's wrong with Jamey?"

Jo shuffled to Frank's side and looped her arm through his. "Patience, old man," she chided gently. "I'm sure they'll tell you as soon as they know anything." She flashed pointed looks at the two paramedics.

"Can you open your mouth for me, little buddy?" Zach asked Jamey. "I need to take a look at your throat. See my flashlight?" The paramedic waved the beam on the floor around Jamey. "I'm going to use this little stick here to help me keep your tongue down, okay? And then I'll look inside your mouth with my light."

Jamey burrowed his face into Drew's chest. He kissed the top of his son's head, his gaze welling with compassion and love. A minute went by as Drew patiently encouraged Jamey to let Zach take a look at him.

"You get to keep the stick afterward," Zach bribed with a grin. He handed the tongue depressor to Jamey to allow him to get familiar with it. "If you're a brave boy and let me look in your mouth, I'll even throw an extra one in for Matty."

Matty shrieked in delight and Jamey suddenly looked a little more interested in conceding. Stephanie chuckled. Pleasing his twin brother was obviously important to Jamey, for he finally assented with a reluctant nod.

"Open wide and say aaah," Zach instructed, gently using the tongue depressor as he shined the flashlight into Jamey's mouth and examined his throat.

"That's my boy," Drew encouraged, patting his son on the back.

Zach pronounced Jamey good and, as promised, handed the tongue depressor over to him. Ben supplied Matty with an identical stick. Before shuffling the boys off to the corner to play, Drew managed to get the sticks away from them, promising them he would help them make puppets.

"His lungs sounded fine," Zach informed the anxious audience of adults. "His throat looks a little red and tender, but nothing serious that I could see. What was it that he choked on, anyway?"

Stephanie held out her hand, palm up. "A piece of hard candy. He must have tried to swallow it and it lodged in his throat instead."

"Hard candy?" Drew exclaimed, his voice tight. "I don't keep any hard candy in the house."

Frank made a strangled sound from deep in his throat and his face went from cherry red to ash gray. He brushed a hand across his hair, causing white tufts to spring to attention.

"It was me," he admitted in a stifled tone. "This is my fault. I'm completely to blame."

Frank's usual outwardly stern nature was now turned on himself. "I could have been responsible for killing my own grandson."

"Frank, dear, take a seat and lower your voice. You don't want the boys to hear you." Jo's voice no longer held that sweet, flirtatious tone to it. She was all business. Even Frank couldn't say no to her.

Not that he intended to. For once, he didn't have a sharp, witty comeback. He looked his age, his face weathered and pronounced wrinkles around his eyes and lips. His breathing was coming in short, strained gasps, and Stephanie thought he might be close to collapsing.

She rushed to the old man's side and, with Jo's help, assisted him to a seat on the couch. She reached for the educational magazine lying on the coffee table and began fanning the old man with it.

She'd expected him to protest, at least a little.

Leave me alone. I can do it myself. That was typical Frank.

Instead, he appeared to welcome the women's help, sighing loudly and squeezing Stephanie's hand to convey his gratitude to her.

"I had the candy in the pocket of my sweater," Frank explained gravely. "You know how Jamey is— he's always trying to pickpocket my lip balm. I really thought that was all he was doing. If I would have known he was—"

He inhaled harshly and then coughed and hacked, jamming his hand into the pocket of the tattered sweater he always wore as if to check for the candy.

"Maybe I really am going senile."

"Nonsense," Jo replied, clucking her tongue at him. "You're the sharpest tool in the shed and you know it. Now stop blaming yourself for something you didn't mean to do, you hear?"

Drew crouched in front of his father and laid a comforting hand on his knee.

"It was an accident, Pop," he said gently, his gaze full of compassion and understanding.

Drew was an extraordinary man, and a loving one. Kind and tender, yet strong and enduring. Stephanie could barely breathe around the emotion swelling in her throat.

"Don't blame yourself, Pop," Drew continued. "It just happened. The Lord has His reasons."

"Yeah," his father agreed, pinching his lips and cringing. "To scare some sense into a stubborn old man who ought to have known better."

"Can't disagree with that one," Jo quipped, feigning a knock to his head with the palm of her hand. "Never in my life have I ever met as stubborn a one as you, Frank Spencer. God has His work cut out for Him getting you to bow the knee to Him."

"Oh, hush, woman," Frank replied, the tender expression on his face at odds with his words. "Me and the Lord, we get along just fine. We've got us an understanding."

And then, just like that, the world was okay again, all thanks to a little help from Jo Murphy. Stephanie probably would have coddled the old man, which she now realized would have been the worst thing she could have done. Frank felt guilty enough. Sympathizing with him would have just made him feel worse than he already did.

Jo and Frank settled in together, probably trading barbs, and Zach and Ben had packed up their supplies and shook Drew's hand in turn, preparing to head out.

"It all turned out for the best," Zach said with a grin. "Thank the Lord that Jamey is safe and sound. Hopefully you guys can take it easy for the rest of the day. Y'all have had enough excitement this morning to last a good, long while."

"I owe a debt of gratitude to Stephanie for saving the day," Drew announced loud enough for everyone to hear. "If God hadn't sent her into our lives, I don't even want to think about where we'd be right now."

Jo beamed at Stephanie. "But He did, didn't He?"

One corner of Drew's lips crept upward. Stephanie found the look very attractive, but then, she found nearly everything Drew did these days attractive.

Her face warmed from all the attention, but she had to admit it felt wonderful to be noticed. And for some inexplicable reason, the fact that it was Drew who had praised her only made her feel that much better. Her stomach flitted around like a dozen butterflies at the thought of anyone who needed her for anything.

A good man who needed *her* to take care of his *family.*

She'd rushed into this job head-first, more concerned

with running away from everything she'd known than about where she was going. She hadn't given much thought as to what lay ahead.

She was thinking about that now.

About a wonderful fifth-grade teacher with the weight of the world on his shoulders, his adorable twins, a cantankerous old man and a vivacious redhead—and yes, even the dog.

As if on cue, Quincy's wet nose burrowed under her elbow. His black muzzle looked as if it had been spray-painted in a perfect circle on his otherwise-tan body. He cocked his square head at her and whined softly, his large brown eyes and the funny, dependable smile on his face somehow making her feel as if everything was right with the world.

"Hey, are you all right?" Drew's deep voice resonated into her consciousness.

Her heart jolted. "I'm fine. Just nerves from the adrenaline, I guess."

He shook his head and his pensive green eyes flickered with emotion. "You had a curious look on your face just now."

She probably had the doe-eyed look of a teenager with her first crush. She certainly felt that way.

"No...really. I'm okay," she assured him.

Without taking his gaze from hers, Drew reached a hand out to stroke the dog's neck and instead covered her hand with his. "Quincy here doesn't seem to think so, and I've discovered he's rarely wrong in cases like this."

Stephanie chuckled at the idea of the dog knowing

what she was thinking. In any case, Drew was trying to make her feel better—and it was working.

"No fair, you guys teaming up on me like that," she protested, shaking her head and grinning.

He tilted his head. "Can't resist us, huh? Too cute for you?"

Stephanie's face flamed. If only he knew....

"I think we should all go to the café and get some supper—take everyone's mind off of what happened. We're all a little shaken up by the events of the day. Food and prayer are always the best answers to whatever ails you—not necessarily in that order." Jo laughed. "Go ahead. Admit it, Stephanie. Doesn't a big, juicy hamburger sound delicious right about now?"

"Jo, I don't think—" Drew started, but he was interrupted by his father, who'd shuffled up only a few moments before, curious as to what everyone was talking about.

"Don't bother arguing with her." Frank wedged his way between Drew and Jo. "The belligerent old woman always gets what she wants in the end."

"And don't *you* forget it, old man," Jo responded, jauntily tossing her chin.

"How can I, what with our weddin' coming up?"

"What?" Drew and Stephanie exclaimed at the same time.

Frank chortled. "You heard me, son. I'm a stubborn old man, but I'm not stupid. It's high time I step up for the woman, don't you think?"

"Well, y-yes, I—" Drew stammered. "You just took me by surprise."

"You ain't the only one," Frank murmured.

Stephanie didn't hesitate to throw her arms around Jo and exclaim her delight. "I prayed," she said. "I'm so excited. Congratulations! I'm so happy for you both."

"Thank you, dear. The scare today reminded us that every day God gives us on this earth is precious," Jo explained. "We oughtn't be wasting it when we could be loving it."

Stephanie's breath caught in her throat as she glanced Drew's way, but he wasn't looking at her. She hadn't a clue how Drew felt about what had been said, but she knew how she felt.

She was in love with Drew Spencer. That was the high and low, the long and short of it.

She wasn't exactly wasting her days as a nanny to the twins, but now she recognized that she wanted more.

She wanted Drew to be in love with her.

"Lunch is on me." Jo's voice rose so everyone in the room could hear, even the paramedics, who were loading their gear in the ambulance. "Burgers all around, and chocolate shakes for the twins. That means everybody—even you boys," Jo said, indicating Zach and Ben.

Zach jogged back up to the doorway, his expression disappointed. "We'd love to, but we're on call. Besides, the men back at the station would be jealous if we took you up on your offer."

"You know that's no excuse. Y'all come around and I'll fix something up for the whole gang."

"Yes, ma'am," exclaimed Ben, his head appearing from behind Zach's shoulder. He rocked his fist forward and smacked his lips. "Best call of the day, by far."

"I'll make it worth your while," Jo promised with a hearty chuckle, expanding her smile to include Stephanie.

"It sounds like we can't refuse," Drew said, laying his hand on Stephanie's shoulder and casting her an amused glance. "Who's up for a burger?"

Chapter Twelve

By the time they'd all eaten a good meal at Cup O' Jo and returned to the house, everyone was back in good spirits again. Jamey was roughhousing with Matty as if nothing had happened, and everyone else was wearing marked expressions of relief and gratitude.

Frank and Jo watched over boys, already playfully bickering about the size of the wedding and how long they should wait before tying the knot. Stephanie joined in the animated conversation while Drew checked his email, a daily habit for him—mostly for work-related reasons, although he didn't really expect to get anything on a Saturday.

He certainly didn't expect to hear from his lawyer. But there it was, in black-and-white on his computer screen—an email from his lawyer with the investigation report attached.

He'd been waiting for this moment. He'd been praying about it, desperate to find the peace he knew he would never feel until he heard the results of the investigation. But now that the report was here, he felt sick to his stomach. He swallowed hard against the burn in his throat and squeezed his eyes shut, trying to contain the apprehension exploding in his gut.

"Drew?" Stephanie approached and laid a comforting hand on his shoulder. "Are you okay?"

He jerked his chin toward the computer screen. "The C.F.I. report. It's here."

Her grip on his shoulder tightened and her expression flooded with concern. "Bad news?"

He gasped for a breath, which came out sounding raspy and ragged. "I don't know yet. I'm afraid to open it."

She nodded, stooping down to look over his shoulder at the computer screen as if to confirm what he had already told her.

"Stupid, huh?" he murmured, looking down at his hands, his fingers still resting on the keyboard.

She shook her head. "No, not at all." She used her palm to tip his chin so he could see the sympathy in her gaze. "I completely understand. The twins mean everything to you. Of course you're terrified." Her compassionate brown eyes welled with tears. "It's frightening how much hinges on this one person's opinion. I know it's the judge who ultimately decides, but I imagine this lady's report will have a lot of influence."

He groaned, pressed his lips tightly together and nodded miserably.

"And I'm not helping, am I? What an inconsiderate comment to make right now. I'm so sorry."

"You're only saying what I'm already thinking in my head." And in a way, her speaking the words aloud *did* help, knowing there was someone who understood how he was feeling right now—and who cared enough to root him on. He'd never needed support as much as he did at this moment. He reached for her hand and grasped it tightly, threading his fingers through hers.

"What do you need me to do?" Her voice had taken on the same quality it had when she'd been saving a choking Jamey—calm, collected and in control. Now he was the one choking, and Stephanie was once again coming to the rescue, just as she had earlier that day with his son.

"Could you ask Pop and Jo to take the boys outside for a while?" He didn't want any of them to see him cry, and he thought he might just, no matter which way the pendulum swung on the report.

He didn't want Stephanie to see him cry, either, but he couldn't find the strength to send her away. He needed her there, just so he wouldn't be all alone. "And then you'll come back?"

She nodded briskly. "Of course."

Drew downloaded the report while Stephanie ushered his family outside, but he didn't open it. Neither did he read the letter his lawyer had sent along with the attachment. He still felt unprepared, not ready even to discover what he was dealing with.

What had the case worker said about them? What if the report was negative? Would he be in danger of losing his children?

Eileen had caught them all off guard the day she visited, from his mad dash scurry around the side of the house and through his bedroom window so he could get dressed appropriately, to the toys the twins had strewn from one end of the living room to the other.

The only constant in the equation was Stephanie—

her steady influence with Eileen and her reassurance that everything had gone as well as could be expected.

Now they both would know if that was, in fact, the truth.

"Well?" she asked, slipping back through the front door after seeing that the kids were busy playing on the lawn. "How is it?"

He grimaced. "I still haven't read it yet."

"Oh." She looked surprised. "Okay."

"Will you do me a favor?"

"Anything." She hadn't hesitated a second before answering. "Whatever you need."

"Pray with me?"

"Of course."

He reached for her hands, and together they knelt on the hardwood floor, their foreheads close as they petitioned the Lord for strength and wisdom to deal with whatever they were about to face.

When they finished praying, Drew felt marginally better, although he was still scared to death. But at least he'd taken a moment to seek God's presence, and remind himself that no matter what the social worker had said about them, God was ultimately in control of what happened. The Lord would never stop taking care of Matty and Jamey.

Drew reached for the Bible he kept next to his desktop computer. "I need to hear this right now. Will you read it for me?"

He turned the dog-eared pages to chapter twentynine of the book of Jeremiah and cleared his throat. He felt a little awkward. He wasn't a preacher, and he didn't usually read Scripture aloud outside of family devotion time. "Um, this is Jeremiah 29:11. *'For I know the plans I have for you,' declares the LORD, 'plans to prosper you and not to harm you, plans to give you hope and a future.'*"

"Well, I say amen to that," Stephanie murmured, squeezing his hand. "Our future—and the twins' futures—are in God's capable hands."

"Right." Drew glanced back at the computer screen, the flashing cursor pounding with the beat of his heart. "We should probably get on with it, then."

"Okay."

"But Stephanie?"

"Hmm?"

"One more favor?"

"Sure. Of course. Anything."

"Read the report first yourself, and then read it aloud to me. I know it's not going to make any difference on the outcome, but it might be easier for me to hear coming from you."

She hesitated. "Are you sure? This is such a private, personal matter. And you—"

"—need your help. Please, Stephanie." His voice cut out halfway through her name. He hoped she wouldn't make him continue to beg.

Her wide gaze met his. She looked unsure of herself, but after a moment, she nodded. "All right, then. I'd better get started, then."

He stood and offered her the chair he'd been seated on and then stood behind her, one hand jammed into the front pocket of his blue jeans and the other leaning on the back of the chair. The cords of his neck and shoulders strained with tension.

Her lips pursed as she carefully scrolled through the document—pages upon pages of information with bold paragraph headings and asterisked lists. She didn't say a word as she read, although she occasionally nodded or made indistinguishable sounds from the back of her throat.

Fire burned through his veins. He was in agony. The sheer length of the report couldn't mean good news, could it? The case worker hadn't even taken any notes while she was at the house. How had she been able to write in such detail about them?

It wouldn't take that many words for Eileen to say she thought they were doing well as a family. The only reason she'd have needed to write at length was if she'd found issues she thought needed to be addressed, right?

He held his breath, wishing Stephanie would read faster, yet relieved that the words on the screen were too blurry for him to read without his glasses. He wanted—needed—to hear Stephanie's summary before he read the whole report on his own. She would let him down easy, prepare him to face whatever was written within the letter.

Even when she finally reached the end of the document, she didn't say a word. Instead, she rubbed her chin thoughtfully and then clicked back to the lawyer's email and started silently perusing that.

Why wasn't she saying anything?

Was it so bad she didn't want to tell him?

Was he in danger of losing his boys?

He pressed his fingers to his incessantly throbbing temple, sure his head was going to burst at any moment. Try as he might, he was unable to get his thoughts to slow down. He paced away from the desk, pivoted and stalked back, feeling like a caged tiger. Feeling like his chest was going to explode from tension.

After what seemed like forever, Stephanie swiveled the chair around and looked up at him, her expression unreadable. All she said was, "Okay."

"What?" Drew pleaded. "What did Eileen say? Are the boys going to be safe? Am I going to be able to fight to keep them with me?"

He had a million other questions for her—like what the case worker had thought of their living situation and her opinion of him as a father, if she thought he was able to care for his children.

But all that paled in comparison to one thing—what was going to happen to the twins?

"She said," Stephanie murmured as she stood and reached for his elbows, and then slid her palms down his forearms until her hands were clasping his, "that from what she observed, you are an incredible father who is doing a fantastic job raising his two sons."

The adrenaline surging through him had him literally quivering. His legs nearly gave out from underneath him. He dropped to his knees, taking Stephanie with him.

"Thank God. Thank You, Jesus." Tears streamed from his eyes, but he didn't care. He pulled Stephanie farther into his embrace and kept thanking God aloud for His grace.

She wrapped her arms around his neck, brushing her fingers through his hair and beaming at him through the tears in her own eyes.

"That was the paraphrased version of the report,"

she said when he allowed her to get a word in edge-wise. She laughed softly and hiccupped back a tear. "You'll probably want to read the whole thing yourself, now that you know that it's good news. Considering the fact that Eileen didn't even take notes, she sure wrote a novel-length report."

"You noticed that, too, huh?" He stood gingerly back to his feet and pulled her up with him. His smile was so wide it was making his face ache, but he didn't care. If he could have grinned any wider, he would have.

The twins were safe!

Or at the very least, he and his lawyer now had a powerful legal tool in their battle for full custody.

"Oh, and by the way," she added, pressing her soft palm against his cheek and beaming up at him. "Your lawyer says he's already heard from your ex-wife's counsel. Apparently they want to set a meeting. Your lawyer seems to think you won't have to go to court at all."

Drew's mood skyrocketed. He whooped and reached for Stephanie's waist, lifting her off her feet and spinning her around and around.

Her laughter was like a meteor shower, threads of brilliant light. When he stopped twirling her and set her back on her feet, their eyes met and locked, and his breath caught at what he saw.

Though she was clearly happy for him—and with him—he detected a hint of sadness in her gaze.

He couldn't imagine why, on a day filled with so much happiness. He only knew he didn't want her to feel that way. This was one of the best moments of his life, and he wanted to share the exhilaration he was feeling with her. He wanted her to feel his joy.

He didn't think about it—there was nothing to think about. There was only the glowing warmth of his heart, the same feeling he wanted to be inside her heart, too.

His gaze dropped to the luscious fullness of her lips, and then to the rapid rhythm of her pulse beating along the line of her delicate neck. He brushed the tip of his finger along that spot on her neck and felt her pulse jump. The spicy, exotic scent of her perfume wafted around him, making his head spin and his heart hammer.

He took his time, hovering his lips over hers, enjoying the experience of her warm breath mixing with his, bonding them together even before their lips met. This wasn't some merely physical attraction overcoming a man's good sense. This was the kind of love he knew he would only find once in a lifetime, the kind of feeling strong enough to trump even his own stubborn stupidity.

He slanted his head and deepened the kiss, satisfied when she immediately responded.

How could he *ever* have encouraged her to leave? He knew better now. He needed her in his life. He'd never felt this way about any woman, even Heather, and he wasn't about to let her go.

He just needed to figure out a way to humble his own pride and ask her to stay.

"What's all the hollering in here?" Frank boomed, rushing in the door as quickly as his cane would allow. "Is everyone all right?"

"Whoa," he said, coming to such a quick stop that

Jo, who'd been right on his heels, nearly plowed into him. "Watch out, woman. Can't you see what's going on here?"

Drew reluctantly broke off the kiss, but he wouldn't allow Stephanie to squirm out of his arms.

"I do see," Jo replied. "And it's about time, if you ask me. Now we can all do some celebrating."

Stephanie turned a shade of bright red. "Yes, we can."

When the twins came running in, she elbowed him just enough to let him know she was truly uncomfortable with the situation. He supposed he had to agree. He needed to make his intentions known to Stephanie before the twins witnessed any public display of affection between them. He didn't want to confuse the boys.

When he released her, she ran straight forward, squealing as she hugged Jo around the shoulders and gave his father a big smacking kiss on the cheek. "We have the best news."

Wait for it, Drew thought, a little bit amused because both Pop and Jo thought Stephanie was going to announce that she and Drew were a couple. If everything went well, that would happen soon enough. In the meantime, he was enjoying how this was playing out. Pop and Jo had jerked his strings enough times.

Stephanie beamed. "A celebration is definitely in order. The C.F.I. report came back and Drew passed with flying colors!"

"That wasn't what I meant," Jo said, shaking her head and chuckling, "but that is certainly good news. Does that mean he gets to keep full custody of the kids?"

"We think so," Stephanie answered, and Drew bit back a grin. She'd said *we.* He wondered if she was aware of it or not, or whether it was just instinctual. Either way, he'd take it as a good sign. "Drew's lawyer says that Heather's counsel has asked for a meeting. He seems to think that means we won't have to go to court."

There was that *we* again. From the knowing grin on Jo's face, she had noticed it, too.

"And about the other news?" Jo pushed.

Stephanie's gaze jerked to the twins, and then to Drew. "What news? There is no other news."

"So we're back to that again, are we?" Frank said. "Take a tip from my book and stop wasting time. God's only given you so many days, son. Don't waste 'em."

Drew didn't know why his father was directing his comments at him. He wasn't the one denying that there wasn't anything between the two of them.

"I think we have more important things to concentrate on right now," Stephanie insisted. Her face was still a bright shade of red, and Drew realized that maybe they were all pushing too hard on her. Maybe if they backed off and gave her room to breathe, she'd be more inclined to admit she might still have feelings for him.

"I think I have a bottle of sparkling cider in the pantry," Drew said, taking the heat off of Stephanie. "I've been saving it just for this day."

"Do we get some, Daddy?" Matty asked, running forward and swinging around his leg.

Drew laughed at his progeny's selective hearing. If he'd been told to pick up his toys, he would have feigned being too far away to hear. But Matty and Jamey loved the bubbles in sparkling cider.

He tousled Matty's hair. "I think it would be okay if you have a glass today. It's a very good day. Jamey, do you want some, too?"

"Yes, yes, yes," came Jamey's excited reply.

"And how about you, Miss Stephie? Are you up for a glass?"

Stephanie had been staring out the window, her arms folded, but now she turned with a steady, genuine smile and a clear, unfettered gaze.

She ran up mimicking the unsteady gait of a preschooler and cried, "Yes, yes, yes. *Please.*"

Chapter Thirteen

"I've been thinking about solutions for you, now that your temporary position with me has almost ended," Drew informed Stephanie as she returned from running errands. He'd apparently been waiting on her, for he'd stepped out from the side of the porch as she approached the front door and had scared her half to death.

Especially because she'd kind of been trying to avoid him for the past couple of days. Frankly, she wasn't sure what to do with him. He went hot and cold on her faster than a bad faucet.

"Is that right?" she murmured. She had been thinking about solutions for herself, too, but she hadn't come up with anything concrete, as of yet. She figured the first thing she needed to do was find housing, and then she would look for a job—beg Jo for a part-time waitressing position, if she had to. She'd spread the news that she was looking for a new place to live around church, but so far she hadn't had any offers.

Drew nodded, looking quite proud of himself. "Yes. I think you should stay."

"In Serendipity?"

"In my garage."

She couldn't have been more shocked if he would have thrust her finger into a light socket. He'd said over and over again that this position had to end, that he couldn't afford to have her living with them anymore.

But his gaze was serious. Determined.

Her breath caught in her throat. "What? I'm not sure I understand what you are saying."

He shrugged as if it was nothing, but it wasn't *nothing*. Her whole world was spinning around the axis of his answer.

"How else can I spell it out for you? I think you should stay with *me*. With us—me, and Pop and the boys."

"Oh. I—"

"Before you say no, consider how much the boys have come to depend on you. They've kind of gotten used to you being around all the time. Our house won't be the same without you, *Miss Stephie*. And not just because you make top-of-the-line kitty pancakes, either, although the kids love those."

"You know I'll visit the twins a lot, even after I'm not living here anymore."

"I'm not sure that's enough." He held his hands up before she'd even thought of anything to say. "I want you to know that I'll do everything I can to help you start a preschool here in Serendipity, even run for town council if I have to."

Her heart felt as if it was going to beat out of her chest. He was saying the words she'd longed to hear—

or almost. For so long he'd been persuading her to leave.

Now he was asking her to stay. But she needed to know why.

"That's very generous," she replied.

"Not as much as you think," he said with a dry chuckle that almost sounded nervous.

"Okay." He hadn't said as much, but she felt there was a condition coming up, and she tensed for it. This wasn't quite the way this scene had played out in her head.

She had to admit it…she'd thought of it. Of Drew asking her to stay. But this wasn't what she'd prayed about and hoped for.

This wasn't any kind of romantic proposition, based on flowery sentiments and feelings that would rival late spring on the Texas prairie. This sounded more like a business proposal.

"I'm not in a position to offer you an actual job, because I can no longer afford to pay you a salary. I know that's what you were looking for—I heard you mention it in church. But the room above the garage is just going to sit there empty after you move out. Since you're planning to stay in town while you get your preschool underway, it seems ridiculous for you to have to look for other accommodations. You're already settled in right here. You may as well stay with us."

"Okay," she said again. She wasn't assenting to his idea as much as acknowledging it.

"You're welcome at our table as often as you can make it. While I can't afford anything in the way of salary, we have plenty of food to go around. Maybe we can make the terms of your room and board some kind of exchange for watching the twins once in a while? They've been begging me to let you stay, and I hate to let them down."

So this *was* a business arrangement. His voice was the controlled tone of a professor, asking for help on behalf of his sons. His proposition hadn't come from any deep feeling on his part, but motivated from not wanting to see his twins hurt.

And she was an idiot to have even thought for one moment that it might be otherwise. She was getting really good at misreading signals. When would she learn that to a man, a kiss or two didn't mean a commitment? Even to a man she respected as much as she did Drew. Clearly she'd read too much into the time they'd spent together.

And that was that. She took a deep breath to calm her racing pulse.

She wasn't the woman of Drew's dreams. She was the nanny. It was as simple as that.

Or, at least, it ought to be. With her, it never would be—but that was kind of beside the point now, wasn't it?

And the worst thing about it was, she wouldn't hesitate a moment to take him up on his proposition, even now that she knew exactly what it was. Even with offering her room and board, he was offering her way more than he would receive in return by having her babysit for him once in a while. She felt guilty considering it. But she wasn't going to turn him down.

"I have a couple of ideas on ways you can make some cash while you're working out the details of the preschool. I wouldn't object at all if you wanted to take in a couple of kids at the house, to babysit over the summer. Your reputation precedes you. You won't find any problem locating a few parents who need day care for their children, as long as you keep the prices reasonable."

"Of course." What did he think, that she would charge New Jersey prices in a Serendipity market? Surely he knew her better than that by now.

"We can announce it at church. Or if you don't want to go that direction, I'm sure you can get a part-time job at the café. Jo's always willing to help a friend in need."

"I accept." He sounded as if he was going to go on forever, trying to set her up so she would stay and help him out with the twins.

He didn't need to continue. She was prepared to do all that and more—clean his house, wash his car...whatever was necessary in order to stay with him, and with his family. She loved every single one of them.

It would break her heart every day to be with Drew and not *be* with him. But wasn't that better than nothing?

He probably didn't know how much he was asking, but she knew how much she was willing to give.

Everything.

For a moment there Drew had thought he'd made an enormous mistake offering her room and board like a tenant, when she was so much more to him. But he'd panicked when he thought of her leaving, even so much as to move down the block, and he felt he needed to be serious in convincing her to stay.

Because if she left, his heart would go with her.

Down the street, across town or across the continent. Wherever she was, that's where his heart would be.

He thought it preferable just to keep her under his roof, even if the arrangement wasn't exactly ideal. Conflicting emotions churned through him as he glanced across the truck cab at Stephanie, but she was looking out the passenger side window.

They'd gone to Sam's Grocery to stock up on supplies. He hadn't expected her to go with him, but she'd insisted. She'd said she needed to feel as if she was doing more to carry her weight, and since she enjoyed shopping, that seemed like as good a place as any to start.

As if she knew he was looking at her, she turned her head. Her eyebrows arched as their eyes met.

"Are there sugarplums dancing in your head?" she asked, pursing her lips in amusement.

He nearly swerved the truck at the look in her eyes. "I beg your pardon?"

She laughed. "Never mind."

He glanced at her and back at the road. If he didn't pay more attention to his driving he was going to get them in an accident, even if he was the only truck on the road. "You say the oddest things sometimes. I can't keep up with you."

"Yes, but that's why you love me."

He stomped on the brakes and turned to face her. "What did you say?"

Her face turned beet-red and she averted her gaze

out the passenger-side window. "Nothing." She paused a moment, and then added, "What a colossally dim-witted thing to say."

He didn't think so. He thought those were the best words he'd ever heard in his life. She'd said "love." She'd only been teasing, but it was the truth. He *did* love her. And if the pretty blush on her cheeks was any-thing to go by, he thought she might care for him, too.

It couldn't get much better than that.

But it could get worse.

Drew immediately noticed the sporty blue Mustang parked in front of his house, even before Stephanie did. A sharp pain spiked in his gut like an ice pick. He didn't know *anybody* in town who owned a car like that. He knew that the fellow was from out of town even before he was close enough to read the rental plates. The guy must be loaded to rent a car like that, consid-ering how far away the nearest car rental place was. He would have had to have driven for miles, and a car like that would guzzle gas.

"Oh, no," Stephanie murmured, burying her face in her palms.

"What?" Drew asked as his body surged with adren-aline. "Who is he?"

Three guesses, and the first two didn't count.

"Ryan. What is he doing here?" Her voice was laced with panic. Drew couldn't imagine how she felt.

What *was* the guy doing here? He had no more busi-ness in Stephanie's life. Drew was going to tell him as much and get him out of here as quickly as possible. He was glad his father had taken the twins out for an afternoon at the park. He wanted to be able to concentrate all his resources on getting this man out of here as quickly as possible.

"Your ex-boyfriend," he ground out, keeping his eye on Stephanie to monitor her reaction.

It wasn't a question. They'd talked about Ryan a lot. He knew enough about the guy to dislike him, just for hurting Stephanie. Her reaction now only served to crank his protective instinct into higher gear.

Ryan wasn't going to hurt Stephanie again.

He turned off the ignition and reached for her hand. He didn't know what to say, so he didn't say anything, waiting for her to take the lead. Only now did he realize just how much he should have *already* said, whether or not he'd thought she'd be ready to hear it. She should have known how he felt about her. But now it was too late to make up for that mistake.

She was trembling, but when she looked up and met his gaze, it was with the calm strength and determination that he so admired in her.

"I've got this one," she assured him, almost but not quite smiling.

"Are you sure? Because I can send the guy packing, if you'd rather. You wouldn't even have to talk to him."

That's what *Drew* would rather do, to be sure. If he could keep Stephanie from having to relive what was clearly one of the most difficult times in her life, he would. He'd step between her and Ryan and protect her from the kind of heartache he had known with Heather. Stephanie was even braver, because Ryan had been physically abusive. Just to meet him face-to-face had to be the hardest thing she'd ever done in her life.

But she wasn't asking him to step in and fight her

battles for her. She was a strong and capable woman, more even than he'd realized until that moment. She was facing down her own past, and her own pain, with more courage than he'd ever shown with Heather.

She tilted her head thoughtfully. "As pleasant as the idea of having you pound him to pieces sounds, I think I'd better take care of this one on my own. I don't know why Ryan is here, but I can guarantee you that he won't be staying long."

Stephanie squeezed his hand and exited the cab, walking toward Ryan with her head held high and her shoulders back. If Drew wasn't mistaken, Ryan was in for a giant surprise. Stephanie wasn't the same woman she'd been when she'd left New Jersey.

She was going to tell Ryan off. Drew only wished he could be around to hear it.

Or maybe that wasn't how this was going to go down.

She *had* been in love with the man…enough to want to marry him. He'd been abusive and over-possessive— could he intimidate her back into his arms? Drew watched as he greeted her animatedly and kissed her on the cheek. She didn't rebuff him as Drew half expected her to do.

What if Ryan was here to make amends? What if he wanted to rekindle their relationship? What if she decided to go back with him?

If Drew could have kicked himself he would have. Why hadn't he taken advantage of the time they'd had alone together today to speak what was really on his mind, to tell her how much he loved her?

Fool.

Stephanie was nodding to Ryan, and then a moment later she was heading back toward the truck. She opened the driver's-side door and leaned her forearms against the top of the frame, smiling down at Drew in a way that made his stomach flip over.

"Just so you know, I'm going to bring Ryan up to my room for a bit. He's flown in all the way from New Jersey to talk to me, so I figure I'll give him the dignity of hearing what he has to say."

"I see," he said, trying not to grind his teeth. He didn't want to know what Ryan was going to say, but he had the gut-wrenching suspicion that he already did.

This was worse than a nightmare. This was a competition, and every male instinct he had wanted to fight for this woman. Maybe not physically, but at least in his heart.

Which was, he realized with a sudden twinge of dejection, virtually all he had to give. Side by side, there wasn't one thing he could offer Stephanie that would even remotely compare to the world of luxury Ryan could provide.

A meager country existence on a fifth grade teacher's salary versus mansions and sports cars and culture. There was no competition in that. The younger man won hands-down.

Ryan was here, wasn't he? He'd flown all the way in from New Jersey to attempt to reconcile with her, or, at least, that's why Drew assumed he was here, and he had to admit that was a point in Ryan's favor. Stephanie had changed. Maybe Ryan had changed, too. Maybe he'd gone to therapy or something. Could abusers ever get beyond that stage?

Drew pounded his fist against the steering wheel. This wasn't stacking up well for him, at least not in his mind.

But the big city life wasn't what she wanted anymore, was it? She'd left Ryan for a reason. And he had broken her heart. He'd physically beat her. She wouldn't go back to him that easily, would she?

She said she loved being in Serendipity, and she certainly cared for his twins. That much Drew knew for certain. She wanted to start a preschool, but he supposed she could do that anywhere—and probably with a lot less effort, if Ryan got behind her and financed her dreams.

Drew wanted to pull Stephanie aside right then and there, take her in his arms and kiss her until she understood how he really felt about her. If only he'd figured that out for himself before he was thrust into a situation where the truth had smacked him in the head....

He wanted to know if she could possibly feel the same way about him, if he had what it took to make her happy. He wanted to give her a diamond ring, even if it took what was left of his meager pension fund to do it.

Last, but definitely not least, he wanted to pack Ryan back in his fancy sports car and point him to the nearest airport.

But that wasn't for him to do. It had to be Stephanie's decision, made without his influence. It was how *she* felt about Ryan that counted here.

He brushed her cheek with his palm. "Whatever happens, Stephanie, I want you to know I'm here. You're safe, do you understand me?"

Her expression was solemn and unsmiling, but she

leaned her cheek into his touch. "Thank you. You'll never know how much that means to me."

Stephanie wasn't comfortable bringing Ryan into her living quarters. The room above the garage was her personal space, her private haven, and having him there seemed as if it was spoiling the atmosphere. It didn't feel that way when Drew visited, but she felt safe with Drew.

Ryan was a different story entirely. The only reason she could stand to be in the same room with him was because she knew Drew was down at the house waiting for her. One scream from her and he'd come running.

Ryan couldn't hold a candle to Drew. Drew was the best man she'd ever known, and he was the man she wanted to spend her future with.

It was past time to put her emotions out in the open, be an adult and own up to them.

But first she had to deal with Ryan.

"I'd offer you something to drink, but as you can see, there's no kitchen in my apartment."

He gave her a look that was just a hair short of a sneer. "Really? Not even a mini-fridge?"

"That isn't necessary. I take meals with the Spencer family at the house."

"At the *big* house?" he asked with a snicker. "Who is Spencer? Your employer? That hick cowboy I saw driving you around."

Stephanie bit her lip and gave him a clipped nod.

"You've been hiding out here for over two months? How did you stand it?"

"I don't need to hide from you anymore," she said

and realized it was true. She wasn't afraid to stand up to Ryan. "I've been working. What do you want, Ryan?" she asked bluntly. She'd learned a few tricks from Drew. Straight-talking was one of them.

"I should think that would be obvious. I came for you." He stepped forward so he was looking down on her, one of his old ploys. It used to work.

She straightened and looked him in the eye. If he thought he was going to intimidate her, he had another think coming. There was a time in her life when she would have been unsettled by his high-handed behavior, by his money, his clout...and his fists.

Not now. He couldn't hurt her. He'd wasted a trip. And the quicker she told him so, the quicker she could throw herself into Drew's arms where she belonged.

"How did you find me?" she asked, knowing even as she said the words that Ryan's power was in his money. "I didn't leave a forwarding address."

"No kidding." He shook his head in an almost violent gesture. "Did you think you could just leave me like that? That I wouldn't find you?"

Her mind flashed back to the fear she'd once lived in and a moment of panic ensued, but she quickly brushed it off, remembering Drew's presence nearby.

"I can't believe you left me." He sounded like a little boy. His voice was almost a whine. He was four years older than she was, but he seemed so immature, especially compared to Drew.

She'd never even loved this man. She hadn't known the meaning of the word. She'd been afraid of him perhaps, and she'd been afraid of being alone. Now she knew she was never alone. God was always with her.

"I'm sorry you've made the trip for nothing. I'm not interested in returning to New Jersey, with or without you."

Ryan's eyebrows shot up, and he actually had the nerve to look surprised. Offended, even. She should have guessed that was how he would react.

But then he nodded, as if he'd come to a sudden understanding. "Oh, I get it. You have some kind of legal obligation to the dude in the truck. You always were a stickler for those kinds of details."

Stephanie wanted to stop him before he got out of hand, but Ryan never gave her the chance. When she opened her mouth to protest, he held out his hand.

"Hush," he barked. "Don't worry about it. I'll take care of it. I'll go down and talk to the guy," he promised with a self-assured nod. "I'm sure we can work this out. And if talking isn't good enough for him, I can always get my lawyers involved."

"No lawyers. Ryan, please," she pleaded, thoroughly exasperated with trying to explain herself to what amounted to a brick wall. "Listen to me just a second."

He flashed her his playboy smile and ran a palm over his neatly-trimmed hair. "Well, you need to hurry if we're going to catch a flight back to New Jersey tonight."

She noted that he didn't apologize for the way he'd treated her before, for the anger and the abuse. For treating her as if she were inferior to him. He had the nerve to wonder why she'd left New Jersey in the first place?

He'd always been controlling and domineering, which was part of the reason Stephanie was not entirely surprised to see him when he showed up at Drew's curb today.

He probably *didn't* understand why she'd left. And now he thought he could come down here and she was just going to waltz back into his arms as if nothing bad had ever happened between them?

She didn't think so. She wasn't sure what he was offering—or what he thought had changed—that he'd suddenly come seeking her out. He might just be here because he didn't like to lose what was his.

Frankly, she didn't care. Her life was here. In Serendipity.

With Drew.

"Look, I'm not sure how to get through to you, but I'm not going anywhere with you. Yes, I had a contract with Drew, but it's up now. And besides, it was a verbal obligation, not a legal one."

His face reddened, and his hands clenched into fists, a sure sign he was getting agitated.

She paused and leveled her gaze on him. "Let me be perfectly clear. I'm staying in Serendipity because I love it here and I want to make it my home, not because I'm obligated by anyone to do so."

His expression was a combination of sheer disbelief mixed with a healthy dose of distaste. He was a snob in the worst way. Stephanie wondered how she could only now be seeing him for the man he truly was.

"You've got to be kidding me. You love this *town?*" Then he stopped and his eyes narrowed with contempt. "Don't tell me. It's that cowboy. *He's* the real reason you want to stay in the middle of nowhere."

"That *cowboy* happens to be an educated teacher,

and I'd appreciate it if you didn't speak about him in that manner," she retorted.

"Educated?" Ryan mocked. "Stephanie, you aren't thinking straight. What can that man give you? Horses? Pigs? A miniscule house and a dozen children? Come on. That's not the life for you."

Stephanie thought of the twins, and of how very little Ryan really knew about her.

"And what about you, Ryan? What can you offer me? Pain and humiliation and heartbreak? You don't know a single thing about me. I'll take the *pigs* and the horses." She couldn't help it if she emphasized that one word just a little bit.

"You really are in love with this guy, aren't you, Stephanie?" Ryan said scornfully, sounding shocked. She, on the other hand, wasn't stunned by the revelation at all.

"Unbelievable."

She was thinking the same thing—how unbelievably blessed she was.

"Why?" she asked. "Because I learned the meaning of faith and family and fell in love with a wonderful man? A man who treats me with respect and kindness, I might add." She looked him square in the eye. "I don't call that unbelievable. I call it a godsend, and I thank Him every day for allowing me to be a part of Drew's life, and the lives of his family."

"I see you've found religion, too."

"Not religion. God. Another benefit to living in Serendipity."

"God. Religion. Whatever. You're out of your mind, girl, you know that? I offer you the world and you turn it down." He scoffed at her. "Well, it's your loss. It wasn't like I was going to marry you, anyway. Take that back to your hick cowboy."

Chapter Fourteen

Drew nearly burst the door down. He knew he shouldn't be listening to a private conversation. He didn't exactly *mean* to overhear what was being said, but since he had, he was outraged about the way Ryan was treating Stephanie. He nearly dropped the tray of iced-tea and cookies he'd been bringing to her and her guest when he heard how unpleasant the young man was being.

So much for Texas hospitality. The sooner Ryan Forsythe left, the better, as far as Drew was concerned.

And then he'd heard Stephanie's bold proclamation. Of course, she didn't know he'd heard what she said—but that only made her declaration more special to him.

She'd said she loved him.

His heart was soaring and his mind was racing. The first thing he was going to do when he got Stephanie alone was to kiss her senseless.

And then he was going to ask her to be his wife.

After he threw Ryan out on his ear. The man was clearly not good at taking hints. Even when she'd directly informed him she wasn't going back with him, he hadn't backed down. Drew had a feeling she hadn't seen the end of the annoying Richie Rich with his slick hair and his sports car. Not unless Drew did something about it.

He backed down the stairs and returned to the kitchen without delivering the snack. If he wasn't mistaken, he'd just heard the end of the conversation between Stephanie and her ex-boyfriend. It was only a matter of time before Ryan would come to him. All he had to do was sit back and wait. A confrontation was looming in the distance, and Drew was more than ready for it.

Just as he suspected, a few minutes later there was a knock at the door. He barely had the screen open before a furious Ryan burst through, looking not nearly as neat and refined as he had been earlier. Apparently being rejected and not having things go exactly as he had expected them to had knocked a little bit of the wind out of his sails.

If Ryan wasn't careful, he was about to get a lot more than just the wind knocked out of him. Drew just needed a few minutes with the man to set him straight about a few things, one way or the other. He prayed God would help him keep a cool temper and sort this out without physical violence, even if his first inclination was to grab the kid by the ear and teach him how to speak to a lady.

The moment he and Ryan began to face off, Stephanie burst through the door, out of breath. "Ryan, please don't bother Drew. There are children in the house. You need to leave."

"Not until I've spoken to Mr. Green Jeans, here," Ryan insisted.

"He can tell me whatever he thinks I need to hear, and then he can be on his way. It's all right, Stephanie," Drew assured her. "The boys are out with my father. I can handle this."

"Yeah. Like you handle her?" Ryan asked with a callous chuckle.

Drew wondered if anyone could see the steam shooting from his ears. "I beg your pardon?"

"I get it. I do," Ryan insisted. "She's nice on the eyes. It's hard not to notice her. A bit of a step up for you, though, isn't she?"

Well, Drew couldn't argue with that.

"I just came in here to warn you about your dear *Stephanie*. You need to know the truth about her, dude," Ryan continued. "Before you get in too tight."

Drew went stiff, trying to breathe through his nose to quench the urge to clench his fists and deck the man. It wasn't easy to restrain himself from at the very least coming out and ripping Ryan to pieces with his words. As an educated man, it would be a simple thing to do.

Turning the other cheek was easier when it was his face being slapped. But when someone offended the woman he loved, it was a different story.

"You've got to watch her like a hawk," Ryan insisted. "Frankly, it's better if you don't get involved with her at all. She's an opportunist. Take it from me. I don't know exactly what she's got on you, dude, but whatever you're offering her, take it back." He shrugged. "I know first-hand how she uses men and then dumps them flat to move on to new prey. She'll take advantage of you if you let her."

Stephanie made a strangled sound and slapped a hand over her mouth, and then went running from the room. Drew reached out to stop her, but he missed.

"Stephanie, wait," he called, but either she didn't hear him or she ignored the sound of his plea over her sobs. He knew Stephanie hadn't had her sights set on Ryan's money. That wasn't what she wanted out of a relationship. All she'd managed to take out of her relationship with Ryan was a few black eyes, and frankly, it was all Drew could do not to give Ryan one now for lying through his teeth just to be cruel.

When he turned back, Ryan was smiling—a downright sinister grin, as far as Drew was concerned. Ryan knew exactly what his words had done, and the kid had the nerve to be proud of it. In fact, Drew realized that was exactly what the other man had aimed for in coming here to talk to Drew in the first place.

It wasn't to warn him. It was to hurt Stephanie.

"You don't get what you want one way so you think you'll just try another, huh?" Drew didn't care if Ryan heard the unveiled threat in his voice. He was furious, and it would be better for Ryan if he knew it.

Ryan's smile became an uncertain frown. Maybe he hadn't expected the old *hick* to have the guts to stand up to him.

He was wrong on that count.

"I don't know what you're talking about."

"Oh, I think you do."

"Well, she had it coming, then." Ryan smirked.

"You besmirch the name of an honest, respectable

woman and you think it's funny?" Drew set his jaw. Control was difficult, but he reminded himself that being able to think his way through things and not simply act with brute force was what set him apart from a man like Ryan.

"Honorable? Who even says that word anymore?"

"I do, that's who. And now, I suggest you remove yourself from my house before you say another word about Stephanie, or anything else, for that matter."

Ryan had the audacity to sneer at Drew, so he took one step, and then another, toward the young man, moving forward until he was looking down on the kid, or rather, glaring down at him. It didn't take long for Ryan to become intimidated and duck his head, cowering like the coward he was.

"As a matter of fact," Drew continued, "I don't just want you out of my house. I want you out of Serendipity. The whole state of Texas, for that matter. And don't even think about coming back."

"Why would I want to come back *here?* I'm so done with this place."

"I'm glad to hear it." Drew opened the front door and pointed to Ryan's fancy rented sports car. "Now, go."

Stephanie was packing her suitcase. She could have screamed at the top of her lungs and it wouldn't have drowned out the rushing sound in her head.

After what Ryan had just told Drew, she had no doubt that it was time for her to leave. Oh, Drew wouldn't throw her out on her ear straight away. He was too nice of a man for that. But even if he didn't immediately take Ryan at his word, the accusations would eventually take root and grow.

Why wouldn't they? Every single thing Ryan had said was true.

She *was* an opportunist, however unintentional. She'd never meant to be a burden on him. But how could Drew not see the way she was using him— his house and his hospitality—as a stepping stone to achieve her own goals and dreams? He had just offered her *free* room and board, and for little more than watching his beautiful children now and again, which she would have been glad to do, anyway.

If that wasn't taking advantage of him, she didn't know what was. She didn't mind watching the twins. She'd be heartbroken when she no longer could. But she had no illusions about who was getting the better end of the deal here, and it wasn't Drew.

She tensed when she heard a knock on her door. If it was Ryan again, she didn't know what she was going to do.

She quickly wiped her tears from her eyes with the corner of her sweater, hoping they wouldn't give her away. The last thing she needed was for Ryan to see her cry. He'd get all the wrong ideas about it and start putting pressure on her again to come away with him.

"Ryan, please. Just leave me alone," she said as she swung the door open.

"Ryan's gone," Drew said, standing at the doorway with his hands in his pockets. "I sent him packing."

Stephanie sighed and brushed a stray tendril of hair off her forehead. "Thank you for that."

He cleared his throat. "No problem." He didn't step

through the threshold, but he did glance over her shoulder. "What are you doing?"

Good old Drew, blunt as always. Her mind flashed back to her first day here, and Mattie's *Who are you?* Now she knew where the little man got his straightforward nature from—his father.

Tears sprang back to her eyes and she swallowed a sob.

"I'm packing. I promise I'll call the airline first thing in the morning to get a flight out of here."

He frowned and leaned against the door jam. "And why would you do that, exactly?"

She was going to start bawling again if he kept peppering her with questions. "You know why."

"Because of what Ryan said."

"Yes, because of what Ryan said," she repeated, hurt and exasperated at having to spell it out for him. "You heard him. I'm an opportunist. You can't deny that I've taken advantage of you."

His gaze darted away, as if he'd been blinded by a camera's flash.

That proved it, then. No doubt about it. Ryan's words had gotten to Drew.

Not that it mattered in the end. Even if nothing Ryan said got to Drew, it had gotten to her, and she was still going to leave. Why had it taken Ryan's coming here for her to realize the great extent to which she'd taken advantage of the man she loved?

"Stephanie." Drew's fingers caressed her cheek, turning her gaze toward him. He was looking right at her, and there was no anger or betrayal in his gaze.

There was—something else.

"Do you think I've used you by having you take care of the twins at all hours of the night and day?" he asked gently.

"No, of course not. That's what you hired me for."

"And the fact that I added my pop into the mix? You didn't feel taken advantage of then?"

"Not in the least."

"What about all the cooking and cleaning you did so I'd be ready for the case worker to visit? Surely that bothered you."

Stephanie moved back to the bed and started folding clothes to put into her suitcase. She didn't know where Drew was going with this, and her heart was aching. Her hands needed something to do. "No. It didn't bother me. You didn't force me to clean for you, I offered. I told you I was happy to do it, and I was."

"Were you? And yet you somehow seem to think that I'll resent you for being here, if not now, then later."

She shook her head, even if that was exactly what she'd been thinking. "Eventually you'll feel that way. You're too kind for your own good, offering me a place to stay and food to eat free of charge."

"Then I rescind my offer."

She hadn't expected that. It was as if he slam-dunked her and then threw her out of bounds. She lost her ability to take a breath, and her throat burned with emotion.

"I'll be gone as soon as possible," she whispered, unable to look him in the eye. She stuffed the rest of the pile of clothes she'd been packing into the suitcase without folding any of them. There was no chance whatsoever of stopping her flood of tears now.

"I will no longer be providing your room and board

for free," Drew repeated succinctly. "There are new conditions."

"Conditions?" Now she was confused. She'd thought he was showing her the proverbial door, if not the literal one.

"Right. I'm going to expect you to keep playing with the twins every day, and reading to them every night before bed. Hand puppets and everything. You'll need to tuck them in at night, and fix any boo-boos they incur during the day. I'll expect you to have tissues and bandages on your person at all times."

Stephanie didn't know what to say. She was in complete and utter shock.

"And you'll have to continue to put up with my father, at least until he and Jo get married and move in together. I know that's asking a lot, but there you have it."

"And if I agree?" She didn't know how she even got the words out. Drew was offering her a second chance to prove herself. She wasn't going to let him down. He'd get all he asked and more. She would never be a burden to him.

"If you agree, I will fulfill my side of the bargain— to provide room and board and help you get that preschool of yours started."

"Then I accept."

His eyes widened and he reached for her hand. He actually looked surprised—and very pleased. Ryan's words must not have had the impact on Drew that she'd originally thought they had.

"You accept?" he asked as if he wasn't sure he'd heard her right.

"Yes, of course. I'd be crazy not to. If you really want me to stay here, I'll continue to be the twins' nanny for as long as you want."

"I—you," Drew stammered. He was a man of few words, but he was rarely at a loss. He cleared his throat and tried again. "I really want you to stay here," he repeated.

When he squeezed her hand, she smiled and nodded.

"But not as the nanny." His smile was so broad and encompassing and hopeful that her heart stirred despite her best efforts to remain impassive. She really did love this man, with every beat of her heart.

"Nanny doesn't quite have the right ring to it," he said, pursing his lips thoughtfully.

"Child care provider?" she offered, wondering why it mattered what she was called. This was Serendipity. Nobody went by titles here.

"I was thinking more like *wife*."

"Drew?" she questioned, afraid she had heard wrong. Her heart was hammering so loud in her ears that she couldn't be certain.

"If you're really willing to marry a cowboy teacher who can't afford to offer you more than a tiny house and a dozen children, then I promise I will be the best husband you could ever imagine. I will love you with everything I have, and protect you with my whole being."

"You forgot the horses and the pigs."

He looked confused. "What?"

"The horses and the pigs. Ryan seemed to think that was part of the deal if I married you. That might be a deal breaker if you can't provide them."

"I think I can manage to get you a horse, if you really want one. But pigs?" Laughing and whooping with joy, he swung her around in circle. When he set her down, he pressed his forehead to hers and gazed into her eyes. His green eyes were gleaming with unabashed love.

"I know I'm asking a lot," he murmured. "Not just for me, but for the twins. You'll become a wife and a mother and a daughter-in-law all in one quick trip down the aisle. Although I can't promise you it will be easy, I guarantee you'll be greeted by that much more love when you make this house your home."

"I didn't even know what the word meant until the day I joined the Spencer household. My life really started on that day, Drew. And then I fell in love with you, only to think it was all over for me when Ryan showed up tonight."

Drew shook his head and tightened his arms around her. "Never, my love."

Somehow when Drew had been swinging her around, they had knocked the suitcase off the bed. Multicolors of fabric pooled around their feet. Before she met Drew she might have considered the haphazard pile of clothes a mess. Now it looked to her like an ocean of rainbows.

Besides, there was plenty of time to tidy up later—after they'd sealed their love with a kiss.

Epilogue

Thirteen. Fourteen. Fifteen. Stephanie counted heads as the children lined up to come in from recess. Fifteen lovely children from ages three to five, all a part of her first-ever Serendipity preschool class. Teaching these kids was better than anything she could have imagined when she'd first conceived the project in her head.

With Drew's help, they not only had the community behind them, but the church. Preschool was being held in the fellowship hall. They'd even allowed her to put up colorful bulletin boards depicting colors and numbers and days of the week, as well as the Bible stories she illustrated every afternoon.

"Story time, children," she called, moving to take her place in the center of the circle so the kids could gather round.

Suddenly she felt a tug on the bottom of her sweater. She looked down to find Matty's big blue eyes staring up at her, with Jamey ever-present at his side.

"Yes, boys?" she asked with a smile. Her love for them had only grown in the months she'd been married to their father.

"We were wondering," Matty began.

"Yes?"

"Do we have to call you Miss Stephie here like the other kids do, or can we just call you Mama?"

"I'd like to know the same thing, little man," said a warm tenor voice from behind Stephanie's shoulder.

Stephanie whirled around, a smile on her face and her heart welling. She wondered if it would always be like this, the tender feelings that were stoked to life every time she heard Drew's voice or saw his handsome face.

"Drew!" she exclaimed. "What are you doing here?"

Drew leaned down and pressed a kiss to her forehead, then pulled a plain brown paper bag from behind his back. "I thought I'd stop by and bring my lovely wife her lunch. You were in such a hurry this morning that you forgot it. Besides, it was a good excuse to see you."

Stephanie beamed at her thoughtful spouse. There was no one like him in this world.

Matty tugged on the corner of her shirt, reminding her that she hadn't yet answered his question.

"I think Mama will be fine," she said with a catch in her voice. She reached for the boys' shoulders and pulled them close to her. With a smile that said more than any words, Drew stepped forward and wrapped his arms around them all, completing the family.

Her family.

* * * * *

Dear Reader,

It's been a lovely journey back to Serendipity, Texas, for me, and I hope for you, too.

Like Stephanie, I have struggled with the issue of self-esteem all my life. I've made the mistake of trying to find my worth through my own good deeds and through what others might think of me. It was only after Christ entered my life that I came to see that through God's plan and purpose for me, I can find out who I truly am, and be happy with myself. True esteem begins and ends with Him.

I hope you'll be encouraged by Drew and Stephanie's story to seek out God's promises and plans for you. God's vision is so much clearer than ours, and His designs so much better!

My thoughts and prayers are on the readers of this book, and hearing from you is a great blessing to me. Please email me at DEBWRTR@aol.com or leave a comment on my fan page on Facebook. I'm also on Twitter @debkaster.

Keep the faith,

Deb Kastner

Questions for Discussion

1. At the beginning of the novel Stephanie had just left her boyfriend and moved across the country to take a position in Serendipity. Do you think she was running away or starting over? Why?

2. Why did Drew think hiring a nanny would help his case in court?

3. Stephanie identified a real need in Serendipity. What was it? How important do you think it was to the town?

4. What are the major themes running throughout this book? Which are important to you, and why?

5. Stephanie had been burned by love, but she was still attracted to Drew. What character traits did Drew possess that appealed to her?

6. If you could meet one character in this book, who would it be? Why?

7. The Christians Stephanie met in Serendipity spoke openly about their faith in their daily lives. Do you talk about God outside church?

8. What was your favorite scene in the book? Explain.

9. Can you think of a Bible story where God intervened and created what might have seemed like a

catastrophe at the time only to turn it into a blessing? (Jonah!)

10. Why do you think Drew didn't want Stephanie to stay in Serendipity permanently?

11. Why do you think Frank and Jo took so long to get together? What might have hindered them from being a couple?

12. Why do you think Stephanie thought Drew would believe Ryan when he accused her of using men?

13. Why do you think Stephanie became involved with a man like Ryan in the first place? What role did her upbringing have in this decision?

14. How did the Spencers change Stephanie's perceptions on what a family was supposed to look like?

15. What is the takeaway value of this book? What will you remember most?

INSPIRATIONAL

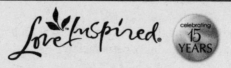

Love Inspired®

celebrating **15** YEARS

COMING NEXT MONTH
AVAILABLE JUNE 19, 2012

MONTANA COWBOY
The McKaslin Clan
Jillian Hart
Montana cowboy Luke McKaslin hits it off with Honor Crosby on a book lovers' website, but will the wealthy city girl fit into his humble small-town life?

HER SURPRISE SISTER
Texas Twins
Marta Perry
If the discovery of a twin sister isn't shocking enough for Violet Colby, imagine her surprise when she finds herself falling for Landon Derringer—her twin's former fiancé!

WILDFLOWER BRIDE IN DRY CREEK
Return to Dry Creek
Janet Tronstad
Security expert Tyler Stone was hired to find runaway heiress Angelina Brighton, but will this assignment turn into a matter of the heart?

THE DOCTOR'S DEVOTION
Eagle Point Emergency
Cheryl Wyatt
When former combat surgeon Mitch Wellington and nurse Lauren Bates find themselves working side by side at a trauma center, they learn that love is the best medicine.

A FAMILY TO CHERISH
Men of Allegany County
Ruth Logan Herne
Former high school sweethearts Cam Calhoun and Meredith Brennan find themselves working on a project together—can they move beyond the past and possibly find a future?

AND FATHER MAKES THREE
Kim Watters
Desperate for a cure for her adopted daughter's leukemia, Elizabeth Randall contacts her daughter's biological father—could Blake Crawford be a match in more ways than one?

Look for these and other Love Inspired books wherever books are sold, including most bookstores, supermarkets, discount stores and drugstores.

LICNM0612

REQUEST YOUR FREE BOOKS!

2 FREE INSPIRATIONAL NOVELS
PLUS 2
FREE
MYSTERY GIFTS

YES! Please send me 2 FREE Love Inspired® novels and my 2 FREE mystery gifts (gifts are worth about $10). After receiving them, if I don't wish to receive any more books, I can return the shipping statement marked "cancel." If I don't cancel, I will receive 6 brand-new novels every month and be billed just $4.49 per book in the U.S. or $4.99 per book in Canada. That's a saving of at least 22% off the cover price. It's quite a bargain! Shipping and handling is just 50¢ per book in the U.S. and 75¢ per book in Canada.* I understand that accepting the 2 free books and gifts places me under no obligation to buy anything. I can always return a shipment and cancel at any time. Even if I never buy another book, the two free books and gifts are mine to keep forever.

105/305 IDN FEGR

Name   (PLEASE PRINT)

Address   Apt. #

City   State/Prov.   Zip/Postal Code

Signature (if under 18, a parent or guardian must sign)

Mail to the **Reader Service:**
IN U.S.A.: P.O. Box 1867, Buffalo, NY 14240-1867
IN CANADA: P.O. Box 609, Fort Erie, Ontario L2A 5X3

Not valid for current subscribers to Love Inspired books.

**Are you a subscriber to Love Inspired books
and want to receive the larger-print edition?
Call 1-800-873-8635 or visit www.ReaderService.com.**

* Terms and prices subject to change without notice. Prices do not include applicable taxes. Sales tax applicable in N.Y. Canadian residents will be charged applicable taxes. Offer not valid in Quebec. This offer is limited to one order per household. All orders subject to credit approval. Credit or debit balances in a customer's account(s) may be offset by any other outstanding balance owed by or to the customer. Please allow 4 to 6 weeks for delivery. Offer available while quantities last.

Your Privacy—The Reader Service is committed to protecting your privacy. Our Privacy Policy is available online at www.ReaderService.com or upon request from the Reader Service.

We make a portion of our mailing list available to reputable third parties that offer products we believe may interest you. If you prefer that we not exchange your name with third parties, or if you wish to clarify or modify your communication preferences, please visit us at www.ReaderService.com/consumerschoice or write to us at Reader Service Preference Service, P.O. Box 9062, Buffalo, NY 14269. Include your complete name and address.

celebrating **15 YEARS**

Fairy tales do come true with fan-favorite author

JILLIAN HART

Honor Crosby never thought she would find a man she
could trust again, especially not in an online book group.
But when Honor finds herself heading to Luke McKaslin's
Montana ranch to see if their chemistry works offline,
her fantasy becomes too real. Can Honor believe in love...
even as she falls for Luke?

Montana Cowboy

THE McKASLIN CLAN

Available July
wherever books are sold.

www.LoveInspiredBooks.com

LI87751

*Violet Colby's life is about to get turned upside down
by a twin sister she's never met.*

**Read on for a preview of HER SURPRISE SISTER
by Marta Perry from Love Inspired Books.**

Violet Colby looked around the Fort Worth coffee shop. She didn't belong here, any more than the sophisticated-looking guy in the corner would belong on the ranch. Expensive suit and tie, a Stetson with not a smudge to mar its perfection—he was big city Texas.

That man's head turned, as if he felt her stare, and she caught the full impact of a pair of icy green eyes before she could look away. She stared down at her coffee.

She heard approaching footsteps.

"What are you doing here?"

Violet looked up, surprised. "What?"

"I said what are you doing here?" He pulled out the chair opposite her and sat down. "I told you I'd be at your apartment in five minutes. So why are you in the coffee shop instead?"

Okay, he was crazy. She started to rise.

"The least you can do is talk to me about it. I still want to marry you." He sounded impatient. "Maddie, why are you acting this way?"

Relief made her limp for an instant. He wasn't crazy.

"I think you've mistaken me for someone else."

He studied her, letting his gaze move from her hair to a face that was bare of makeup, to her Western shirt and well-worn jeans.

Finally he shook his head. "You're not Maddie Wallace, are you?"

"No. Now that we have that straight, I'll be going."

"Wait. It's uncanny." A line formed between his eyebrows. "Look, my name is Landon Derringer. If you'll be patient for a few minutes, I think you'll find it worthwhile." He flipped open his cell phone.

"Maddie? This is Landon. I'm over at the Coffee Stop, and there's someone here you have to meet.

"Okay," he said finally. "Right. We'll be here."

Violet glanced at her watch. "I'll give you five minutes, no more."

"Good." He rose. "I'll get you a refill."

"That's not—"

But he'd already gone to the counter. She glanced at her watch again as he came back with the coffee.

He glanced at the door. "You won't have long to wait. She's here."

The door swung open, and a woman stepped inside. Slim, chic, sophisticated. And other than that, Violet's exact double.

To unravel the mystery, pick up HER SURPRISE SISTER, the first of the TEXAS TWINS series from Love Inspired Books.

Available July 2012

SHLIEXP0712